MW01224918

MAKING BETTER LIVES

WYSE Series in Social Anthropology

Editors:
James Laidlaw, William Wyse Professor of Social Anthropology, University of Cambridge, and Fellow of King's College, Cambridge
Joel Robbins, Sigrid Rausing Professor of Social Anthropology, University of Cambridge, and Fellow of Trinity College, Cambridge

Social Anthropology is a vibrant discipline of relevance to many areas – economics, politics, business, humanities, health and public policy. This series, published in association with the Cambridge William Wyse Chair in Social Anthropology, focuses on key interventions in Social Anthropology, based on innovative theory and research of relevance to contemporary social issues and debates. Former holders of the William Wyse Chair have included Meyer Fortes, Jack Goody, Ernest Gellner and Marilyn Strathern, all of whom have advanced the frontiers of the discipline. This series intends to develop and foster that tradition.

Recent volumes:

For a full volume listing, please see the series page on our website:
https://www.berghahnbooks.com/series/wyse

Making Better Lives

Hope, Freedom and Home-Making among People Sleeping Rough in Paris

Johannes Lenhard

berghahn
NEW YORK • OXFORD
www.berghahnbooks.com

First published in 2022 by
Berghahn Books
www.berghahnbooks.com

Library of Congress Cataloging-in-Publication Data
Names: Lenhard, Johannes (Ethnologist), author.
Title: Making better lives : hope, freedom and home-making among people
  sleeping rough in Paris / Johannes Lenhard.
Description: New York : Berghahn Books, 2022. | Series: WYSE series in
  social anthropology ; volume 11 | Includes bibliographical references
  and index.
Identifiers: LCCN 2021040519 (print) | LCCN 2021040520 (ebook) | ISBN
  9781800733671 (hardback) | ISBN 9781800733688 (ebook)
Subjects: LCSH: Homeless persons--France--Paris--Social conditions. |
  Homeless persons--Substance use--France--Paris. | Shelters for the
  homeless--France--Paris.
Classification: LCC HV4556.P37 L46 2022 (print) | LCC HV4556.P37
  (ebook) | DDC 362.5/920944361--dc23
LC record available at https://lccn.loc.gov/2021040519
LC ebook record available at https://lccn.loc.gov/2021040520

British Library Cataloguing in Publication Data
A catalogue record for this book is available from the British Library

ISBN 978-1-80073-367-1 hardback
ISBN 978-1-80073-368-8 ebook
https://doi.org/10.3167/9781800733671

Contents

Figures

Preface
A Personal Down and Out in London and Paris

In 2011, I met Mike[1] for the first time right in front of the same Tesco supermarket where he still stood almost every day eight years later. The small shop was just a couple of minutes south-west of Shoreditch High Street station and was a very busy spot frequented by the many people who visited Spitalfields Market. When I first saw Mike, he wasn't asking for anything. Every now and then, I saw someone stop and chat with him. Mike had deep, droopy eyes and a full head of grey hair, normally hidden under a thick, black hat, even in summer. His small body was either wrapped in a big coat or protruding out of a long, grey t-shirt. Mike didn't seem to be a person of moderation; his face was either covered in the thick, grey wool of a long beard or totally clean-shaven. For weeks at a time, he went without shaving and then, from one day to the next, he was hairless. Only later did I find out that this was his way of saving money on razors.

For weeks, I didn't realize Mike was begging, despite living nearby and walking past him regularly. He stood outside the supermarket, greeting people as they walked past him. Many seemed to know him, addressed him by his name, came out with a little present – a piece of cheese, some sweets. He was friendly to everyone, but never explicitly asked for anything. Sometimes, I saw him speak to people before they entered the supermarket; some would inquire whether he wanted anything in particular that day. Did people just know that he was begging? Yes, Mike looked rough – his clothes were shabby, his beard was mostly in a bad state, his eyes were unsteady – and he stood in front of a supermarket for hours at a time. What else could he be doing?

I didn't know how to approach him at first. Simply giving him money – without him asking for it – seemed like a weird thing to do. I saw him many times, walked by him, heard him speak to other people, looked at him. I had never really spoken to someone begging on the street. But there was something about Mike, the humbleness of his approach, the unobtrusiveness of his begging, that made me sympathetic in a way I had not been before. Mike became my first informant before I even knew what an informant was.

***

I was doing a postgraduate degree in sociology and had just moved into an ex-council housing flat just west of Spitalfields Market in East London. Back in 2011, before the gentrification of recent years, Shoreditch High Street was still reasonably cheap and cheerful. Going to Mike's Tesco to buy groceries became a ritual I enjoyed. I was curious about this new city I had moved to. What did it mean for a city to develop? What did the artists do to make a space more liveable and what came after them? I was interested in finding the 'frontier': where was East London still rough? Where was it totally comfortable already? Between sociology classes, I explored the area on long walks alone, progressively moving farther from the centre, farther from the City of London, the financial hub. I would often stop to get a 50p packet of crisps at Mike's Tesco on my way out or a final packet on my way back to my little apartment. So Mike had become a regular sight on these tours through my new neighbourhood. Even before I started to talk to him, I had begun to notice more and more people begging: under the newly opened bridge leading to Shoreditch High Street Overground station, right in front of the station's entrance, next to the Tesco cash machine on the High Street, outside what was then a petrol station, in the little street opposite the Albion café. There seemed to be spots that people used regularly. I didn't always see the same people in the same spots, but the same faces repeatedly showed up in the neighbourhood. A map of people and places formed in my mind as I started to notice regularities, routines and what seemed like a carousel of begging spots people used throughout the day.

When you walk through Central London, you can barely turn a corner without seeing somebody sitting on the sidewalk, often with a sign, sometimes with a sleeping bag behind them. In 2019, before Covid-19 hit, there were about 150,000 people who were classed as belonging to the category of core homelessness, that is, 'people who are rough sleeping or in "quasi rough sleeping" situations (such as sleeping in cars, tents, public transport) ... squatting and occupation of non-residential buildings; staying in hostels ... and unsuitable "temporary accommodation"' in the UK, the vast majority in London (Fitzpatrick et al. 2019: xvi). About 3,500 people were sleeping rough in the capital, a number that has risen by more than 160 per cent since 2010 (and by 25 per cent compared to 2017 alone) (Fitzpatrick et al. 2019: xvii). But most of the time we don't *really* see any of these people. They are not part of our perception of the city. On the one hand, they are not supposed to be part of it. They are seen as a nuisance (Courtenay 2017) and pushed out of the centre with zoning laws and injunctions to prevent nuisance or annoyance (IPNAs), particularly in the UK.[2] On the other hand, the public consciousness chooses to 'forget' about them: we don't want to be confronted with too much misery, so we opt to not 'see' such misery, effectively banning it (Langegger and Koester 2016; Minnery and Greenhalgh 2007). Admitting the presence of homeless people would mean admitting that society is doing something wrong. How is it possible that there are still people on the street in this day and age? They must all be Roma, come from Eastern Europe, Syria, Afghanistan or Africa, or be on the street of their own choosing. In any case, it is the responsibility of the government, not the individual citizen. There are many excuses, all of which have the same result: homeless people and people who beg are mostly excluded from the public's sight.

For the longest time, particularly while living in small German cities, I was the same; I opted to not see homeless people. What could I do about all of their suffering? This was not a conscious decision, of course. It felt normal that I didn't *see* homeless people, that they weren't part of my world. Nobody in my life – at home, in school, even at university – ever really talked about it. People were not all that concerned about homelessness, poverty and inequality when I was coming of age in Germany in the 2000s. Only upon moving to London did I become aware of my partial blindness. But it wasn't its pervasiveness or the high visibility of people on the street that made me think about homelessness. It was the subtle approach personified by Mike that paradoxically changed my perception. The suffering of the people I regularly saw on the street – often showcased in a way that was supposed to make passers-by feel pity, to make them give money – was too much to bear. It was easier to cut it out completely. With Mike, it was different. He appeared to be 'one of us', just lingering for a little longer in front of a supermarket. I had registered him as a person before I understood that he was homeless. Whether consciously or not, Mike compelled me to recognize him and subsequently take him and his issues and problems seriously.

This shift in my own perception, precipitated by Mike, led to what became the basis for this monograph: more than seven years of intensive anthropological investigation of homelessness, culminating in two years of doctoral fieldwork in Paris between 2014 and 2016. At first, my sociological explorations, which started with Mike, were driven by an interest in the giving encounter between the homeless person begging and members of the public. Do the two interrelated activities of begging and giving lead to relationships? I found that people like Mike were indeed trying to obtain money – and had all kinds of tactics to convince people to give – but they were also keen to find a listening ear, somebody who would spend some time with them.[3]

During two subsequent summers, I conducted further fieldwork with homeless people in London, first diving deeper into the group around Mike, whom I had first met in 2012, and afterwards in a set of homeless shelters of people with mental health issues. I looked at relationships among homeless people, at friendship and conflict, and I also learnt about the prevalence of drugs among my East London group of informants (Lenhard 2017). In 2014, while working with homeless people with mental health issues in three homeless hostels in the King's Cross area, I became interested in questions of choice and freedom. Despite being put under enormous pressure by several government initiatives known under the umbrella name of 'personalisation' (SCIE 2010; McNicoll 2013), choice was often more of a burden than a desire for my informants. 'Freedom in dependence' – being able to rely on the decision of the social worker – was often more achievable.

After three consecutive summers spent studying homelessness in London, my curiosity regarding the problems faced by homeless people was not at all fulfilled. At the beginning of my doctoral degree, I decided to switch my field site to another European capital, Paris. Historically, France has been more deeply involved in providing federal resources for social services, healthcare, unemployment support and social housing (Lévy-Vroelant 2015). Moreover, it had not effected the same kind of privatization and 'personalisation' of services for homeless people as the UK and had mostly avoided the demonization of homeless people and their legal ban from public spaces (FEANTSA 2007; Edwards and Revauger 2018). Hence, my experiences in Paris would be different to my experiences in London, both on the street and in institutions. While this monograph will focus on Paris, my observations in London shaped my way of accessing the new field site. What follows is a detailed account of two years of encounters with people I met in Paris: some of them were different to those I had met in the UK; many others were very similar. In much of the literature on homeless people, the focus is on their suffering; what I saw, however, went far beyond that: the people I met on the streets of both Paris and London were energetic and active – they had agency that other commentators often don't ascribe to homeless people in their studies. What I set out to document is how people on the streets of Paris are struggling to survive, make a living and create a better life.

Notes

1. I have used pseudonyms for both individuals and organizations in this volume.
2. IPNAs were introduced in the UK in March 2015 (Crisis 2017).
3. See Lenhard 2014; begging is the main focus in chapter 1, as well as in Lenhard (2021).

Acknowledgements

The people most crucial to this project are the people I met on the streets of London, Paris and most recently Cambridge, people who became my friends. Thank you for letting me into your lives over the last ten years.

Thank you also to the different members of staff at Freedom, Sun and Emo and to Linn and Priyanka for being my research assistants for a while.

I also want to thank people who have helped to shape drafts of this manuscript, particularly Chris, but also Eana, Nikita, Farhan, everyone in the Cambridge writing-up seminar and the EHESS exchange seminar in Paris. Many thanks also to the post-docs in my new home, the Max Planck Centre for the Study of Ethics, Economy and Social Change, for helping me finesse some of the crucial arguments in this volume.

Without my supervisor James, I would not have even started this project; thank you for your kindness and patience. Thank you also to Harri and Matt for commenting on my work throughout the writing process. A special thank you to Joel, who provided valuable feedback, particularly when I was finalizing this manuscript.

Thanks also to the organizations that funded the project, the Cusanuswerk in Germany, as well as King's College, Cambridge, the Cambridge Trusts and recently the Max Planck Cambridge Centre for Ethics, Economy and Social Change.

Lastly, thank you to Rebecca for hosting me at Tanglewood, where I finalized the first version of this monograph, and to Chris Hann for repeatedly hosting me in Halle, where I worked on my revisions.

Part I

INTRODUCTIONS

Introduction
People Sleeping Rough at the Gare du Nord

Walter's legs were impressive. They looked young, almost hairless – as is the case for many old men – but very muscular. Whenever I saw him, he would be wearing shorts; was he proud of his legs? The muscles were the result of walking around all day. 'Sometimes I walk 20 km per day. Always up and down and back and forth and in this or that direction.'

Walter came to Paris from the Netherlands and was in his early seventies when I met him at the Gare du Nord, Europe's biggest train station. He had travelled a lot during his life and had worked in Germany for a while. It was easy for us to communicate as we shared a common language. When I first started going to the day centre for homeless people, Freedom, just a stone's throw from the station, I spent a lot of time with Walter because I was the only person he could talk to. I quickly learnt that Walter had originally come from the Netherlands with a woman; they had met in the Netherlands, but she was half German and half Dutch. Neither of them had a job; they lived together on the streets of Paris for almost two years, but, in May 2015, she left him for an Algerian man. Walter was not inclined to admit his sadness; he never complained, instead moving forward, he explained, just as he kept on walking.

He was a rather quiet character, a silent mountain. I never saw him getting angry. He liked the street and slept on benches in the 10th arrondissement during the time when we saw each other regularly. Sometimes I found him at République, sometimes on the Boulevard Magenta leading from the station down to the big plaza. He wasn't ready for a room of his own yet ('There are too many rules. I don't need one. There is no freedom') and preferred his active life of walking all day, every day. But he was full of hope, despite all the problems in his life.

And Walter had good reason to be hopeful: he was nearing his official retirement age and, having worked for a significant amount of his life, he could expect a decent pension from the Dutch government. He already had a Dutch identity card, the first step towards being able to claim the money. His head was shaved in the picture, which had been taken only a couple of years previous, and his face was not hidden by a massive, wild grey beard, as it was when we met. The card was his insurance, as he told me, and his way out: 'Yeah, they [the French police] checked me three times. If you don't have a card they take you to their office and ask you questions. And I need the card to get the money.'

He came to the day centre most days and checked in with his *assistant social* [social worker] almost every week: 'When can we go to the bank and get my money?' He only needed a French bank account to resume communication with the Dutch government about his pension; with his identity card and the address that Freedom provided for him in the form of a pigeonhole, the matter could progress quickly. Walter was very keen indeed: 'When I get the money, I can leave.' However, he was dependent on the help of his *assistant social* in order to reopen the bank account. Months passed during which we waited for the right document to arrive from the Netherlands, confirming Walter's pension payments. He grew increasingly impatient and annoyed with the 'system' and its representatives – but he wouldn't give up; he relentlessly chased me and whoever else he could get hold of at Freedom's day centre – volunteers and staff alike.

Just as Walter's days were filled with continuous walking, his struggle to get his money involved continuous hustling, perpetual asking, demanding and trying. Eventually, it paid off. I was with him and his *assistant social* when the letter arrived from the Netherlands – he was to be paid €900 per month until the end of his life – and when his bank account was reopened, allowing him to receive the payments.

***

Like Walter, many of the people I encountered on the streets of Paris during my two years of ethnographic fieldwork between 2014 and 2016 were actively struggling, trying to achieve small goals, such as getting an appointment with their *assistants sociaux* to go to the bank, or bigger and more future-oriented ones, such as accessing their pensions. Although, according to official statistics,[1] the majority of the approximately 30,000 homeless people in Paris were living in temporary accommodation (e.g. hostels, hotels, emergency shelters), most of my informants were roofless according to the ETHOS (European Typology of Homelessness and Housing Exclusion) categorization of the European Federation of National Organizations Working with the Homeless (FEANTSA): 'people living rough [with] no access to 24h accommodation / no abode' and 'people staying in a night shelter' (Edgar et al. 2004; FEANTSA 2006: 1). In France, this sub-group of homeless people is called *sans-abris* [without shelter]. These people have neither a permanent shelter nor an income; they are most affected by mental health issues and drug and alcohol addiction and they are least supported and engaged with by charities and other sources of help (Laporte et al. 2015; Laporte and Chauvin 2010; Grinman et al. 2010; Hodder, Teesson and Buhrich 1998). In early 2019, about 3,600 people were identified as *sans-abris* in Paris.[2]

Following on from my London investigations, I studied the daily lives of a loose group of about thirty *sans-abris* on the streets of Paris, following a core group of informants in a variety of different contexts. Unlike earlier work on homelessness in general (Jencks 1995; McNaughton 2008; Desjarlais 1997; Bourgois and Schonberg 2009) and homelessness in Paris and France in particular (Declerck 2003; Garnier-Muller 2000; Zeneidi-Henry 2002), I found that my informants were actively struggling along (Desjarlais 1994), driven by the hope for a better life. Joel Robbins (2013, 2015) argues that anthropology in recent decades has involved a lot of what he calls an analysis of the 'suffering slot'. Within this 'anthropology of suffering', homeless people have been described as half-dead zombies affected by illness – both physical and mental[3] – as 'the useless' (Garnier-Muller 2000) and as 'dopefiends' (Bourgois and Schonberg 2009). Often, these descriptions seek to understand the reasons for homelessness, marginalization and exclusion through the lenses of inequality, structural violence and social suffering (Singer 2006; Bourgois 2002; Bourgois and Schonberg 2009). In *Naufragés*, the most prominent French example of this genre, ethnologist and psychoanalyst Patrick Declerck describes the 'clochardisation' [immiseration] of people on the streets of Paris in the 1980s and 1990s and the impossibility of their reintegration into any kind of mainstream society. My observations in Paris mirror many of these findings: although heterogeneous, homelessness is very much the product of a structural malfunction of the social, economic and welfare system – producing inequality and poverty, as well as a lack of affordable housing – paired with various events on the individual level – mental or physical disease and/or personal and family issues, such as divorce, death or domestic violence.[4]

But my aim in this monograph is not to follow this tradition, which has given rise to many important research documents and fostered understanding of the reasons for homelessness and the conditions homeless people endure on the street. I believe that focusing solely on the structural suffering, exclusions and marginalisations of the people thus affected is of limited value for at least two reasons: firstly, and most importantly, the people I met on the street did often not conceive of their situation as one of suffering. Paul Ricœur defines suffering as 'the reduction, even the destruction of the capacity for acting, of being-able-to-act' (Ricœur 1992: 190). I found that my informants were heavily invested in actions rather than being passively affected and pacified by structures. It is these active practices that I will describe in this monograph, following my informants' trajectory from living *sans abri* on the street through various institutions – day centres, needle exchanges, homeless shelters. Secondly, focusing on the negative aspects of the lives of people on the street naturally produces an incomplete picture. Homeless people, like recovering alcoholics, people affected by HIV or people suffering from poverty and restructuring programmes in developing countries, are not always consumed by their lack of resources, shelter, relationships and intimacy (Zigon 2005; Farmer 2005; Ferguson 2015). They do not even necessarily lack all of the above (e.g. Lenhard 2014; Lenhard 2017). I conclude from my two years of observations among homeless people in Paris that re-ascribing agency to them is crucial; they are, individually and in groups, independently and with the support of different kinds of *assistants sociaux*, actively striving to survive.

They use techniques of the self – practices that 'permit individuals to effect ... operations on the[mselves] ... so as to transform themselves ... to attain a certain state of ... happiness' (Foucault 1997b: 177) – to create better lives for themselves. While some of these struggles are focused on short-term survival (Part II), others are future-focused and longer term (Part III). This monograph is about these different practices and techniques.

Mapping on to Jonathan Parry and Maurice Bloch's (1989) classic distinction between short- and long-term transactional orders, I observed my informants engaging in two distinct but related sets of processes of home-making in different settings. The two spheres are differentiated by two temporally distinct affects of hope. On the one hand, almost all of the homeless people I met wanted to leave the street behind in the long term: to return to their families, find jobs, become French citizens. On the other hand, they were dependent on short-term, immediate survival on a day-to-day basis. As a result, they engaged in short-term, daily home-making activities, such as the labour of begging (chapter 1), the work of shelter-making (chapter 2) and drug taking (chapter 3). These shorter-term practices and processes are the focus in Part II of this volume.

But not all of these activities focused on immediate survival contributed to their long-term desires, plans and hopes. At times, 'the individual will become so embroiled in the short-term cycle that he will ignore the demands of the long cycle' (Parry and Bloch 1989: 27) – for instance, through an effect of addiction that I call 'drug time'. However, I describe these activities as part of the non-linear trajectory towards what my informants considered a better life, both now and in the future. In Part III, we follow my informants along this imagined longer-term trajectory or pathway, leaving the street often with the aid of different institutions. From the help they receive in harm-reduction facilities for substance users (chapter 4) and day centres (chapter 5) to arriving in mid-term accommodation (chapter 6), I will focus on how their longer-term hopes are unearthed, reflected upon and worked towards, mostly aided by different *assistants sociaux.*

This shift in focus to the activity, agency and 'techniques of the self' (Foucault 1997) of homeless people, as opposed to their suffering, is significant because the alternative observations I offer could inform policy decisions. I am providing a starting point for supporting people in their own practices and devising creative ways of dealing with homelessness. While I understand the often politically motivated decisions of earlier scholars of homelessness to portray the deeply negative aspects of living on the street, I am complementing that picture with glimpses of hope amid the suffering. As Cheryl Mattingly writes, with reference to her research on chronically ill people in the United States: 'Hope as an existential problem takes cultural and structural root as it is shaped by the poverty, racism and bodily suffering' (Mattingly 2010: 6). She goes on to argue that 'hope emerges as a paradoxical temporal practice and a strenuous moral project' and 'involves the practice of creating, or trying to create, lives worth living even in the midst of suffering' (ibid.).

In the following chapters, I will describe how my informants, such as Alex from Germany, Barut from Bulgaria or François from France, 'struggle along', in Robert Desjarlais's words, in Paris, unpacking what Mattingly calls practices of hope (Desjarlais 1994). Accompanying these individuals on the street and following them through the institutional landscapes of soup kitchens, drop-in centres, government institutions and homeless shelters, I will describe how they make choices that influence whether they have a better and freer life on and ultimately also off the street.

Street-Level Ethnography at the Gare du Nord

I spent two years in Paris between September 2014 and 2016 doing fieldwork with a loose group of about thirty homeless[5] people. Unlike most other ethnographic studies of homelessness both in France (Garnier-Muller 2000; Declerck 2003) and internationally (Desjarlais 1997; Hall 2003), my starting point was the street; thus, my research mostly concerns people who are roofless and sleeping rough. I identified the Gare du Nord – Europe's busiest railway station, with more than 700,000 passengers per day – as my main field site for three interrelated reasons: it is a central site for homeless people both during the day and at night in Paris (APUR 2011); it is the first point of arrival (and departure) for many immigrants (Kleinman 2012, 2019); and the large number of travellers and tourists constitute a good source of begging money for homeless people (see chapter 1). A 2011 study by the Atelier Parisien d'Urbanisme (APUR) describes the homeless population at the Gare du Nord as highly diverse, but also a good approximation of the population captured by the national statistical study (APUR 2011; Yaouancq and Duée 2013): among the 600 people counted by APUR, many were immigrants from Iraq, Afghanistan and India, but there were also Roma; many had alcohol problems and struggled with *toxicomanie* [drug addiction]; most were single men.

For the first three months of my fieldwork, I spent my days and evenings walking around the area between Gare du Magenta in the east, Barbès in the west, Place de la République in the south and Stalingrad in the north, observing people whom I at first assumed and later confirmed were homeless. I only slowly started speaking to people whom I had seen several times at 'their spots', in part because my French was only just developing. My first contacts were members of a group that had formed around Natasha, a woman of Algerian descent in her sixties who had managed to amass an array of varied followers. When I first arrived, Natasha and her mostly male companions would always sit in the same spot opposite the main entrance to the Gare du Nord, just in front of the *Quick* fast-food restaurant. Natasha was one of the maternal figures I encountered in my fieldwork; over the course of two years, she introduced me to many other individuals, including Sabal, a Punjabi who became one of my main informants.

By following people like Natasha and Sabal on their 'mobility paths' (Wolch and Rowe 1992) through the city, I extended not only my network of informants, but also my field site beyond the direct vicinity of the station. It was also through Natasha that I first learnt about Freedom, the homeless institution running several drop-in centres, street tours and a homeless hostel, at which I spent many days volunteering during my two years. Although I got to know Carl, as well as other informants of mine, on the street, I followed him on a long trajectory: I observed him begging (chapter 1), but we also spent many hours at Freedom's day centre (chapter 5) and at a drop-in facility for people with alcohol problems (chapter 4). I even visited him during the winter of 2015 in his hotel room, sponsored by the city of Paris, and went with him on his first day at a new shelter in early 2016 (chapter 6).

My approach to the field as a fluid site that was defined by the routines and daily processes in which my informants engaged produced a varied image of what homelessness looks like in Paris. I observed what rooflessness is – being, and particularly sleeping, on the street – but also how people were dependent on working *with* institutions such as Freedom – in day centres, on street tours, in vans distributing risk-reduction material to drug users – and what being on the *inside* of institutions does to people in, for instance, homeless shelters (chapter 6). However, this fluidity also came with certain problems. On the one hand, the lack of structure in my approach to the field left some parts of it undiscovered. I had only very little contact with women on the street; only three of my core group of around thirty informants were female. Not only do women often navigate the social care system more quickly, but there are also more institutions focusing on supporting women in their efforts to move away from the street (Passaro 1996; Russell 2011). In France, only about 5 per cent of *sans-abris* were women in 2016 (Seuret 2016). On the other hand, like children – often called 'jeunes en errance' [wandering youngsters] (Pimor 2014) – homeless women are more likely to be invisible and inaccessible on the street, making them harder to include in ethnographic research.[6] For similar reasons, I was not able to engage with Roma people, who are very prevalent on the streets of Paris; the language barrier made communicating with them complicated and they were mostly part of closed social groups, unwilling to engage with outsiders (Messing 2014). To address the question of language briefly, I spoke a mixture of French, German and English with my informants. In this monograph, I sometimes quote the original language used for clarity, but I always provide my own translation. All my field notes were taken either in English or in French, which I translated into English for my field journal as soon as possible. While many of my informants were (at least originally) migrants, I did not engage with many Syrian, Iraqi, Afghan or other more recent refugees (Sanyal 2017; Freedman 2017). Their geographies of daily life, as well as the support they received, differed widely from the ones I was engaged in with my homeless informants. Different NGOs and government institutions to the ones with which I volunteered were involved in helping refugees, mainly with their legal and health problems.

The fluidity of my own role[7] in the field – anthropologist, friend, volunteer – also gave rise to uncertainty. Negotiating transparency and my own position while constantly switching between different roles further complicated my responsibility to protect marginalized research participants (Lee 1993; Power 2002). On the one hand, my position as a volunteer for several organizations gave me credibility beyond the volunteering context, making it easier to engage people; on the other hand, I had to be careful to make my position clear in order not to abuse the trust of my informants. As social workers and volunteers often act as gatekeepers for research on vulnerable populations, it was beneficial for me to become such a gatekeeper (Goode 2000). But I deemed it important to avoid what might be described as semi-covert research[8] and repeatedly informed the people I engaged with of my identity as an information-gathering researcher.[9]

The equal treatment, anonymity and security of my informants were always of the greatest importance. I observed many criminal acts – the sale and consumption of drugs, the theft of goods, violence – that made it particularly important for me to protect the identities of the people I worked with (Lee 1993; Denzin 2009). For that reason, I never filmed anything, nor did I take audio recordings of any of the homeless people I encountered (Esterberg 2001: 73). Only the interviews with experts – mainly social work professionals at the institutions in which I volunteered – were recorded and transcribed. Notes were my main form of data generation; they were usually taken 'after the fact', with the result that many of my quotes are not verbatim (ibid.). In addition, I have given all of my informants pseudonyms and some of their biographies have been changed slightly in order to protect their identities further. To guard my own personal safety in the field, I made sure to mostly stay in public spaces with my informants, to not get involved in any criminal activities myself and to mostly avoid being with high or aggressively drunk people. For the same reasons, I never slept outside or on the street.

Homelessness (Research) in France: Definition Problems

André Gueslin's historical overview helps to put homelessness in France into its wider historical context (Gueslin 2013). The original idea of the *pauvres errants* [poor wanderers] dates back to the Middle Ages, when homeless people were demonized and mainly received only religious aid. From the fifteenth century onwards, a repressive penal system centred on what were called *hôpitaux généraux* [mental and poor people hospitals] not only labelled *vagabonds* and *mendiants* [beggars] as delinquent, but also made it easier to institutionally exclude them. The 'good poor' were those who wanted to work. Poverty became a crime in the legal statutes of the nineteenth and twentieth centuries, especially with the penal code of 1810. A *vagabond* could go to prison for ten to thirty days if he (or she) was without home, work and resources. The notion of the *sans domicile fixe* (SDF) first arose in the nineteenth century, but became commonplace in the 1980s after the establishment of an even stricter and more comprehensive system of restricting homeless people through the BAPSA (*brigade d'assistance aux personnes sans-abri* [assistance unit for homeless people]) and early homeless shelters, such as Nanterre, which is described in Declerck's (2003) famous ethnographical study. SDF were defined as people who sleep on the street or privatized public space and are dependent on assistance (Gueslin 2013: 407).

Only in 1994, with the change of the legal code, is there evidence of a radical rethinking of how to deal with homelessness in France. Begging and *vagabondage* were removed from the list of crimes; they could no longer be punished with imprisonment. But homelessness has continued to be seen as a phenomenon that needs to be pushed into the suburbs and away from city centres on the basis of excuses such as health risks. Around the time the legal code was changed, however, media and public awareness shifted, giving rise to a wealth of NGOs and organizations, such as the Restaurants du Cœur and Emmaüs, which support the population of SDF. In the early 2000s, the government followed suit and introduced its own financial support system. The RMA (*Revenu minimum d'activité*), the RSA (*Revenu de solidarité active*) and the RMI (*Revenu minimum d'insertion*), established in 2003, 2008 and 1988 respectively, provided a minimum, regular income to long-term unemployed people for the first time. These changes in how homelessness is viewed in France slowly influenced how homelessness was defined.

Today, the official definition for a homeless person provided by the French statistical institute (INSEE) is based solely on the person's shelter the previous night: a person's status as homeless, according to the 2016 INSEE definition, is based on their being in a temporary hostel or a space that is not supposed to be inhabited (the street, emergency accommodation).[10] Similarly, in 2008, the UN Statistical Division defined two categories of homelessness, roughly mapping onto the differentiation between roofless (people on the street) and homeless (people living in shelters or temporary accommodation) (OHCHR 2008). Even the European homeless organization FEANTSA's lauded and widely adapted ETHOS definition ultimately only includes thirteen different types of inadequate housing, from roofless to overcrowded situations, and does not take into account any other circumstance of homelessness beyond the sleeping location (FEANTSA 2006).

The definitions above – which are mostly focused on the absence of something – mirror Edwin Heathcote's description of life on the street as the ultimate absence of home: 'we fear the idea of homelessness, it means a life on the streets, of not having a place to sleep, to eat, to be. Our home is our base, a place that roots us to the earth, to the city or the landscape; it gives us permanence and stability and allows us to build a life around it and within it' (Heathcote 2012: 7).[11] Instead of focusing on place alone, I propose the idea of home and subsequently homelessness as connected to a continuous process of the *making* of home.

In reference to her research on students establishing their first homes after leaving their parents' houses, Irene Cieraad conceives of home as exactly this kind of ongoing process:

> reinventing home is an ongoing process of linking the present to the past and the future. It entails not only remembering past homes but also projecting future homes. Away from home, whether traveling, migrating or living in lodgings, one becomes more aware of the main of the home one has left behind, temporarily or for good. (Cieraad 2006: 99; 2010)

Also introducing a temporal dimension that I will further develop in subsequent chapters (chapters 1 and 6), I follow Cieraad by emphasizing home-making. The focus on activity, routine and practice is more in line with an anthropology of the good as distinct from the suffering. Seconding critiques of home as defined solely by its functions and standardized, socially defined structure (Douglas 1991; Veness 1993), the notion of home as a process allows me to zoom in on the active struggles to make a home – such as the act of shelter-making (chapter 2) or the act of earning money by begging (chapter 1). It allows us rethink and enrich the category by providing ethnographic examples of home (making) on the street as a creative activity (rather than passive suffering).

It was only in 2015 that the UN Human Rights Council (HRC) admitted the problems I outlined above regarding the purely negative definition of homelessness as the lack of (adequate) housing (Human Rights Council 2015: 4, 5). The inclusion of the more positive view of homelessness as also involving being active and surviving, 'work[ing] hard to establish and build homes', as the HRC puts it, coincides with my observations on the streets of Paris and provides another anchor and motivation for the complementary view I seek to establish in this monograph.[12]

***

The historical lack of attention paid to certain aspects of homelessness is not confined to the abstract, international level of bureaucracy, but is also evident in accounts of homelessness in France. More narrative-based accounts such as Ann Webb's or Hubert Prolongeau's provide a vivid picture of a single homeless life in Paris (Webb 2012; Prolongeau 1993). Webb, for instance, describes in detail issues that my informants struggled with, too: accepting one's homelessness (chapter 1), the influence of the social worker (chapter 5) or the prevalence of drug and alcohol issues on the street (chapter 3). Like George Orwell's (2001) classic work, however, they are neither analytic nor structured; rather, they are merely anecdotal and, as such, are only of limited value for academic scholarship.

An important canon of work focuses on attitudes towards homeless people and the relationship between homeless people, the public and the state. Most recently, Marie Loison-Leruste (2014) and Stéphane Rullac (2005) considered the idea of a 'culture of homelessness' in France and – on the basis of deviant studies – the exclusion of homeless people from public space and opinion. Rullac (2005) goes on to explore ethnographically the Samu Social, the biggest support provider for homeless people in Paris. As I mentioned before, such institutional – as opposed to street-based – studies are very common in France.

Declerck's classic account of the emergency shelter at Nanterre is only the most well-known example of such a study. Yann Benoist (2009) updated Declerck's study twenty years later, focusing particularly on how the groups of visitors have changed and comparing the shelter to a total institution (Goffman 1991). More medically influenced – and often policy-driven – work has been conducted on mental health institutions for homeless people, particularly in Paris (Marpsat 2007; Kovess and Lazarus 2001). Pascal Noblet (2014) studied the Enfants de Don Quichotte, another organization that specializes in providing support for homeless people; Corinne Chaput-Le Bars and Arnaud Morange (2014) recently examined the successes and problems associated with the French variant of housing first (*lodgement d'abord*), comparing it to its Canadian predecessor; Pascale Pichon (2014) conducted a study of the SIAO, something every applicant for temporary housing has to go through, comparing it with the equivalent systems in the UK and Switzerland (see chapter 5).

I depart from the above studies in at least two respects: firstly, my initial focus was the street; the institutions included in this study – the day centre, the 'drug van', the homeless shelter – were part of my informants' daily geography, accessed mostly while continuing to sleep rough. Secondly, I was mainly interested in the activeness of my informants, rather than institutional intricacies. Institutions only feature insofar as they have a crucial impact on my informants' practices. In the French literature, two studies, in particular, served as starting points for me: Djemila Zeneidi-Henry's elaboration of how homeless people make 'their' city in Bordeaux and Anne Garnier-Muller's study of homeless people making a life in Paris (Zeneidi-Henry 2002; Garnier-Muller 2000). In both studies – despite their often more geographical focus – the ethnography of the street plays a strong role. The guiding question for both authors seems to have been similar to my own: how do homeless people actually survive?

The common thesis in most of the French accounts – as well as in the most prominent international accounts of homelessness – is that homeless people want to leave the street behind because they suffer. What I observed in Paris supports this thesis, but also adds an important dimension that I describe as the focus on home-making. Most of my informants were working – to different degrees – on leaving the street in the longer term, but the prospect of and hope for this eventuality was supplemented by shorter-term daily home-making activities on the street. As I will describe in detail in the next chapter, 'Frame', which links hopes and home both in the long and short term, my informants were, in Desjarlais's words, 'struggling along', that is, approximating certain aspects of home on the street on a daily basis and also taking small steps towards the bigger hope of leaving the street.

Many of these activities are related to a view of life on the street not only as one of suffering but also as one of creative engagement with one's surrounding and conscious strategizing, in Mattingly's sense.[13] As Mark W. Flanagan argues with reference to his homeless informants with addiction problems, many 'viscerally experienced hope ... hope was experienced in deeply emotional ways and thus assigned meaning' beyond the pessimistic 'creature living' usually assigned with living on the street (Flanagan 2012: 57). It is in this sense that my informants were working on creating a better life.

A Better Life on the Street

Robbins (2013) characterizes anthropology since 1980 as focused on the 'suffering slot'. Reframing the commonplace earlier analyses of the anthropological subject as 'other' or 'savage', new studies of trauma, violence and colonization brought an understanding of the universal experience of suffering to the fore (ibid.: 453). The anthropology of social suffering also extends to medical anthropology, where narratives of individual chronic pain, loss, trauma and structural violence are linked to problems in the collective structure of society (e.g. Scheper-Hughes and Bourgois 2003; Farmer 2004; Biehl 2005). In the literature on homelessness, similar issues come to the fore in accounts such as Declerck's *Naufragés* and Philippe Bourgois and Jeff Schonberg's *Righteous Dopefiend*. Bourgois and Schonberg explicitly describe the symbolic violence of public health outreach as unfair; the physical suffering of 'being cold, wet, filthy, hungry, and exhausted' through detailed ethnographic accounts; the gendered suffering of, for instance, mothers of homeless children; the de facto apartheid in the American labour market and the influence on children of the lack of a father, to give just a few examples.[14] These descriptions, although graphic at times, are subtle and don't have an air of pornographic voyeurism to them; however, they often stop there, with the suffering.

C. Jason Throop (2015) deals with the issues associated with writing about suffering slightly differently in his ethnography of the Yapese communities of Micronesia. While the Yapese are struggling with historical suppression by various forms of colonial rule – struggling to overcome past suffering (*gaafgow*) – their daily life also revolves around trying to be happy (*falfalaen'*): 'Suffering was thus generally deemed virtuous by local standards to the extent that it helped to orient individuals, families, and communities to future horizons of possibility and past legacies of effortful sacrifice. In so doing, suffering defines extended horizons of experience, and accordingly gives rise to possibilities for hope' (ibid.: 57). For the Yapese, happiness and suffering ebb and flow, often appear in quick succession and are both always limited and precarious, for instance, during hard work.[15]

It is this kind of synthesis and the sensitivity to both sides of the coin – suffering and efforts to be better – that I document in this volume, too. In his analysis, Robbins points out a tripartite way forward in what he calls the anthropology of the good: new studies advancing this agenda could either focus on value, morality and well-being (Laidlaw 2014; Zigon 2011; Lambek 2010; Robbins 2007); empathy, care and the gift (Throop 2007; Mol 2008; Winance 2010) or time, future and hope (Bear 2014; Crapanzano 2003; Green 2012; Mattingly 2010; Miyazaki 2006). The chapters in this volume can be related to these three fields, but first and foremost follow the logic of what is often called the 'homeless pathway' (Clapham 2003; Clapham et al. 2014), from surviving on the street to moving into longer-term housing, supported by various institutions along the way. Although this path was not linear for most of my informants, many did see it as a motivation for achieving their own hopes. The clear and structured way forward, as presented, for instance, by their *assistant social*, was part of my informants' narrative of hope regarding a longer-term home.

Starting with the theoretically grounded 'Frame' chapter, the question of how people 'successfully create a good beyond what is presently given in their lives' (Robbins 2013: 458) is a thread that runs through the chapters in this monograph. Part of Robbins's third categorization of the new 'anthropology of the good' – time, change, hope – the question of how to create a better situation over time becomes central, particularly in my informants' dealings with support institutions. Mirroring what Jonathan Lear describes as radical hope or 'hope for revival' (Lear 2006: 95), my informants were forced to experience a different kind of hope, more immediate and short term, geared towards survival. Lear describes – mostly from a philosophical point of view based on certain historical and ethnographic snippets – how the North American Indigenous tribe the Crow lost every idea of sense – and the good life – when they were confined to reservations and when buffalos were going extinct in their territory. Based on a conception of happiness and value that centred on being courageous, their structure in life lost all sense when being courageous – hunting, defending one's territory, etc. – lost its meaning. Lear describes how the Crow went on to 'find new ways' (ibid.: 64), 'giv[ing] up almost everything they understand about the good life' (ibid.: 92).

For my informants, a somewhat comparable situation arose on the street. Having lost almost everything – social relations, material stability, employment, often also the familiar context of a home country or city – a reorientation was necessary in order to survive. In the short term, the radically new environment of being roofless on the streets of Paris – in a different country, for many – demanded the generation of a similarly radical hope. I describe the great significance of daily and short-term home-making activities – home as a process – in the lives of my informants.

At the same time – and here my account differs from Lear's – most of my informants had hopes about their (future) home, which were often connected to memories of an idealized past home country. They were hoping for a future remaking of their remembered home. These hopes often fitted into collectively perceived (and idealized) ideas of home as my informants would have known it in the past. In this sense, their long-term hope was not radical, but conformed with a life off the street, a life that many of them had previously known. This kind of hope was based on an often nostalgic longing for an ideal-ized past, but was further encouraged in the various institutions, described in Part III, that figured strongly in my informants' lives.

In Part II (chapters 1, 2 and 3), directly related to Robbins's first field of value, morality and wellbeing, I focus on daily short-term home-making prac-tices as part of the project to create a better life. It is this part of my observa-tions that relates most to a better understanding of ordinary ethics (Lambek 2010; Das 2012). How exactly do people earn money through begging and accessing the infrastructure of the city? Chapter 1 is concerned with the par-ticularities of what I call, following Hannah Arendt (1998), the labour of begging: being visible and invisible at the right moments, flipping the script of one's narrative (Carr 2011), performing neediness and deservingness and building up networks of regulars are all part of the hopeful labour of making money through begging. Like begging, shelter-making can in this sense be described as an often reflected-upon (hence ethical) act of daily home-mak-ing. Thinking through the ideal location, the complications arising from the securitization of public space ('anti-homeless architecture'), the actual making of different types of open and closed shelters – from *abri ouvert* and *abri couvert* to *abri fermé* (Pichon 2002) and ultimately also the competition for space – were all part of the processual (and often cyclical) character of shelter-making for my informants.

Chapter 3 and 4 focus on the role of drugs in my informants' lives. I portray what are perceived at times to be the positive effects of drugs and alcohol – for-getting, the perception of control – as part of my informants' daily, short-term home-making activities. As I described elsewhere, drugs are often seen as *giving* something while demanding a big sacrifice from the user (Lenhard 2017). For people like Barut, the substances were initially a means of taking back control over their minds and hence part of their short-term home-making. Only in the longer term did the negative influence mostly associated with addiction develop. All three of these activities – begging, shelter-making and taking drugs – can be described by what I will theorize as 'short-term hopes for' and 'practices of' home-making marking in Part II. These activities are more relevant to immedi-ate survival than a long-term project, while also being necessary for the possibil-ity of the latter, which was formed more directly in the institutional context to which the attention shifts in the third part of the volume.

The observation of everyday home-making practices also permeates chap-ters 4–6, in which Robbins's second axis – care and the gift – plays a more important role. Starting in chapter 4, institutions and their care-giving func-tionality become more prominent. Through long-term fieldwork with both a needle-exchange organization, which also provides heroin substitutes and other medication, and a drop-in centre for homeless people with alcohol addiction run by Freedom, I observed the flip side of the short-term focus on drug-taking for my informants. The care provided in both these institutions often came in the form of physical care – for the body – as well as the mental space for and exercise of thinking (reflectively and consciously) about the future. It is here that I first observed my informants giving in to support and switching their focus from the short to the longer term.

In chapter 5, I describe the ways in which my informants engage with a homeless day centre run by the Catholic organization Freedom through various core activities: street tours, activities in the *salle* [main room in the drop-in centre], using the showers and washing machines and the crucial one-to-one social work encounters. While the street tours – classical outreach work, following the same route every week, visiting homeless people at their spots – were carried out with *mains nues* (empty hands) as an almost free (but imperfect) gift, accessing the drop-in centre, with its coffee, physical warmth and security and the playing of games, followed a logic of 'silent' sharing (Widlok 2013). Taking a shower was reserved for the most destitute and using the washing machine was restricted to a handful of people per day – here, conditionality was stricter. The sought-after one-to-one social work was really only provided to those who demonstrated a willingness to engage and change (Mauss 2001; Sahlins 2004). In these encounters, a *projet de vie*, a concrete way forward, was formulated that provided guidance towards a better future.

However, even being admitted to temporary shelters, such as Valley of Hope (VoH) – the primary focus of my sixth and last chapter – did not guarantee that a better future would materialize. Drawing mainly on ethnographic observations from three months of living at the *centre d'hébergement de stabilisation* that I call VoH, the structures and routines proposed by staff and *bénévoles* constituted what Morgan Clarke recently called rules as technologies of the self (Clarke 2015, following Foucault 1997). Intricate rules – no drinking inside the centre, how to clean the bathroom, how to use the bins, when and where to shop, when to eat together – were often implemented by signs and meetings. In this sense, the environment of the shelter was, in Clarke's words, 'ruly'. Following rules and repeating routines established a practical project aimed towards achieving the good life (leaving the street context behind, advancing on the ladder towards independent housing). The idea was that the rules became part of the person by being learnt or relearnt. Conflicts occurred, however, as a result of the tension between 'being a good shelter resident' and other desires related to drinking and socializing. For some inhabitants, learning the rules of *habiter ensemble* [living together] at Freedom's shelter Valley of Hope was not easy – or wasn't desirable – so that the project of the good life achieved through the rules as techniques of the self often collapsed anew. Hence, many of my informants went backwards on their pathways, at times back on to the streets, where their struggles would mostly continue.

The aim of moving through the different contexts within this volume, whilst always remaining aware of the ambiguities of the practices, routines and techniques both used by my informants and proposed by members of staff and volunteers in institutional contexts, is to complement the idea of homelessness often exclusively described in terms of suffering. I am presenting a version of how my informants, aided by various kinds of *assistants sociaux*, struggled towards a better life both in the short and longer term. As Robbins claims, the 'nature of the good lives is different in different places' (Robbins 2015: 229). In this book, I am describing its nature in a place where no good life is expected at all.

Notes

1. In 2012, 28,800 people in Paris were officially defined as *sans domicile* [homeless] by the French statistical agency, an increase of 84 per cent from 2001 (Pierre-Marie et al. 2014). Most of these people were male (59 per cent), single (67 per cent) and foreign (55 per cent) (ibid.: 2). The large majority (>85 per cent) lived in temporary accommodation (30 per cent in hotels, 15 per cent in social apartments, 41 per cent in homeless shelters (Yaouancq and Duée 2013).
2. Paris.fr 2019; this number is likely comparable to the number of *sans-abris* when I conducted my research between 2014 and 2016.
3. See Declerck 2003, particularly his own illustrations and drawings.
4. See Neale 1997, Peressini 2009, Fitzpatrick 2005.
5. Henceforth, I will use 'homeless' and 'roofless' interchangeably, as most of my informants belonged to the wider category of homelessness, as well as the narrower one of rooflessness.
6. See Fournier 2017, Herschkorn-Barnu 2014. This quasi-absence of women also resulted in me being more or less unable to observe gender relations and sexuality. None of my main informants – to my knowledge – engaged in any kind of partnership or had regular sexual interactions. Sex work – despite being known as a common form of money-making on the street – was not visible to me during my fieldwork.
7. I am further reflecting on the boundaries of these different roles in a book chapter in *Home* (Lenhard and Samanani 2019), with a particular focus on my home-making as a researcher.
8. Ward (2008) uses this term.
9. Denzin 1968; Israel and Hay 2006; since illegal activities – such as drug dealing and theft – were only a marginal focus of my study, I was able to avoid covert methods of obtaining data.
10. INSEE 2016: 'une personne est qualifiée de "sans-domicile" un jour donné si la nuit précédente elle a eu recours à un service d'hébergement ou si elle a dormi dans un lieu non prévu pour l'habitation (*rue, abri de fortune*).'
11. See also see Seele 2011: 108.
12. By focusing on this, however, I am importantly not implying that my informants were *not* homeless, but merely stressing their activeness and agency in a situation of poverty and desolation.
13. Through notions of, for instance, resistance and endurance, certain studies of (social) suffering think this activeness through at least partly (see Kleinman, Das and Lock 1997). They usually stop short of going beyond the notion of suffering and the role (globalized) institutions have in this.
14. See specifically in Bourgois and Schonberg 2016: 107, 113ff, 135, 159ff, 188ff.
15. See also Hage 2003: 20.

Frame
Hoping for Home

I want to do something with my life. I want to have a job I like and a group of people I like spending time with, and just a good life. ... I don't need a big pay cheque, but I want to be paid well enough. I want to have a good job. I want to work, and I would be happy to work hard. ... I want to start thinking about that now. What can I do when I have my passport?

—Pascal

In spring 2016, Pascal and I were sitting in a big waiting room of the Lariboisière Hospital, right behind the Gare du Nord. I had come with Pascal to translate what the doctors had to say about his cramps, which had been keeping him up for many nights. While waiting, Pascal started to talk about his hopes, about what he wanted to do once he got off the street again. He talked about a life that resembled one he had previously lived.

Pascal was born in the Democratic Republic of Congo twenty-three years ago, but he lived in Germany from his first birthday. His parents had missed the opportunity to get him a German passport and instead regularly renewed his right to stay there. He went to school in the Rhine area and lived with his mother. His father, a salesman, travelled frequently; it was perhaps this absence that led to his parents' divorce. Eventually, Pascal moved to Munich to undertake an apprenticeship in electrical engineering, an education that made it easy for him to get a job and establish a stable social world of colleagues and friends afterwards. He often talked about going out and buying weed with his 'mates'.

It was only when he got into legal trouble two years previous – he spent four months in prison for repeatedly refusing to pay a public transportation fine – that cracks started to appear in this secure shell. The authorities suddenly refused to renew his right to stay. He and his family panicked at the prospect of years of court procedures that they wouldn't be able to afford and Pascal decided to move to France to apply for asylum using a fake Congolese identity. Pascal and his family thought that undergoing this process in another European country would be the quickest way of getting a European passport, which would allow him to travel back to Germany freely. Although the original plan was for Pascal to stay with relatives in Paris, he has been on the streets since his arrival in late 2014, living through three-month cycle after three-month cycle on his *titre de séjour* [temporary right to stay].

About one year after his arrival in France, his application for asylum was denied. His relatives in France – one of whom was his father's new wife – were still not happy to have Pascal stay with them, so he continued to sleep outside. At least there was still hope where his legal case was concerned as he was able to repeal the original court decision. Subsequently, he found a Congolese-French lawyer who specialized in cases like his. The lawyer demanded payment under the table to make Pascal's narrative more 'believable' and, for several hundred euro, agreed to reinvent Pascal's story, casting him as a political refugee. His parents – despite being separated – originally supported Pascal in this undertaking and paid some of the additional costs, not least because the lawyer was well known for his positive track record:

> I hope that my invitation [for the tribunal, to discuss his refugee case a second time] will arrive over the next couple of days. My lawyer is good. He won a couple of cases already. I hope he can push me through as well. He knows my story and he said he will help me and say everything [in court].

In spring 2016, however, Pascal was growing tired and fed up. The lawyer didn't seem to be making any progress and he was in constant conflict with his parents because his case wasn't advancing quickly enough in their view. Living on the street involved a daily struggle for money and shelter amidst violent competition with other people on the street. He wanted to leave that all behind:

> I have to leave this thing [the street]. And if you want to leave you have to leave fully. I might come back to see you and things but when I get my room I will need to take this in my hands. I need to think about my future.

He imagined what this future might look like in many other conversations with me, during moments of relative calm and security – talking to me over lunch or sitting in a chair in the warmth of the homeless day centre Freedom (see chapter 5). But these moments were often overshadowed by other, more pressing or immediate concerns that took over his thinking:

> The weekend is the most horrible part. You don't have anything to do. If you don't have friends, like real friends – the others are too different – there is nothing you can do. ... But then when they [the social workers] at Freedom ask me about my *projet* [*projet de vie*; project in life] I don't know. It's a stupid question. I have enough problems at the moment. Do you really think I want to think about my future work life now? I need to think about where I sleep and piss and shit – and you are asking me about my *projet*?

***

This glimpse into Pascal's recent past, as well as the immediate problems he faced when I first met him in 2015 and the future he dreamt of, brings to the fore the tension at the core of this volume: short-term hopes versus long-term hopes, immediate home-making and surviving on the street versus planning for the future ahead. These categories are in turn related to two different kinds of home that I will respectively call home-as-process and home-as-ideal-homeland. Pascal thinks about his family, about his friends, about his former life, about Germany as a place he wants to return to *in the long term*. While it was origi-nally a home he escaped from, because of trouble with the police and adminis-tration, his best memories date back to his time in Germany. He doesn't want to stay in France – where his relatives don't want to engage with him at all – and sees his future in Germany. Coming from the field of migration studies, Cathrine Brun and Anita Fábos (2015: 13) define this idea of what they call 'HOME' as the 'geopolitics of nation and homeland'. This conceptualization of home is particu-larly fitting in the context of homelessness in Paris generally and my research specifically: while more than 50 per cent of homeless people in Paris are not French nationals,[1] more than 70 per cent of my informants were migrants, which also reflects the diverse nature of the area around the Gare du Nord (Kleinman 2019). As we will see, for people like Pascal, but also Sabal and Alex – who were likewise migrants – this background brings with it a strong desire to return to the left-behind homeland, linked to a view back, to the past.

Pascal's situation demands less of a focus on the politics of the homeland and the role of the state. More important for him is the movement back into the cultural environment of his past. However, the past is often idealized by people who have left the homeland behind, as in Pascal's case. When Pascal talks about his former life and the life he imagines going back to, he tends to forget about the negative aspects: his divorced parents and the consequent challenging family situation, his marijuana consumption, his unhappiness in his job as an electrical worker and particularly his complicated legal situation without a passport in Germany. During Pascal's Paris days, Germany largely became, in his mind, an ideal homeland. He imagined it – and talked about it – as a place where he was free to do what he wanted (like smoke weed), was materially secure (with a job and an apartment), was surrounded by friends and family (his siblings), and was speaking *his* language (German) and eating *his* food.

While being connected to memories and the past, this notion of home-as-ideal-homeland is simultaneously directed towards the future. Pascal says in the epigraph to this chapter: 'I want to do something with my life.' He 'wants', he desires, he dreams, he hopes. I will use this last category – hope – as an analyti-cal frame with which to turn from the past-inspired future orientation of the above aspect of home to a different facet of it (Crapanzano 2003; Zigon 2009).

I will describe two – often competing, conflicting and meandering – forms of home-as-process in the shorter term (Part II): one concerning daily survival in the short term and one made up of steps leading towards the long-term hoped-for home-as-ideal-homeland. Pascal makes this conflict clear when he states 'I need to think about where I sleep and piss and shit – and you are asking me about my *projet*?' while he knows what he wants to do and where he wants to go in the longer term (get a passport, return to his home country Germany) and tries to translate this hope into manageable everyday steps as he survives on the streets of Paris, he often finds himself caught up in poverty, lack, uncertainty, fear and insufficiency.

His focus on the future of an ideal-homeland necessitates defining smaller goals on his way towards this future: to start with, he needs identity papers and the help of a lawyer; he also needs a room to stay in, then perhaps a modest job and a supportive group of people around him. These compartmentalized, more future-orientated home-making practices are one dimension of home-as-process in the present. Pascal's daily hopes are stepping stones leading towards his long-term hope of returning to a home in Germany. They make up what is referred to above as Pascal's *projet de vie*: his step-by-step trajectory away from the street, developed with his *assistant social* [social worker] at Freedom (see chapter 5).

But everyday life also affects Pascal in unforeseen ways and demands sometimes competing home-making practices. Living on the street without a fixed place to sleep, shower or go to the toilet, in the short term he is often preoccupied with constructing daily routines and navigating and 'ordering' (Douglas 2001) the infrastructures of the city: making money (chapter 1), finding shelter (chapter 2) and dealing with setbacks like the denial of his refugee application. Thus, the long-term hopes of a home are overwhelmed by a focus on daily hopes of survival or, in other cases, forgetting – when high or drunk (chapter 3) – leads not to a straightforward upwards and outward trajectory, but rather to an at best meandering path. These shorter-term practices will be the focus of Part II of this monograph.

As I already briefly mentioned, the two temporal spheres I observed map onto a classical anthropological distinction proposed by Parry and Bloch in 1989. Summing up contributions to their famous volume on money and exchange, they differentiate two spheres of transactional orders: 'a world ... in which men engage with strangers in a myriad of short-term transactions and where individual competition, if not sharp practice, is acceptable; and a world which is oriented towards the longer-term goals of reproducing the household' (Parry and Bloch 1989:23). While the focus of the short term is often individual appropriation and sensuous enjoyment, the long term can be conceptualized as a restorative cycle of long-term reproduction. Ideally, the first set of practices would be subordinate to and contribute to the second, but, as with my informants, there is a fear that the ideal scenario will not work out: 'the individual will become so embroiled in the short-term cycle that he will ignore the demands of the long cycle' (ibid.: 27). What happens if, for instance, my informants become consumed by their addictions or other short-term survival practices, such as begging? What kind of support is necessary to help them refocus on the longer term? On the other hand, how do short-term practices contribute to the ability to look ahead?

In this section, drawing on Pascal's and others' thoughts and hopes about home, I will dissect the ambiguous constructions of home as future-tense idealized longing and as a present-tense process of survival in increments.

Hoping for the Idealized Homeland: From the Past into the Future

I met Sabal very early on in my fieldwork, in December 2014. It was late at night and he was sitting just a stone's throw away from the main entrance of the Gare du Nord with his friend and fellow Punjabi Bouti. When I approached them, I noticed that their conditions were not good: they were sitting on the pavement without blankets or even cardboard, wrapped in a thin piece of cloth, pressed against each other and intermittently falling asleep apparently as a result of alcohol and fatigue. As I learnt later, both Sabal and Bouti had already spent a considerable amount of time in Paris. But even after having been in the city for more than a year, Sabal's French was not good enough to converse with me. On that cold winter night when we first met, he addressed me solely in English: 'Please – I am hungry. Can you help me? Please?' As I observed over time, he mostly spoke Punjabi and was surrounded by a group of Punjabi-speaking people, including Bouti. Sabal had come to France after escaping from an Indian prison. After periods in South Korea and Italy – in which countries he also spent time in prison – he arrived in France in 2013.

I didn't notice the bracelet Sabal was wearing for quite a while. It was unpretentious: an unembellished iron bracelet around his right wrist. It was a *kara*, one of the signs of being an initiated member of the Sikh religion. Sabal was a firm believer, which translated into a certain confidence about himself: 'I know I am a good person and that God loves me. I will find a way out of here. God will help me.' Sabal hadn't lost his hope and the longing to 'get out of here', leaving the street and, ultimately, France behind. Unlike Bouti, who was not married, Sabal had a strong reason to go back: his wife and young daughter were still in India waiting for him. 'I haven't seen her in almost six years. I haven't talked to her for almost a year. I want to be with her. But I will. God will help me.' His dreams took him further: 'When I am back home, I want to send my daughter to Canada. I know it's expensive but I want to.' He also said he missed the Golden Temple close to his house. The thought seemed to keep him alive. He made plans that included Bouti: 'We will both go home, won't we?' Bouti doesn't answer. But Sabal goes on: 'I will take you to my house and we will go to the temple together.'

***

For Sabal – as for the group of about six Punjabi Indians around him – home was connected to his nation of origin. His long-term hopes related to returning to his family, his wife and little daughter, and the Golden Temple, which was, for him, emblematic of his religion. For Sabal, his country – and the

Punjab region in particular – was connected to a past that seemed to be the only stability in his life, in the form of familiar memories and his religious community, but also a site of violence and hatred, as a result of which he had ended up in prison. He missed his house, his comparative material wealth in India, practising his rituals, speaking his language and eating food he knew well. In France, he understood himself as a person who was waiting to return to India once the attempts to prosecute him there came to an end.

Sabal's idea of home as connected to the homeland figures strongly in the social science literature on migration and refugees. In her study of refugees in Georgia, Brun (2015) found that return and repatriation were of great importance to the people she worked with, who had escaped from the Georgian war in the late 1990s. Home is related, first of all, to an 'absence' of 'social relations and practices possible to enact in the familiar home environment' (ibid.: 7); it is associated with a feeling of nostalgia for the home of the past: 'people long for the home they lost' (ibid.). Like Sabal, Brun's informants thought of home primarily as a (lost) homeland, both in the sense of a country and a cultural routine – including food, language, people and especially family. Home might therefore be understood as a place we depart from and have a desire to return to (Hobsbawm 1991).

Family (see Jones 1995) and religion are particularly significant in Sabal's idea of home; he continuously spoke about both his daughter and the Golden Temple. Abstracting these notions from the problems and ambiguities he faced in India in both realms – his religion wouldn't allow him to drink[2] and his family was suffering as a result of his 'sinning' – Sabal had built up an idealized version of this home on the basis of his memories. Temporal and spatial distance allowed him to think of his home as a rosy conjunction of family life (his wife and daughter), relative wealth (his house) and religious contentedness (his temple). This idealized version resembles Pascal's perception of home back in Germany: access to his family, a secure job with a pay cheque, a solid network of friends, a house, identity papers.

How is this idea of an ideal home constructed by homeless people? In their review of the literature on homelessness and home, Peter Kellett and Jeanne Moore (2003) position the notion of ideal home in between personal and collective-cultural memory and desire. The ideal home is the result of both Pascal's and Sabal's own memories of what might have been a happy childhood, as well as the social – or cultural – ideal of the typical home. On the one hand, both experienced this type of home in the past and 'cutting off' the more unpleasant aspects seems, in their cases, to have been a relatively easy exercise. The past was something that Pascal and Sabal wanted to remember and go back to (Brun and Fábos 2015). Sabal's memories of the temple and his descriptions of his house in the village of his childhood or Pascal's tales of many nights out with his friends and his loving memory of his siblings pay tribute to this. Home is, in this sense, anchored in a personal past.

On the other hand, an ideal type of home can be described as a social construction. In the context of my informants in Paris, this construction was shaped mainly by two forces: an incorporated idea of normality and the personification of norms communicated by the *assistants sociaux* and charity personnel at institutions such as day centres or homeless shelters. Pascal's case worker at Freedom, for instance, would encourage him to think in terms of 'normalcy': reconnect with your family and do everything that will allow you to return. Similar advice was given to Sabal by staff at Freedom: he wouldn't easily be able to access social care in France, so his best chance was to return to India, where people were waiting for him. Both Pascal and Sabal took these suggestions seriously, making them part of their *projets de vie*, worked out with their *assistants sociaux* at Freedom. Hence, the construction of the ideal was often the result of a personal past and social norms. A personal set of cleansed, nostalgic, longing memories of a (better) past home are merged with socially given *and* (institutionally) supported pillars of home to bring about the home-as-ideal-homeland. The hoped- and longed-for home is, in this sense, born from memories and positioned in the future.

***

For Alex, a similarly complex construction of an ideal home has led to a desire for a very specific type of homeland, his adopted *Heimat*, France. When I met him, Alex – a man in his late forties who was born in Kosovo but has spent more than a decade in France – was ardent about his French identity, his right to French citizenship and the support received from the French state. In the 1990s and early 2000s, Alex had spent more than ten years living and, most of the time, working in France. After the Kosovo War ended, Alex travelled to Lyon and was granted a *titre de séjour* [right to stay] for one year, which allowed him to take up work, mainly in construction and the manufacturing industry. During that first year, he met his future wife. His right to stay was fragile, but it was renewed every year during his eight-year marriage. When he and his wife separated, Alex ended up on the street for the first time. He spent one year *sans abri* [without shelter] in Lyon until the couple officially divorced. Subsequently, he was expelled from France and sent back to Kosovo. Alex stayed in his home town, where he had grown up, for almost two years before embarking on a new attempt to 'return' to France in 2013. He ended up spending time in Hungary, Austria and Kosovo again before he arrived in Germany in late 2014. 'They were nice in Germany but I didn't want to stay. I don't speak the language and I kept telling them: France, France, France.' Eventually, he was able to convince the German administration to put him on a train to Paris rather than sending him back to Kosovo.

During his decade in Lyon, Alex missed the chance to become a French citizen. 'I don't even know. They renewed my right to stay every year and I didn't think any further. I was happy.' In 2015, when I first met him, this possibility was all he could think about: on 23 November 2015, Alex missed a scheduled appointment with the Prefecture de Police in Paris, the institution with the power to grant him the right to stay. 'It was my chance, I know. I missed it. I missed it.' He also knew that he had messed up previously, in a way that might prevent him from ever getting a French passport: 'When I came last year, I registered under a different name. I took a different identity. I know it was stupid but I just wanted to get in.' He didn't want to give up, though, and still adamantly trusted French goodwill and institutional precision: 'But they have to answer me. I want my papers. If not in Paris, then in Lyon. I don't want to go back. Now I am ready. I will fight. I don't usually get violent, but now I am ready. They have to hit me first and I will hit them back. I don't know any mercy.'

For Alex, the idea of home as homeland did not apply to his original home country, Kosovo, but to his adopted home, France. He didn't like to think about or talk about his early life, his past in Kosovo. Unlike Sabal and Pascal, Alex was not able to cleanse his memory sufficiently to construct an ideal home out of Kosovo. Instead, he worked with a different part of his past to construct this ideal home: his years in France. Since 2010, he has repeatedly attempted to return, but when he was eventually allowed back into the country, it seemed as if his ideal state would not come to be. Home related not only to a particular space and certain things associated with that space, such as language; it also related to a certain way of life. Alex was hoping for a European passport, for citizenship; he was longing for a life with social security and benefits, in an apartment paid for by the French government if possible. His personal life – finding a new family – would come after that. His ideal home did not involve returning to Kosovo – a place he associated with the war and loss – rather, he dreamt about arriving at, and returning to, a found home anchored in a specific and idealized part of his past. He was meandering towards this ideal, with stops in Kosovo, Germany, France – a constant geographical back and forth.

***

The three examples above present us with intermingled versions of home as a place to return to and a place to long for. For Pascal and Sabal, home is to be found in their home countries – in Germany and India respectively – but these countries, or certain parts of them, appear as idealized places constructed out of cleansed memories. In contrast, Alex's particular version of France shines brightly as a welfare state able to support him, one that would give him benefits and tangible rights as a citizen. All three narratives are strongly linked to a longing for a certain part of each person's personal past.

For most of my informants, the first version of home – what I call home-as-ideal-homeland – points towards a future and comes from the past; it constitutes a goal to be reached, often constructed from memory and (past) ideas of ideal homes. I argue that explicitly focusing on this dimension of time will allow me, in the remainder of this section, to extend my initial categorization of home into the two contrasting spheres: the past-inspired but future-oriented home and home-as-process in the present. I will introduce hope as an analytical category in this respect.

Hoping for Home in the Future Tense

Sabal's dream of returning to India, Alex's longing for a place in France and Pascal's desire to be reunited with his family were not about an immediate tomorrow. They were desires nurtured over extended periods of time. Sabal hadn't been to India for over a decade; Pascal had left Germany more than two years prior to us meeting; Alex had been trying to return to France for over five years. They constitute long-term hopes for home. Sara Ahmed (1999) supports this view of home as something in the longer-term future in her study of migrants' writing, particularly Asian women living in Britain. She found that home is often a destination, somewhere to travel to:

> the space which is most like home, which is most comfortable and familiar, is not the space of inhabitance – I am here – but the very space in which one finds the self as almost, but not quite, at home. In such a space, the subject has a destination, an itinerary, indeed a future, but in having such as destination, has not yet arrived. (Ahmed 1999: 331)

According to Ahmed, home is quintessentially not about the present, but about one's hopes, about making home in an imagined place where one has *not yet arrived* (Bloch 1995; Moore 2000: 212). I want to follow Vincent Crapanzano (2003) and Jarrett Zigon (2009) in linking the category of home closely to the future by positioning hope as a driving force behind it. Crapanzano promotes a dichotomized view of hope as in between 'active desire' and 'positive resignation'. He concludes his theoretical analysis of the category of hope in a way that recalls Pascal's hopes for home. He describes hope as being about 'opening the future' and a 'movement forward' (Crapanzano 2003: 15). Pascal's longer-term hopes for home, for a passport and for a return to his maternal family are a driving force directed towards a long-term future. Pascal's hopes are, in Lauren Berlant's sense, 'optimistic' and provide a meaning, motivating him to 'keep on living on and to look forward to being in the world' (Berlant 2011: 33).

Zigon (2009: 258) describes this facet of hope as a 'temporal orientation of conscious and intentional action'. Working in post-Soviet Moscow with people rehabilitating from drug addictions, Zigon is careful to think less about hope's passive/active stance and more about its temporality, with its 'intentional and creative use of the past and the future' (ibid.). I want to follow up on this and differentiate along lines of temporality, between the long-term hope for home-as-ideal-homeland and what I will call daily hopes, translated into the home-making activities of home-as-process.

Long-term hope and daily hope do not easily fit into the passive/active dichotomy as both can be motivating and forward-driving, involving perseverance and change. The first facet of hope as a long-term prospect of home – often an idealized homeland – was, for my informants, linked to a (personal and/or collective) past, but pointed towards the future (Mallett 2004; Massey

1992). Quotidian hopes could, on the one hand, be the everyday processes and activities aimed towards fulfilling this long-term longing and hence be active steps in the present. But they can also seem to be more focused on waiting, continuity and daily survival (Schielke 2015; Jeffrey 2010), rather than being steps on 'a linear path of time toward the better future' (Zigon 2009: 257). They can resemble Zigon's second notion of hope as an 'existential stance of being-in-the-world' that 'allows one to keep going or persevere through one's life' (ibid.: 258; Jeffrey 2010: 5). However – and here I am departing from Zigon – my informants sometimes worked against their long-term hopes, setting themselves back through a continuous focus on the 'distraction' of a high brought about by drugs and alcohol. Some of their 'purposeless timepass' (Jeffrey 2010) was not entirely useless – at least initially. As I will describe in chapter 3, for instance, some of the men I worked with saw the short-term focus – or what, in the context of drug addiction, I call 'drug time' – as something positive: it initially gave them a certain sense of control and the opportunity (and illusion) of being able to forget.

I will, in the last part of this section, further examine the different types of hope for home. I will look at future-oriented long-term hope (for home in the idealized homeland) as it is translated into the endpoint of a *projet de vie* and then broken down into daily life on the street in what I call home-as-process.

Home-as-Process: The Ambiguity of Hope

Since the day I met Pascal, sometime in early 2015, his most urgent concern was leaving the street. A room in a temporary shelter, which Pascal saw as a first step in that direction, might eventually be given to him by the charity Freedom, which he had been visiting on a daily basis for several months. The Catholic organization's drop-in centre is based in the north of Paris, only about a ten-minute walk from the Gare du Nord. Pascal arrived every morning around 10AM after having found his way from the parking deck at La Défense, where he spent his nights with his closest acquaintance, a Polish man his age called Lobo. He had found a temporary shelter at the parking garage he went to each night, though he did not feel very safe there ('There are all these French teenagers; it's not safe. I am afraid they are going to steal stuff'). However, it was better than the street, the pavement, and it was also better than the train in which the two of them used to sleep ('You never knew when the security there would throw you out'). When sleeping at the parking deck with Lobo, two levels down from the busy squares of the financial district, Pascal would prepare his bed using piles of pillows, cardboard, his sleeping bag and plastic bags.

Freedom was where Pascal was able to relax:

> I have become a big gamer there [at *Freedom*] ... I like going there, drinking my milk coffee. ... It is the only space where I can really relax. It is more or less a place where I can relax. Where there is a little bit of normality. ... That's where time passes most

quickly. From 9–12AM – I almost don't notice it. ... When you are doing Freedom ...,
you have something to do. It makes it much easier.

Pascal was also keen on thinking more concretely about his prospects of
finding a job:

> I don't know the system here. They have these 'formations' but they only take six or
> nine months, not three years like in Germany. I want to start thinking about that
> now. I can't use any of my German qualifications. So I don't know how to find any-
> thing. I was thinking about the SNCF [French train company]. You talk to tourists
> and tell them where to go. But then you don't really earn anything and, I don't know,
> it's not really a good job.

When I left Paris in the summer of 2016, some of this thinking had already
been put into practice: he had started an apprenticeship course and was
granted a second court hearing regarding his asylum case. With the help of his
assistant social, he had found a temporary shelter, La Péniche, where he would
be able to stay for several years, if need be.

Let me recap: Pascal's long-term hope was for a home (Germany as the
homeland) that would come with identity papers, a place to stay, a job and a
relationship with his family. I called this his long-term hope for home-as-
ideal-homeland; this was his future-oriented, reflected-upon hope for home.
In the immediate short term, however, Pascal was – with the support of his
assistant social – able to break his ideal down into manageable portions of
daily home-making that seemed to lead towards the goal of leaving the street.
To start with, he made an effort to find a sheltered place to sleep every night,
first in the train, then at La Défense and eventually at La Péniche. He also
formed much clearer ideas about what kind of a job he might be able to pick
up while in France, started an apprenticeship and made progress in his asylum
case. He created everyday 'normality' in the form of routines and repeating
rhythms by going to Freedom for coffee, games and warmth every day. These
routines were part of Pascal's daily home-making activities and, as such, part
of his daily practices of 'happiness' (Walker 2015: 5; Vigh 2015 on emplace-
ment; Englund 2006). While working on realizing his future hope for an ideal
home in Germany, Pascal – on a daily basis – was constructing approxima-
tions and temporary homes in physical and emotional forms. Like many of the
other homeless people in Paris that I will present in this volume, Pascal was
not merely waiting for something to happen, for his ideal future to materialize;
he was working towards it by breaking it down into little chunks, which would,
hopefully, ultimately add up, while also contributing to his daily survival.

In more general terms, Pascal, Sabal, Alex and the large majority of the
people I worked with were living in conditions of material scarcity; neither
money, food nor shelter were reliably available, forcing them to focus on these
quintessential parts of home again and again. In Part II of this volume (chapters 1–3), I will describe in further detail how home was made on a day-to-day
basis – what I call home-as-process. Brun and Fábos (2015) position the idea

of home-as-process at the centre of their categorization. They describe it as a set of everyday practices; 'such practices involve both material and imaginative notions of home and may be improvements or even investments to temporary dwellings; they include the daily routines that people undertake … and the social connections people make' (Brun and Fábos 2015:12; Botticello 2007, Veness 1993). Home-as-process does not have to relate to a fixed structure, but can relate to practices and routines, as exemplified by Pascal's description above; it comes in the form of a 'highly complex system of ordered relations with place, an order that orientates us in space, in time, and in society' (Dovey 1985: 39). As for Pascal, who went to the homeless centre at 9AM every morning and ordered his day around the centre's opening hours, giving a temporal order to the day, as well as the environment, was a key part of his daily home-making. I find the culmination of this focus on order – and routine – in Mary Douglas's definition of home:

> home is always a localizable idea. Home is located in space but it is not necessarily a fixed space. It does not need bricks and mortar, it can be a wagon, a caravan, a board, or a tent. It need not be a large space, but space there must be, for home starts by bringing some space under control. (Douglas 1991: 289)

Thus, home, in this sense, relates to the process of controlling a particular space, finding a structure and regular rhythms, and constructing routines (Easthope 2004: 135; O'Mahony 2013). This takes us away from the past and the future and back to the present. It takes us away from long-term hopes, shifting the focus to everyday activities and what I call daily hopes.

Pascal's long-term hopes were broken down into daily hopes, stepping stones in the *projet de vie* leading towards a return to his homeland Germany. The daily processes are meant to add up. However, I will illustrate, through the story of Barut, how this can be much more ambiguous. Barut's focus on daily, short-term hopes, such as drug-taking and the begging cycle associated with it, distracted him from his long-term longing for home (with his family). Hence, for Barut, daily home-making sometimes worked against long-term hopes for home.

***

While, for Pascal, long-term and daily hopes often led in the same direction, they were opposed – at least temporarily – for many, including Barut. Berlant reminds us that hopes in general can be ambiguous, alternately enabling and disabling us and sometimes doing both at once (Berlant 2007: 35). Long-term hopes do not necessarily break down into daily hopes. Particularly in situations of suffering and poverty, the ability to hope can be lost (Throop 2015: 50); one can become trapped or focus on short-term moments of happiness, such as, for instance, the high that a drug or alcohol can provide. The influence of law enforcement can also play a large part in this conflict, causing people to become 'stuck' in the present. Daily hopes can then become debilitating and stifling. Barut's story will allow me to focus on the role played by drugs, as objects of daily hopes, in his life on the street.

Barut was from Bulgaria. Before coming to Paris to live with his brother, who has a secure job in real estate there, Barut had worked in construction in Spain for ten years. By 2015, he had been in Paris for five years, most of which had been spent on the street – between begging at the Gare du Nord, shooting up in front of the Lariboisière Hospital and sleeping at La Défense. As a result of his high dependence on drugs, neither his brother in Paris nor his father in Bulgaria spoke to him anymore. Over time, I saw Barut take every drug he could get hold of. The basis of his 'drug diet' was methadone, a substitute for heroin that he received free from Sun, a charity devoted to risk-reduction measures for people struggling with drug addiction. If he was able to earn enough money begging in the train station, Barut also smoked crack because of the 'small high' he got from it and because it kept him going – it kept him awake and fended off thoughts of his failures holding on to jobs and a more stable life. He also injected Skenan, a morphine-based drug available from pharmacies that was usually given out to cancer patients, but that was easily available on the secondary market on the streets behind the train station.

However, like Pascal, Barut wanted to quit the drugs. I met him late one night in April 2016, more towards the west of Paris. He was sitting in a niche between two houses in the pitch dark, totally alone. At first, he didn't recognize me and asked me for money. He was embarrassed when he realized who I was. When I sat down with him, he started humming a tune. It was the beginning of 'Under the Bridge' by the Red Hot Chili Peppers. Barut went on to explain his thoughts:

> I sit here on my own. I feel lonely. There is so much stuff going on down there [Gare du Nord] and I just came up here to be alone. I want to change ... I want to leave this life and get clean.

Barut wanted to change – wanted to leave 'them' (his group of acquaintances) and 'there' (the train station where he spends most of his time) behind. He 'knew' that he was able to get clean; he had undergone drug rehabilitation before when he was in Spain and a couple of years previous in Paris: 'This [the street] is not for me. I should be somewhere else. I know I can do it.' He was confident about his own will and also, in a way, about what he conceived of as his destiny. He felt that he *should* be somewhere else; he shouldn't be lonely and dependent on a city as his 'only friend'.

For Barut, the translation of his long-term longing to leave the street and the drugs behind into practical and everyday actions was complicated. Taking drugs was one of the daily home-making practices with which he removed himself from time, living according to the drug cycle (what I call 'drug time'): it was both a consolation for him and a constant source of frustration. He wanted to forget where he was, his situation and his lack of contact with his family, his lack of a network of friends or a stable and secure shelter – in short, his lack of a home. In moments like the one described above, he realized that drugs were not the solution, that they only temporarily helped him to push away his long-term hopes by replacing them with a feeling generated by a substance. Barut knew that the substances were not only little more than a cover-up, but also that they were keeping him on the street. They generated a routine and an order for him – and, in this sense, a home – which were all-encompassing and time- and thought-consuming, what I describe as the cycle of addiction time: making enough money for the next shot, 'scoring' the drugs, shooting up, getting a beer, making money again.

In spring 2016 and also later that year, I saw Barut take more drugs than ever – sometimes spending up to three days on the street without sleep while on crack. However, his long-term hopes to leave – the way he talks about them, the way he seems to feel about them and how his 'failure' makes him sad and angry – did not go away. They were only 'on hold', as he put it, while he focused on a present dominated by daily hopes and practices, which, in his case, often worked against his long-term hopes.

***

Drinking – or, in Barut's case, taking drugs – can be about forgetting. It can induce a 'fleeting state of being' happy (Throop 2015), while at the same time threatening both his immediate and his longer-term wellbeing. Barut was often exclusively focused on the daily hopes and the organization necessary to feel 'high'. This orderly routine was home-as-process in the present for Barut, but, unlike in Pascal's case, it did not accord with or lead to his long-term hope to leave the street. Barut's daily hopes and moments of happiness were not connecting him to the future; they were not contributing to his long-term hopes. On the contrary, they severed the connection to the past and future and resulted in him living according to addiction time, as a result of which he felt greater despair.

Two factors contributed to the emergence of moments of epiphany, as described above, when the long-term hope of leaving the street came back into focus: his own original suffering in the form of his lack of a home (money, shelter, family, security) and the suffering induced by taking the drugs (which were physically hurtful and mentally stifling). The two sources of suffering could turn into a driving force. Barut was fed up with his addiction. He was aware of how it separated him from his family and kept him on the street. While striving for happiness was firstly translated into daily, short-term 'highs' on drugs, it also eventually manifested itself in a second temporality of an imagined future home.

Conclusion

I have established the analytical frame within which the chapters of this volume operate. What does home look like for the people I worked with on the streets of Paris, who are regularly called homeless, *sans-abris* and *sans domicile fixe*? Through the narratives of Pascal, Sabal, Alex and Barut, I have explored various dimensions of this question and arrived at curiously entangled ideas of home – in *home-as-ideal-homeland* and *home-as-process* – and different temporalities of hope. The main ambiguity underlying the remainder of this volume is the constant struggle between the two notions of home and their respective temporal directions. While home-as-ideal-homeland is situated in a past-inspired future, home-as-process is situated in the present. The notion of hope connects the two. The two can come together, as in Pascal's case, with the hope for a return to the ideal homeland broken down into steps leading towards that goal, daily hopes adding up in home-as-process, or they can work against each other, at least temporarily, as in the case of Barut, struggling with addition and how it seems at first to help him to order his thoughts, but keeps him stuck in the short term – what I will call 'addiction time'.

The following two parts give rise to two overarching questions: in Part II, I will observe how people operationalize short-term hopes. How do people construct their meandering and at times interrupted paths? In chapters 1–3, I examine short-term survival, the individual ordering practices of begging, shelter-making and drug taking. In Part III, the focus will shift to how longer-term hopes come back into focus, mostly with the help of *assistants sociaux*. How did my informants connect to institutional support and their *projets de vie*?

Notes

1. APUR 2015: 10; while it is acknowledged that a proportion of migrant homeless people are in Paris without papers and should technically be registered as refugees, the APUR study explicitly states that the exact percentage is unknown. The proportion in my group of informants was relatively small, certainly under 10 per cent.
2. On the contrary, he engaged heavily in drinking while he was in France.

Part II

SHORT-TERM HOPES
SURVIVING THE STREET

1

Labour with, off and on the Street

François is woken up by park wardens every morning. He sleeps on the steps under the roof of a little garden shed in the playground right next to the Saint Vincent de Paul church. 'It depends on the time of the year, but they usually open the park around 7AM and they know I'm there. They leave me alone but I have to get up.' In 2015, François spent most of his days between this park, the Gare du Nord and the Leader Price supermarket. Once up, he walked from the park – which became busy later in the day with school kids playing football, adolescents smoking weed and people playing cards – to the Leader Price up the road. 'They open at 7:30AM. And the beer there is the cheapest, anyway.' When I first met François, I was unsure about whether we would get along. He was an outspoken, loud and rowdy Frenchman in his mid-fifties. He joked around – particularly with the young women on outreach tours[1] who visited him regularly – and made fun of the world around him. He loved to sing French *chansons*. His voice was pleasant, smoky; it felt like the street itself was singing when he recounted the tales of Yves Montand and Edith Piaf. François considered himself a *gitan* [French gypsy], a traveller of the world who never rested in any given place for too long. Over eight years previous, after a decade-long relationship during which he fathered three children (the names of whom he had tattooed on his arms), he left his family behind to return to the road. His life since then has been spent between Paris and the *banlieues*, begging, drinking and singing.

He tried to ensure that he always had enough money left for at least one beer in the morning. The extra strong 8.5 per cent can was 65 cents at the Leader Price supermarket. Thereafter, his day at the train station commenced; 300 metres up the road, the main entrance of the Gare du Nord, with its shiny new statue of a red angel-bear, lured him in. His daily work centred around the busy entrances of the station; money was gathered from taxi drivers, metro and train passengers, tourists and shop owners. Over the course of several hours, François meandered between his resting spots – next to a small Monop supermarket west of the station, on the corner of a branch of the Caisse d'Epargne bank south of it or right outside the eastern entrance – and the Leader Price.

Occasionally, he jumped up to ask passers-by for money more directly or to empty his bladder in one of the public urinals positioned at every corner of the station at that time. However, he was always on the watch: for people who would give him money and for cigarettes on the floor, butts that were still burning and contained some tobacco to smoke, carelessly thrown away by people entering the station. He was constantly working with the resources the city provided: money given to him by passers-by, the spot where the park guards let him sleep, forgotten or discarded cigarettes, shed roofs, taxi drivers, public toilets, supermarkets. François was working not only on, but with and off the street, using the resources it provided.

***

The Red Hot Chili Peppers' song 'Under the Bridge', referred to by Barut, is perhaps the most lyrical description of the complexities of surviving and making money on the street, and makes explicit the most common problem of this way of life: my informants were challenged by material poverty, as well as loneliness, social isolation and often exclusion from the formal economy (Gaetz and O'Grady 2002). On a daily basis, future-oriented hopes have to be broken down or even suspended for survival practices that frequently involve the city, the 'only friend' available. The future has to withdraw to the background to allow a focus on the immediate – which, in turn, is paradoxically the only way to make the future possible at all. The focus in this chapter will be on the daily practices and routines around making money and more broadly using the infrastructure of the city, which is conveyed by Arendt's notion of *labour* (Arendt 1998). Arendt defines labour as a process that produces 'vital necessities' and assures individual survival (ibid.: 7, 47). Unlike work,[2] the product of which is always material (ibid.: 86, 93), it leaves nothing behind, is unproductive. Labour is never-ending and repetitive (ibid.: 102) and, as such, cyclical, because the need to consume – the second movement in the endless cycle of labour – is never satisfied. Labourers are, according to Arendt, bound up by the necessity of daily survival. She likens labour to the 'menial servant' (ibid.: 93); in antiquity, it was the way of life of the slave. But, unlike her ancient predecessors, she doesn't completely view labour as something one needs to rid oneself of. She believes, on the contrary, that 'the perfect elimination of the pain and effort of labour would not only rob biological life of its most natural pleasures but deprive the specifically human life of its very liveliness and vitality' (ibid.: 120). Labour – and the balance between pain and repetition, but also its direct link to the need to consume (ibid.: 134) – is an essential part of the human condition.

Following Arendt's conceptualization, I describe begging – and making use of the city's infrastructure – as a process of labour.[3] My informants begged to survive; they didn't produce anything of lasting value or importance beyond ensuring their immediate ability to consume in a repetitive circuit. Thus, begging is categorically unproductive – unlike the work of shelter-making, which involves creating a material home, at least temporarily (see chapter 2). Without romanticizing the pain and suffering associated with the daily labour of begging for my informants, I also follow Arendt in her more optimistic conception of labour as fundamental to one's life. The pain of labouring is often balanced by rewards. Ethnographically, labour was directly linked to the environment of the city and public infrastructure – supermarkets, toilets, warm waiting rooms. The key operation I observed as part of this labour of hope (Pedersen 2012; see also Zigon 2005) was managing visibility. At times, the labouring practices of homeless people consisted in making themselves visible to the public – by portraying neediness and deservingness or by using connections to regulars – to make money from passers-by; at other times, they involved becoming invisible and blending in to gain access to warmth, microwaves and benches; and they always crossed the line between physical and emotional labour.

Consuming Lives

Arendt describes labour and consumption as two parts of the same cyclical movement (Arendt 1998: 96). Before I consider the labour involved in making money, let me initially address the question of what this money is *spent* on. There is no general statistical survey on the consumption patterns of homeless people in Paris.[4] However, some indication of these patterns can be derived from other data.

A significant amount of homeless people's money is spent on alcohol and drugs. In their most recent overview of the available data on homeless people in Paris, APUR (2011) concludes that, based on data from the Samu Social, almost 30 per cent of all homeless people in Paris struggle with at least one kind of addiction, excluding tobacco (Laporte and Chauvin 2009). The same study claims that the two train stations in the north of Paris – which were the focus point of my fieldwork – are marked by a very high prevalence of both alcohol addiction and *toxicomanie* (hard drugs) (ibid.: 8). This reflects my observation that, among my group of informants – who were all begging and living on the street, another condition associated with high rates of addiction (Gaetz and O'Grady 2002) – up to 90 per cent were regularly consuming large quantities of beer or wine and around 50 per cent regularly consumed marijuana and/or morphine, crack and other pills.

Five concrete examples will illustrate this point and introduce further areas of spending, such as food, cigarettes, daily hygiene products and housing. François might serve as a good example of a relatively representative pattern. Most of the money he made on an average day – between €10 and €20 – was spent on wine (he drank cheap bottles of rosé, at one litre for under €3), cigarettes, food and the occasional bottle of shampoo, bar of soap or item of clothing. Carl had a very similar consumption pattern, though wine was substituted with beer (he needed about ten cans of strong beer a day) and marijuana was a major additional expense; hence, his budget per day was slightly bigger (between €20 and €30). Sabal and most others in his group, including Natasha, mainly consumed wine, beer, hot food and occasionally marijuana too. I found only slightly different patterns among the group around Barut, all of whom not only smoked weed regularly, but also regularly injected or smoked hard drugs (heroin substitutes, crack – see chapter 3) and took pills in addition to the alcohol. This added between €10 and €50, depending on the quantity of drugs consumed.

Food distribution, in particular, was very well taken care of by the public administration and the charity sector in Paris, meaning that only a small proportion of earnings was spent on food. In 2010, more than three million lunches and dinners were distributed in Paris (APUR 2011); most of these were given out through *food bons*, pre-packaged lunch or dinner boxes or in soup kitchens, such as the Restaurant du Cœur or the Armée du Salut. In an earlier study, about 25 per cent of people living on the street claimed the *bons*, while 29 per cent would regularly eat from the distributed boxes (Brousse, de la Rochère and Mass 2002). In a similar way, showers and simple hygiene products (soap, shampoo, shaving kits, underwear) were available for free in Paris from institutions such as the municipally run Bains et Douches (eighteen free-to-use centres in Paris) or the Croix Rouge [Red Cross], as well as in various day centres.

In what might be the best and most comprehensive ethnographic overview of street homelessness in Paris to date, Anne Garnier-Muller (2000) situates her group of informants in a similar network of institutions that homeless people visit to access specific services: she finds that more than 30 per cent of her informants regularly visited soup kitchens, for instance; roughly the same number also visited other institutions, such as day centres, which helped with both the provision of food and with hygiene (ibid.: 181). While a small group regularly received payment for work, both legally and on the black market (about 15 per cent, according to official statistics on Paris (Emmanuelli and Landrieu 2006)), some people sold homeless newspapers (such as *Macadam, Le Réverbère, La Rue* and *L'Itinérant*) or received money from the government. The RMI (*Revenu minimum d'insertion* [minimum income for the purpose of inclusion]), while available to a larger number of individuals, was only taken up by about 20 per cent of Garnier-Muller's informants; 40% refused public support altogether and instead engaged in what Garnier-Muller calls illicit (stealing, dealing drugs) or tolerated (begging, black-market work) sources of income. According to her estimate, about 80 per cent of the income made by people on the street came from such illicit or tolerated activities (Garnier-Muller 2000: 160). Turning to the most important of these tolerated sources of daily income, she claims that about 70 per cent of the people she encountered regularly earned their money by begging (ibid.: 164).

Money, Money, Money: The Labour of *Mendicité*

It was the end of the summer of 2015. François and I were sitting in front of the glass façade in the western part of the Gare du Nord, close to the departure lounges for the Eurostar trains. It was getting late, but the summer had not fully disappeared and it was still bright outside. 'I will show you how I work now. Come with me.' I had just explained to François who I was and that I was interested in learning about his 'survival strategies' when he decided it was a good time to show me around his workplace. The station was busy and one taxi after another drove up in front of it. François was headed towards the first taxi in the queue. He walked to the end of the row of cars on Rue Lafayette and knocked on the driver's window. The man looked up at him and shook his head. François wasn't too persistent; somehow, he knew – from years of experience, perhaps –whom he could make money from. Confidence was key. The next car had its window open. François addressed the man inside:

> 'T'as une petite pièce ou une cigarette, chef?' [Do you have change or a cigarette, boss?]
> > 'Je n'fume pas. Mais, tiens.' [I don't smoke but take this.]
> > [hands over a 50c coin]
> > 'Merci, chef.' [Thanks, boss.]

The donor nodded at him as François slowly walked to the next car, a smile on his face. Before addressing the taxi driver, he looked at me: 'Not too hard, is it?' The row of about twenty cars brought in €1.50 and two cigarettes, all for less than ten minutes of work.

Begging was by far the most common income-creating activity – or work (*travail*), as François called it – among my informants.[5] Turning oneself into a needy and deserving person involved physical effort – walking around, sitting on the pavement, monotonously repeating the same sentence and the same narrative – and emotional labour – overcoming shame and embarrassment, making up narratives,[6] supporting these narratives through appearance, creating a network of regulars.[7] The act of begging, repeated every day, also started with concrete decisions: which spot to choose? Whom to approach? This is where the labour began.

Choosing the Right Location

Carl, who had been a soldier in the German special forces for over eight years – travelling the world before being injured and traumatized in a grenade attack in Afghanistan – introduced me to an important dimension of the begging process. I will also describe how crucial self-presentation through language and clothing was, but the first decision concerned location, the begging spot: what made one location better suited than another? For the longest time, the Gare de l'Est was Carl's preferred venue not only due to the fast trains arriving from Germany, carrying a lot of potential revenue in the form of German tourists visiting Paris, but also because of the train station's architecture:

> The big entrance – 200, 250 m with the taxis – where you can walk along in about 10 minutes and in exactly the same interval the people you just asked have already

disappeared into the train station again. ... Most are there for the length of one ciga-
rette. ... My strategy is to not stand on one spot but to walk around. You can ask
100–150 people in 10 minutes or something like that.

Doing round after round without asking the same people twice, Carl was
easily able to make €10 or €20 at the station in the course of a morning or afternoon. Enough people were streaming in and out of the two neighbouring stations, the Gare de l'Est and the Gare du Nord, to produce a large crowd of
potential donors. While Carl preferred the closed circuit of the Gare de l'Est,
others such as Barut chose to walk from west to east, following the long axis of
the Gare du Nord. My informants consciously thought about their route, testing
new routes in an attempt to maximize the outcome while minimizing effort.

A second factor that made certain locations preferable was the availability
of givers, in particular regular givers, ideally with their purses or wallets
already in their hands. Carl developed a special connection to a second venue,
closer to the Gare du Nord. Every day at around the same time – about 5.30PM,
when people left the offices in the area and were on their way home – he positioned himself right next to a bakery just south of the park, next to the Saint
Vincent de Paul church. It was a busy street that led down to the *Grands
Boulevards* which attracted people *en masse*. While not all of the people he
asked knew him, a significant number became regulars over time. They would
sometimes see him every day and get to know him little by little with advanta-
geous outcomes:

> After some days, some people got to know me. And then they gave me money
> without me even asking them. Then it's easy. ... You talk to them a little – like at the
> bakery. Short conversations.

The bakery and its customers provided two favourable components for
Carl's begging work: the bakery was frequented by both a changing set of
people over short time cycles and returning cohorts over longer time cycles.
People would only come once a day, but they came every day – or at least
several days a week. This made it easy for Carl to become acquainted with the
regulars, who in turn were more likely to give him money.[8] This also meant less
effort in terms of asking people and walking around and explaining himself,
with a higher level of income thanks to the personal connections developed
over time. Additionally, people came to the bakery with the intention of
spending money and Carl would catch them either as they were about to open
their purses or wallets to buy something or when they came out of the bakery
with change in their hands.[9] The barrier of having to make an extra effort to
give a donation was thus minimalized.

Indeed, regulars play a key part in begging (Lankenau 1999: 312, 314).
Mirroring what I found during my previous work on relationships with regulars
in London (Lenhard 2014), they fulfil an important social role (they form dyadic
relationships with people on the street), as well as a material function. Investing

in regulars as part of the labouring process – like capital investments – would pay off over time. Most importantly, such investments reduce the amount of labour that needs to be put into asking the next time around.

Other informants of mine banked on similar locations, where regularity was paired with a preparedness to spend money. The Punjabis around Sabal often positioned themselves outside either bank branches or supermarkets, as did François; a changing group of people camped close to a tobacco shop inside the Gare du Nord; another group centred around Natasha – whom I will introduce in the next section – always sat outside the busy fast-food restaurant Quick on the opposite side of the street to the station's main entrance.

As I will argue below, procuring money through begging can be considered labour in Arendt's sense of the word. As a practice of making home-as-process, the choice of the best location, the begging spot, as well as engaging people and overcoming certain hostile feelings – both in the potential donor and in my informants themselves – necessitates overcoming one's shame and embarrassment and at times the creative and clever construction of narratives or scripts. Where to stand, and when, was something that my informants learnt from experience and was often thought through with efficiency in mind. I will now turn to the stories and the presentation of self that are crucial in the begging encounter. How did my informants display and balance neediness and deservingness, the two most important attributes in the process of begging? What role did a network of regulars play? How did my informants' skills develop over time?

Emotional and Physical Labour

Carl: It is also dependent on the weather, the time of the day. It is easier to ask at night because you are less present. Working when the sun is shining is much harder for me. It is embarrassing. ... It is really exhausting to use the same sentence all day long, completely monotonously. And to walk around. Physically, you are really exhausted after two, three hours. ... Bad moods, no motivation – all this puts extra pressure on it.

Pascal: I have never done anything like this before – begging. It's only punks and Roma who ask for money in Germany. It was this ... pride. They don't see you as equal. I always refused. Didn't want to do it. Until this one day. Lalo [Pascal's Polish friend] told me if you want to smoke, you have to beg [*Taxi machen*]. I didn't have a choice. The first day – on this street opposite the park – I barely asked people. I didn't make any money, not a cent, no. Only in the end, 10 cents from a man. ... I got rid of my shame. I accepted that I was on the street, that I was homeless [*obdachlos*]. ... After this day, I went begging every day for one month. It became easier. ... But I am still looking when I ask people. ... When begging I need beer, at least two. To lose my sense of shame. Two beers, then a [piece of] chewing gum.

While Carl was concerned about both the exhaustion associated with walking around and constantly asking people for money and the embarrassment of asking, Pascal was focused on the second aspect. Pascal, a newcomer to the world of begging and the street in general, explained how his pride and shame made it hard for him to beg at first. Begging marked him as dependent and ultimately as poor and homeless. He didn't want people to know that he was on the street. He didn't want people to put him into that category. Overcoming shame and embarrassment and accepting the categorization of 'homeless' required psychological labour, often enabled by marijuana or alcohol – which had to be concealed, for instance, by using gum. Pascal felt inhibited:

> That's my biggest fear, to go down as a real hard-core homeless person. The shame. ... Perhaps it is a question of my mentality. The others live with it. ... They don't have respect. ... I couldn't beg in the metro. Ekki [a Finnish man in Pascal's circle of acquaintances] does. ... I often see how people joke about him: 'Regard lui, regard là!' [*sic*] [Look at him, look there!] They laugh about him, how he is begging. I couldn't do that.

Pascal was aware of the inferior position he was in when asking people for money. The risk of categorization and the implied social hierarchy that came with 'outing himself' as homeless worried him. He wanted to fight against what Georg Simmel (1908) considers the quintessential feature of being poor: 'What makes one poor is not the lack of means. The poor person ... is the individual who receives assistance because of this lack of means' (ibid.: 140). A sense that he belonged *outside* of the group of homeless people, of the ones who were assisted, was important for Pascal's feeling of self-worth, but also as a tactic. Below, I will elaborate on how Pascal and others managed to keep up a façade through the use of clothes (Smiley and Middlemass 2016), but words, stories and narratives were the most important part of this labour. Pascal used the potential ambiguity of his own standing in relation to the group of donors as a way of hustling.

A clever hustle – part of the 'art of deception ... changing the rule of the game and misdirecting the audience in order to "get over" [to get their money]' (Williams and Milton 2015: 5) – is key to one's success as a beggar. The goal is to convince people to give to you without being too forceful and intrusive. In fact, linguistically speaking, *mendicité* [begging] is etymologically related to *mensonge* [lie], further strengthening the connection between hustling as deception (lying, making up certain facts, displaying only part of the truth about oneself) and the labour of begging. Pascal learnt over time, after numerous days of trial and error, which part of himself to present in which situations, while at the same time trying to be true to his identity. He was learning how to hustle people without necessarily revealing his homelessness by forging personal connections.[10]

Even more relevant in relation to narrative being the most important part of the begging encounter is the concept of the 'script'. In the context of US drug treatment programmes, E. Summerson Carr (2006, 2011) explains how language is used by patients to get what they want – often a certain prescribed drug – rather than what they need. Users in the outpatient programme in the American Midwest would engage in what was called 'flipping the script': 'clients' linguistic interactions with therapists were commonly characterized by carefully constructed, institutionally astute, and strategic performances rather than simple acts of self-reference' (Summerson Carr 2011: 196). In other words, they told the doctors what they wanted to hear in a verbal performance, mimicking a certain kind of recovering client without being honest about their actual inner state (ibid.: 188ff, 213). Over time, people learn which ways of speaking – which scripts or hustles – work and which don't, as they engage with more and more institutions and individuals. These scripts – narrated and performed presentations of certain aspects of the self, as I will further describe below – are part of the emotional labour involved in begging.

Arlie Russell Hochschild (1983; see also Wharton 2009) categorizes emotional labour as labour that is face-to-face (or voice-to-voice) and that aims to produce 'an emotional state in another person – gratitude or fear, for example' (Hochschild 1983: 147). While his study focuses on trained Delta flight attendants, doctors, lawyers and salesmen, at least part of my informants' labour fits into this category. Emotional labour is labour that goes beyond 'suppress[ing] feelings of frustration, anger or fear' and is about 'the production of a state of mind in others' (ibid.: 154, 156). While there is no employer managing staff members' emotional states in the case of my informants (an important element in Hochschild's study), I find his categorization useful when paired with 'scripts'. My informants engaged in both *repressive* emotional labour, by suppressing emotions of shame and embarrassment, and *expressive* emotional labour, by displaying deservingness and neediness and evoking sympathy in the givers (Hoang 2010). As we will see below, learnt 'scripts' – in their core form of a spoken narrative and supported through appearance and clothing – are crafted as a tool of expressive emotional labour. They are used to solicit money from people by evoking sympathy.

I observed how expressive 'scripts' focused particularly on three axes that balance each other: neediness, deservingness and personal connection (ad hoc or in networks over time). Potential givers are more likely to give when they understand that the person begging *needs* their personal help; most want to make sure that the person is *deserving* of their help and won't spend the money on drugs or alcohol; and they are more likely to engage with the person when they feel a personal *connection*. Ideally, all three come together, but at times one of the missing elements might need to be compensated for by another. I will work through these three axes – what I see as the core of the labour of begging through scripts and hustles – by focusing mainly on language and narrative, but also physical presentation, in the following section. My informants learnt over time which scripts worked in which situations and which axes to focus on with whom; they developed the skills of labour with, on and off the street.

Neediness

Let me present a different perspective on an observation I made above. Early on in my fieldwork, in the winter of 2014, I took a late-night tour around the back of the Gare du Nord – a site that was, at that time, unfamiliar to me. It was around midnight and it was a little wet out. I had just come from observing people running around in the station and decided, on the way home, to walk down the road towards Rue Lafayette. On the corner of the Caisse d'Epargne bank, two men in their late thirties were sitting on the ground. One of them spoke only English, while the other had relatively good French. They were both originally from India and had already spent some time in Paris. Within a minute or so, the one who spoke English to me directed my attention to his foot. Even in the dark of the night, I was able to see how bad the skin looked. Not only was it black from the dirt of the street – he was wearing neither shoes nor socks – but it was also strangely wrinkled, almost as if the skin was broken into little pieces. He explained to me how much it itched and that it hurt when he scratched it. Finally, they asked me if they could have some money to get into a room for the night. The other man was constantly looking at me with his dark eyes, his head bent down. I almost couldn't bear to face the two of them; I was appalled to see them sitting there like that, in desperate need of shelter, medical care, help. I felt that I had to help. On that night, I broke my usual rule of not giving to people I didn't know. I gave some money to the two men and walked back home.

That was the first time I met Sabal and Bouti and it was one of the only times I was convinced to give money to as yet unknown informants. What was different in the situation I described? I perceived the two Punjabi men as acutely in need of my help on that night – because of their illness, their apparent neediness – a feeling that was aggravated by the visibility of their bad health, their lack of hygiene, the weather, the state of their clothes. I was also influenced by the fact that the two didn't really seem to speak French, that they looked foreign and lost.

Studies in other contexts[11] show that even more extreme forms of displayed neediness are an important part of the begging encounter. Stephen E. Lankenau (1999: 290, 305), in his analysis of panhandlers in Washington, DC, observed how his informants 'manipulate[d] signs and symbols to demonstrate ... need' by adapting their dress code and shaping their public persona to earn what Candace Clarke (1997) calls 'sympathy credits'. The aim was always to appear in such a way that one's sympathy margin was high: 'Panhandlers that do not look impoverished may unwittingly drain their sympathy margin and receive fewer contributions' (Lankenau 1999: 307). The emotional (and physical) labour of appearing needy is not necessarily enough to solicit gifts, however; people also needed to be perceived as 'deserving' of a contribution (or 'respectable', in Lankenau's words), which brings us to the second axis of the begging narrative.

Deservingness

Excuse me, I am really sorry to bother you, but I don't know what to do anymore. I tried to reach my family but nobody is picking up the phone, and somebody has stolen my wallet, so I can't take out any more money or go to the bank. I don't live far away, and I only need €5.30 to pay for my train there. Would you be able to help me? I would be so grateful to you. I am really sorry to bother you.

For Camilla, a young Eastern European woman doing her rounds at the Gare du Nord, asking people for money for a train fare, the most important part of her spiel was looking the part. For several days in a row, I observed how she interacted with people. Her approach was based on people taking her to be 'one of them'. I observed Camilla use a variation of the above story very successfully over several days addressing people at the Gare du Nord. Her narrative was only one part of her presentation, which was dependent on her looking 'as if' she had actually just lost her wallet on the way home. Whenever I saw her, her hair was combed and her clothes were in good shape, particularly her shoes – the item of clothing under the most pressure for homeless people. She always carried a handbag – small in comparison to the bigger bags that many of the other people living on the street would have with them, containing all the necessities of life. She fitted in very well with the general crowd of tourists and commuters at the Gare du Nord.

In her begging encounter, Camilla balances neediness with what I call deservingness. People are more likely to give if they think the person begging is not only needy but also deserving of their gift. A common hindrance, for instance, is the perception that homeless people will spend donated money on drugs or alcohol (McIntosh and Erskine 2000). In this sense, many of my informants, like Camilla, considered bodily hygiene and the cleanliness of clothing beneficial to both their health and their begging labour. Hygiene – shaving one's beard, showering regularly, washing and changing clothes – is part of one's presentability.

Camilla engaged in what Judith G. Gonyea and Kelly Melekis (2016), in their study of homeless women in Boston, described as 'passing': some of their informants presented themselves in a certain way (using a 'script' both verbally and visually) to pass as what they call a 'normal' person as opposed to a user of a homeless shelter, both in relation to members of the (potentially giving) public and professionals, such as healthcare providers. Camilla wanted to be visible – she was trying to get the attention of passers-by to ask them for money – but *not* as a homeless person. While I will go on to further explore moments when invisibility can be the aim – usually to access semi-public infrastructure, such as shops, benches or microwaves – being invisible for Camilla is about not being perceived as undeserving or as homeless.

In an interview, Carl further elaborated on deservingness and how he made it easier for people to judge him as a deserving person. For him, a successful script was about the right presentation. He would make an effort to display certain parts of his identity – his orderliness – but hide others, such as his alcohol consumption:

> You need to be able to make contact with people before you actually ask them for money. ... I don't like it when people see me with beer. I take a quick break to drink – 10–15 minutes.

While he himself likes to choose the people he asks – mostly addressing white people of both sexes and black women, on the basis of his experience – he also wants to make it easier for them to see that he is orderly, well dressed and not aggressive, dirty or drunk. He wants to appear deserving of donations and as if he won't spend the money he receives on alcohol (despite the fact that he, like Pascal, did like to drink whilst begging). Alcohol would decrease his deservingness and, as a result, his income.

All of my informants had to deal with the question of how to balance neediness and deservingness. Both are part of what Erving Goffman (1959) calls 'impression management' and David A. Snow and Leon Anderson (1993) term 'identity work': my informants engaged in a constant effort to 'anticipate, project, define, interpret, assess, accept, resist and modify images of self' (Dietz, Prus and Shaffir 1994: 60). Rather than acting in accordance with their own perception of the self, my informants were trying to appease the expectation of potential givers (Erickson 1995). Appearing 'too needy' – scruffy, unwashed, with ripped clothes – could put off potential givers. Appearing 'too deserving' might raise questions about their neediness. I found that elaborate narratives, such as Camilla's, were one way of addressing this balance. Another way was to overcome these initial, first-contact considerations in the mind of the giver and to build up a network of personal connections.

Personal Connection

Pascal was very good at building on the third axis – personal connection based on certain commonalities with donors – and cleverly adapted his 'scripts' to do so. He had learnt how to craft the narrative he presented to potential donors in order to achieve the desired result. In the following example, he was very successful because he shared his country of birth, a language, an interest in marijuana and a similar age with a group of young German donors and, later, a Congolese woman:

> It was a crazy day. There were Germans – living in Paris – young Germans who wanted to buy marijuana and I got it for them and they bought me stuff for €10. ... Then just before going back to the train [where he was sleeping at the time] there was this young woman in front of the train station. I asked her: 'Where is the Rue de Rocroy?' It is the street where Freedom is, but I wanted to start the conversation somehow. She offered to lead me there with the GPS. 'Where are you from?' 'From Congo.' *Bäm.* And I immediately dropped my SDF [homeless] story and used the story of someone who shares a home country, comes from the Congo. ... I never

thought anything would happen. ... She asked me. I didn't ask her; she asked: 'Do you have time? Do you have anything to do? Don't you want to go to a hotel with me?' ... *Rambazamba*. ... That's the kind of days you have when you make taxi. Crazy days.

Not only is this experience an example of how scripts are consciously used and changed depending on the situation in order to build temporary personal connections, it also shows how Pascal's relationship to begging has changed since he first started begging. He was able to experience positive feelings when he was successful, when the work went well. This success – firstly the procurement of money and marijuana, secondly a night at a hotel – was not random, but a consequence of the presentation of Pascal's story. Pascal himself admits that he *consciously* changed his story from that of a needy homeless person to that of somebody who shares a country of origin to forge a relationship with the second donor. Since he started begging, Pascal had developed important skills to increase his level of success. He had become more attuned – through what Summerson Carr calls 'metalinguistic labour' and experience in the field – to which 'script', which part of his narrative, identity or life – being German or Congolese, for instance – was going to help him earn money. In this instance, he quickly switched from a more direct narrative of a needy, young homeless man to building ad-hoc connections (with the Germans and the Congolese woman). The third axis – connection – was enough to make the encounter successful and offset any potentially less convincing displays of neediness or deservingness.

***

For Natasha, too, begging revolved around building personal connections with potential donors. Natasha is of Algerian descent but has lived in France most of her life. In 2015, Natasha was in her late sixties. I first met her early in 2015 in front of Quick, the French equivalent of McDonalds, opposite the main entrance of the Gare du Nord; I came to understand that this was her usual spot. Natasha always wore a woollen hat, even in the summer, from under which her dark brown eyes would look up at you when you talked to her. Her voice was deep and kind. It didn't quite seem to match her diminutive body, but perhaps years on the street had given her an inner gravity, a weightiness and depth that radiated out through her voice. Natasha shared an important commonality with many of her donors: the Arabic language. The language she shared with many of the street merchants, delivery people and passers-by to whom she spoke created an immediate connection – binding Natasha and these individuals together in an intimate bond of sharing. Bringing these bonds to the fore was important for making money.

On the other hand, Natasha's way of connecting was more long-term and less situational and included more of what we could call networking. She fully relied on her regulars. She had spent more than a decade in the Gare du Nord area and hence had an extensive network of people who were willing to help.

She didn't make up a script of deservingness or neediness, but rather employed a script of 'having something in common'. She talked about the past, how she grew up in Algeria before coming to Paris with her parents and seven siblings when she was still very young. She talked about her criminal career after she moved out of home at the age of seventeen, leading her into prison, as well as a disastrous marriage, which resulted in three children who have all grown up and apart. She didn't see them anymore and they likely didn't know what their mother was doing. Her tone became more cheerful when she started talking about her friends, the people that had accompanied her during her two decades on the streets.

But importantly, Natasha used connections she had created over years of begging on the streets and deepened them by sharing personal details, secrets. Hence, she was able to beg almost without moving, often without even asking people to give to her. She called people by their names, joked with them as they walked past and engaged in small talk about the weather, her life and the police. Very rarely, and usually only towards the end of a conversation, would she ask for money directly. She waited for the moment when the person was ready to walk away after having stopped to talk. She used this moment of inse-curity and vulnerability when the person was disentangling him- or herself from the conversation to make her advance. More often than not, it worked. Natasha was needy and deserving *enough* for people to give to her, but the key factor in her begging encounter was this personal contact.

Natasha had spent many years developing her network of people by the time I met her. She knew the police and several homeless associations had folders with her name on it; the merchants regularly gave her money, cigarettes and food. Altogether, the network Natasha had developed was more potent and easier to work than a continuous display of neediness and deservingness. Natasha's skill as a begging woman consisted less of narratives and scripts and more of continuous investment (of time and labour) in her network.

Begging as Labour

Unlike other forms of labour in what is often called the informal economy (Hart 1973), my informants' economic engagements in begging cannot be understood as a kind of 'waiting room' from which they would eventually return to the formal economy (Breman 2013). In most cases, my informants were long-term unemployed people for whom begging was not a mere transi-tory activity but an occupation. They (especially François) described it as their labour (French 'travail', German 'Arbeit' or English 'job'). In my analysis, I also need to go one step beyond what, in terms of the informal economy or 'side-walk work' (Breman 2013; Venkatesh 2006; Duneier 2000; Stewart 1997), is still very much linked to temporary but contracted forms of black-market activity, such as trading, wholesale, workshops, agriculture or rural industrial work, such as diamond cutting. In comparison to these activities, begging does not demand the stamp 'job' (or work) as it is perceived by the public as asking money for nothing (Simmel 1908). In order to get away from a distinction between real and unreal labour (Grint and Nixon 2015; Strangleman and Warren 2008), I argue that begging is important for my informants not only as a means of making money, but also as a way of structuring and ordering their day and daily life, and thus contributes to making a home on the street. Alexander Kwesi Kassah (2008), for instance, focuses on people begging in Ghana and how begging contributes to their self-worth, rather than just serving as a means of income generation. Begging is part of my informants' daily, short-term ordering and structuring; they see it as a means to an end that is ultimately necessary to enable them to envision the longer-term future.

***

In her ethnographic study of people begging and selling magazines on the Paris metro, Vanessa Stettinger (2003) divides her informants into two groups: the ones who worked (*travail*) and the ones who were merely surviving (*survie*). While she describes the former as engaging in a routine with a specific, structured project and an aim for the future in mind, the latter deployed a present-focused, order-less, day-to-day engagement with their economic activity. As a starting point, Stettinger's distinction maps onto my analysis of hope and the future in the 'Frame' chapter. I argued that my informants were situationally moving between two poles: a future-oriented long-term hope for the ideal home(land) and the necessity of daily living, with daily hope translating into home-as-process. It is here, on the conceptual level of daily hope and home-as-process, that Stettinger's analysis of work connects with what I observed.

As I already suggested, daily hopes can develop in both of the ways that Stettinger describes. It is easy to write off begging as present-oriented and existing in and for the moment, but I argue that begging, in many instances, resembles structured labour (a job or *travail*), involving skills that are learnt and developed over time: the labour of building personal relationships and developing networks (Natasha); the labour of choosing a spot (Carl); the emotional labour of suppressing the shame and embarrassment associated with asking people for money (Pascal); the physical labour of standing, walking or sitting, searching for potential givers; the labour of passing as 'one of us' by staying clean and consciously dressing up (Camilla); and, most importantly, the labour of building narratives and scripts to display deservingness and neediness and to build personal connections (Pascal, Sabal).

On a general level, all of the above activities contribute to 'making a life on the street' and thus to the process of home-making. Begging is not merely an order-less, day-to-day survival practice but often a consciously thought-out, planned routine with 'scripts' that have been learnt, revised and optimized over months and even years. Begging, for my informants, was future-oriented – not necessarily in the sense that they would save money for a certain purpose,[12] but in its concrete contribution to survival and hence the continuation of life and hope. Begging was part of a set of practices – including shelter-making (chapter 2) – that constituted the daily lives of my informants. This daily life is the necessary basis for imagining a future. People on the street are forced to spend most of their energy on being in what seems like a present-oriented state – begging, drinking, sleeping rough – while often this is the only way they can keep the future, the long-term hope for home, open. I want to take begging in this sense more seriously by categorizing it as labour and as a form of ordering one's day and world[13] and creating both a sense of self-worth and income.

While the labour my informants engaged in was future-oriented and structured in the above sense (comparable to what Stettinger calls *travail*, keeping the future open), it also resembled what Morten Axel Pedersen calls the 'work [in my case, labour] of hope'. Describing people struggling ('muddling through') at the lower end of society in urban Mongolia, Pedersen observes his informants 'practicing hope' in that they were aware of the unrealistic nature of their hopes (most of them wished to have a well-paid, stable job or a secure material life). Their daily job – which took the form of meeting people, pursuing creditors, talking money out of people, convincing people to postpone the payback date for a debt – was not about reaching a goal; it was, in Stettinger's sense, about surviving (*survie*) and continuing to live life (Pedersen 2012: 11). For them, plans (or what I called 'long-term hopes' for 'ideal homes' in chapter 1) did not have to be about realizable goals in a far-off future; they did not have to be broken down into step-by-step actionable goals. Rather, they often involved 'hoping for the magical manifestation of "profit"' (ibid.: 104). Pedersen's informants didn't necessarily strive towards something tangible and, as he claims, they 'did not want to be practical' (ibid.: 7); instead, they practised hope by continuously doing things that were 'active, intersubjective, and … social' (ibid.: 111). The activity itself was hoping, which kept them busy and gave them something to do and as such kept the future open.

My informants were similarly engaged in begging as a way of surviving and thereby 'keeping the future open' in the simple sense of staying alive. It was not part of a long-term strategic plan, but rather the daily necessity of continuing life. My informants did not think about the future every time they were begging. Some of their goals and hopes – Alex's longing for material support from the French welfare system, for instance – were unrealistic, too, and they were often aware of that. Hence, begging – and the other practices I am about to describe – was both about *travail* and *survie*, about labouring towards a hopeful future and simply surviving in the present for a future to come. My informants did not necessarily break down the desires they had to return to their homeland, for instance, into daily steps either. While I will, in chapter 5, further consider how institutions, in general, and *assistants sociaux*, in particular, helped some of my informants (notably Carl and Pascal) to define daily hopes as steps towards their long-term hopes, begging is not necessarily thought of as part of the *projet de vie* translated into a structured trajectory.

Begging as the 'labour of hope' is about survival, without a clear aim, as well as being a learnt, structured, routinized and often consciously thought-out practice. It is both the more present-based activity that only focuses on daily survival (Day, Papataxiarchis and Stewart 1999: 2), on the one hand, and a future-oriented, structured undertaking in the sense of keeping the body alive and creating time for things to unfold, to work towards the *projet de vie*.

***

When I asked Carl's opinion of begging as a job, he introduced another dimension to the debate: *its perception from the outside*.

> Johannes: Why would this [begging] not be called work?

> Carl: There is no social acceptance. For 99 per cent of the people, you are the last piece of shit. And that's how they treat you.

Carl sees a problem in the nature of begging, in that it is an activity that people look down on. From this perspective, he argues that begging could not be described as work.[14] I have already explained how, with different practices – displaying neediness and deservingness, forging connections, producing scripts – Carl and my other informants tried to overcome precisely this problem of negative regard and social acceptance. Begging ultimately involves various ways of becoming visible *in a good enough light* for the public. In contrast to other activities that people on the street engage in to make money – such as theft, violence and drug dealing, which I will discuss in subsequent chapters[15] – my informants had to learn how to be visible in order to beg. The following sections introduce other activities related to procuring goods on the street that involve public infrastructure, focusing on their role in home-as-process as well as the problem of restricted access, in which the skill of invisibility plays a more important role.

Producing Invisibility: Microwaves, Benches and Toilets

Begging and receiving gifts in a direct, one-to-one way from the public is not the only way of obtaining food and other daily necessities, nor is it the only available type of 'labour' in the sense outlined above. Urban infrastructure in and around the train station was an important part of people's daily home-making and contributed to activities of food procuration and preparation, hygiene and relaxation. Many of these activities involved the ambiguous semi-public spaces of shops and the station. How can someone who is not a customer use the microwave in a supermarket or the bench in a waiting room? The labour of scripting, of creating a narrative, is, in these instances, very similar to the begging encounters described above. Being friendly and clean might be one approach; making friends with key stakeholders another. However, unlike soliciting gifts, many of the practices aimed at accessing infrastructure are not about being visible to the public but about rendering oneself invisible. I will return to the trope of 'passing as' (Gonyea and Melekis 2016) and 'blending in' (Hodgetts, Stolte and Chamberlain 2010) to describe this second skill my informants learnt on the street.

Darius and Pawi, who spent most of their time over several months in mid- to late 2015 begging in front of the Monoprix supermarket south of the station, for instance, had not only chosen the spot because of the high number of potential givers, but also because of the staff at the supermarket. Pawi and Darius mostly obtained food not from passers-by but from the supermarket's bin, which was 'replenished' by the staff every day. At around 7PM every night, one of the supermarket employees came out with a big bag of items that were about to expire, which could include anything from fresh salad to sandwiches and cheese to fruit and ready-made dishes. Staff would allow Darius and Pawi and others from the group of Polish friends to take as much as they wanted. Here, the display of deservingness to key gatekeepers – not being aggressive or dirty right in front of the supermarket – played an important role, as in more active begging encounters. Passing as a member of the public, however, was the labour that my informants engaged in when entering the supermarket.

Every now and then, a piece of *steak haché* [raw burger patty] could be found in the bags thrown into the bin. The patty could not be consumed raw, so the Polish men had to find a way to cook it. The first time this happened, Pawi walked nervously back into the shop with the patty to put it into the microwave for Monoprix customers. As it turned out, however, it was accept- able for them to make use of the infrastructure as long as they didn't disturb any of the other customers. He explained to me:

> Most of them [the staff at Monoprix] are fine with us coming in. The black lady even gives us the food bag without putting it into the bin. We can use the microwave, no problem. We only need to be careful with the other customers.

Pawi and others, in similar contexts, often tapped into 'publicly' available infrastructure. This infrastructure was usually only intended for the private customers of the shop, just as you would usually only receive plastic cutlery at Monoprix if you bought something to eat at the supermarket. Pawi was able to get around the barrier of not having bought anything by making a conscious effort:

> We are clean and friendly. We are here every day, all the time. We talk to the people. We try to cooperate. And then we choose who to talk to. They are not all nice, but some.

Pawi and the others had to carefully manage how they were perceived as deserving by key stakeholders, as well as managing their visibility to the public, in order to access the bins and the microwave. On the one hand, successfully accessing the desired resources necessitated appearing deserving to the staff in the supermarket, as in many begging encounters: displaying cleanliness and politeness allowed them to build cooperative connections over time. On the other hand, it was important to pass as a member of the public – and be invisible as a homeless person – to be let into the supermarket to use the microwave. Pawi needed to avoid 'being labelled as a member of the low-status group of "the homeless"' (Gonyea and Melekis 2016: 74). He tried to hide his homelessness so as not to disturb legitimate customers – which would have negatively impacted his network of staff gatekeepers. By being clean, presentable, quiet and neither smelly nor rough-looking, Pawi and the others were able to blend in with the public, thus rendering themselves invisible (Donley and Jackson 2014: 51).

***

A similar effort was necessary if Sabal wanted to use the toilets in the McDonalds opposite the Gare du Nord or the warm waiting room in the Gare de l'Est. Both venues were protected by security – in one case, the private security of McDonalds; in the other, SNCF ticket inspectors. Sabal explained how he dealt with these access issues:

> The people know me there. The security guards. I am clean and nice and I always say hello. I go every day. Several times sometimes. They let me because I don't do anything.

Sabal's strategy mirrors what Pawi's: he firstly made himself invisible by not leaving any traces and not being loud, violent or aggressive. He tried to fit into the regular crowd of customers. Secondly, he cleared his path by being a regular, by getting to know the people involved through continuous interaction. Gatekeepers knew him because he always used the same spots to beg, go to the toilet or buy beer and food. Sabal needed to be visible to the right people (gatekeepers) 'in the good way' of being known as needy and deserving. He became a familiar face to security guards who negotiated access to venues such as the McDonalds. As in the begging encounter, wherein people like Natasha were dependent on a network of regulars, Sabal depended on getting to know (being visible to) certain people in order to gain access. Reversing the movement of begging, however, in this case, it was him who visited them and the infrastructure they guarded.

At other times – again, in an important parallel with begging for money – performing neediness was the most effective approach in soliciting access. Warmth is one of the most sought-after attributes of a place, in the material and literal sense of a heated place to sit and relax. During the winter months, the main hall of the Gare du Nord was no such place. Only slightly warmer than the sub-zero temperatures outside, the thick stone walls were not enough to warm you after a night spent in the cold. The Gare de l'Est provided an alternative in the form of a heated waiting room. This room in the far west of the station was reserved for passengers with a ticket. Initial access was not limited, but SNCF staff would regularly come in to check the tickets of the waiting passengers. Usage was dependent on your status as a customer. Again, Sabal could regularly get past this barrier and had access to the warmth and comfort of the benches behind the automatic door. This process involved the emotional labour of taking the risk of being found out, as well as his ability to convince people of his neediness and deservingness.

I was with him once when we were checked by an SNCF guard. The uniformed member of staff announced the reason for his visit loudly as he entered the room: 'Les tickets, s'il vous plaît' [Tickets, please]. We were sitting relatively far away from the door; we both knew that we could easily be kicked out, but we took the risk and didn't get up. As the man approached us, Sabal looked at him, nodding:

> Good afternoon, Sir. I don't have a ticket. But I am homeless. I don't disturb anyone. I am clean. I am very cold. But I will leave soon.

The security guard allowed us to stay – he didn't scrutinize us any further – and we did, in fact, leave after another couple of minutes. I can only speculate about why that guard did not police the venue more forcefully: Sabal's politeness was surely a contributing factor; it might also have been his status as a regular visitor that made him more deserving, though he didn't tell me whether he knew that particular guard.

In general, it seemed possible to negotiate access if you were able to 'press the right buttons': manage your visibility to the right people and appear needy and deserving if necessary. As I have already highlighted, the labour involved in these practices of access was not necessarily physical but emotional and psychological. The negotiations of access involved the ability to deal with one's shame and possible disappointment, the ability to cope with one's fear of being rejected and guard one's invisibility, and the ability to 'pass' and 'blend in'. If addressed by a guard in such situations, the same three principles were at work as in the begging encounter: once rendered visible, it was important to display neediness (no money, no access to other toilets or warmth) and deservingness (being clean and quiet, trying to fit in) and to avail of one's personal connections and networks (knowing the guard). Rather than presenting oneself as a deserving and needy homeless person, however, access was often negotiated on the basis of passing invisibly – as if one were a member of the general public. Over time, a certain knowledge was built up, a certain knowhow regarding how to stretch the rules of access to the infrastructure of the city. Over time, my informants learnt how to develop the right skills, rendering themselves visible or invisible, to be a successful homeless labourer.

Conclusion

My focus in this chapter has been on the labour of begging in which my rough-sleeping informants engaged. I described how my informants learnt to balance neediness and deservingness, as well as personal connections – what I termed the three main axes of successful begging – involving both physical and emotional labour: the labour of walking around for hours, asking dozens of people and being rejected. It is about constructing and supporting narratives of deservingness and neediness in scripts, covering up one's status as a homeless person and passing 'as if'. Overall, begging and accessing valuable infrastructure around the train station centred on the management of visibility.

This labour of begging, I argue, is ultimately about hope. It is an outgrowth of the hope that is, at times, future-oriented, structured. At other times, the labour itself is hope; less about the future, more about doing *something* in the present, keeping busy with something in the short term and thus keeping the future open. My informants' labour (Millar 2008: 35) was destabilized by life on the street, which demanded an irregular and flexible, rather than wage-producing post-Fordist, kind of occupation. It involves the necessity of unstructured *survie*, but also the conscious development of the skills of a more orderly *travail* (Stettinger 2000). It allows homeless people to struggle along and make home on a daily basis, keeping the (hopeful) future open with and on the street (Pedersen 2012; Desjarlais 1994). In the next chapter, I will turn my attention towards activities relating to the literal work of home- and shelter-making, focusing on the problematic nexus of sleeping and being policed away.

Notes

1. Many NGOs, including Freedom – as well as the Samu Social, the Croix Rouge, the Secours Catholique – or institutional actors, such as the BAPSA (*brigade d'assistance aux personnes sans-abri* [a French police unit established to help homeless people]) undertook street tours (*tournées rues, maraudes*), during which people would walk around the city visiting people on the street. Altogether, twenty-seven different organizations were involved in the coordination of these tours (in 2010, APUR 2011: 15). Often, they would offer hot drinks and food, as well as help with accessing day centres, soup kitchens and the like. I will return to outreach teams in chapter 5.
2. I will elaborate on Arendt's definition of 'work' in the next chapter in the context of shelter-making and *habiter*, which, I argue, resembles her notion of 'work'.
3. As this is an analytical description that does not map neatly onto both of my informants' usage of the word or the more commonplace way of saying things, certain expressions ('workplace', 'Let me show you how I work') will slip in. In such cases, the usage is either idiomatic or based on my informants' expressions.
4. An indication of food consumption (via nutritional intake) comes from a clinical study conducted by France L. Malmauret et al. (2002) (see Sprake, Russell and Barker 2013 for UK); two older studies looked at the consumption patterns of homeless people in the US (Hill and Stamey 1990; Hill 2003), mirroring my observations later in this chapter.
5. Gaetz and O'Grady 2002; in line with my arguments, they conclude that in contrast to the culture of poverty/new underclass arguments (e.g. Murray 1990), people on the

street are not avoiding work, but exert an enormous effort to engage in economic activities.

6. This is how I understand Summerson Carr's (2011) use of the term 'scripts'.
7. This is closely linked to Arendt's notion of action.
8. See Garnier-Muller 2000: 175; Prolongeau 1993: 163ff; Lenhard 2014: 98ff.
9. This mirrors a recent debate between virtue ethicists and situationalists. Kwame Anthony Appiah (2008), for instance, describes a situation in which a person helps another at least partly because of a 'whiff of my favorite perfume' (45). He claims, following the situationists, that 'if the psychological claims are right, very often, when we credit people with compassion as a character trait, we're wrong. They are just in a good mood' (ibid.: 45). In this sense, Carl and others understood these circumstantial factors – standing in front of the bakery, sitting in front of the supermarket. They did undergo the emotional labour involved in this analysis.
10. I will go on to describe how Pascal claimed to be both German and Congolese in different situations as part of his hustle.
11. Sheila C. Moeschen (2008), for instance, provides an overview of feigned disability among people begging in twentieth-century America, while David C. Schak (1988) focuses on disabled people begging in contemporary China.
12. Although this happened as well. Carl, for instance, in advance of his son's birthday early in 2016, made a conscious effort to put money away to buy him presents. Similarly, Pascal would save money during his time on the street to rent a hotel room, which he did regularly.
13. This is part of what Douglas (1991) calls orderly home-making.
14. On an abstract level, this negative view of begging as work could be related to its one-sided nature (not giving anything in return; Gregory 1982) or the dependent nature of the encounter (Simmel 1908). Carl didn't explain his judgment any further, however.
15. See also Desjarlais 1997; Duneier 2000; Bourgois 2002.

2

Habiter
Making Shelter when Sleeping Rough

My informants were navigating between what are, according to the ETHOS definition (Edgar et al. 2007; Edgar, Doherty and Meert 2004), the two most extreme categories of homelessness: they were sleeping rough without a stable dwelling at their disposal (what ETHOS calls 'roofless') or they lived in temporary accommodation, such as shelters and hostels, without a legal right of exclusive possession or adequate private and personal space ('houseless'). This chapter is about the struggle of being roofless, of living in public or external space, or staying intermittently in emergency night shelters (*centres d'hébergement d'urgence*, or CHUs, as they are called in France). According to statistics published by the French Office for Statistics, about 10 per cent of homeless people (*sans domicile*) fit into this category (*sans-abris*). One in five of the people surveyed slept outside; the others would habitually find refuge in parking lots, hallways, train and metro stations, or other covered spaces (Yaouancq et al. 2013; Sheehan 2010: 551; Herring 2014: 306).

As one of the core daily home-making activities and a necessity for short-term survival, how does making a shelter (*abri*) take place around the Gare du Nord? After having discussed the intricacies of daily processes of money-making focused on the labour of begging in the last chapter, this chapter will focus on the self-created spaces in which my informants spent their days – and, especially, their nights. While the physical shelter is only one part of home and hence just one aspect of home-making, it is what is most often associated with homelessness and the way out of it (Houard 2011; Loison-Leruste et al. 2009). The same question arises repeatedly, often daily (Pichon 2002: 12): where will I sleep tonight? The process of shelter-making is perpetual and cyclical and it is hard to routinize as a result of regular conflicts with security forces or other homeless people in one's own group. This leads individuals to move around relentlessly (Bergamaschi and Francesconi 2008).

To draw again on Arendt's distinction between labour and work, I argue that it is this process of *habiter*, of physical shelter-making, that is part of the daily *work* of my informants. While they engage in the (physical and emotional) labour of making money described in the previous chapter, the process of *habiter* is an engagement with the world of things. My informants worked on producing something of durability and permanence, a shelter that was used in the medium term and not consumed (so that it disappeared) immediately. The product of the work of *habiter* was a new thing – a place to stay for the night – and in this sense a human artefact (Arendt 2008: 94). Arendt herself describes how 'the most important task of the human artifice ... is to offer mortals a dwelling place more permanent and more stable' (ibid.: 152). For her, tilling the soil is one of those tasks that 'performed year in year out will eventually transform the wilderness into cultivated land' (ibid.: 138). While my informants were not tilling the soil of train stations or parking lots (non-places that were part of the ordered wilderness, in Arendt's terminology), they were engaging in comparable activities of ordering and physically transforming space. The outcome was always physical, provided a certain *abri* [shelter] and was at least semi-permanent – my informants would stay in one place for up to several months. However, Arendt doesn't capture in her definition of work the processual and cyclical character of the work my informants engaged in, which, for both Tim Cresswell (2004: 37) and Doreen Massey (2005: 9), is an inherent part of the ever-changing nature of any place: the never complete cycle of finding–making–losing the shelter is the focus in this chapter.

***

Many studies have looked at the institutional context of shelter-making in France and beyond, focusing on emergency shelters (CHUs),[1] medium-term temporary shelters[2] or precarious housing more generally[3]. Sleeping rough and rooflessness have not been dominant subjects of discussion in the French context beyond questions of how to rehouse rough sleepers (Gardella 2014; Marpsat and Firdion 2000; Bruneteaux 2005), medical conditions on the street (Laporte and Chauvin 2008; Girard, Estecahandy and Chauvin 2009) or the more general problem of exclusion (Jérôme 2002; Dambuyant-Wargny 2004). I will engage with work that focuses on the 'inhabitation' (*habiter*) of public spaces (or what Augé (2008) calls non-places) by homeless people in Paris (Lion 2015; Pichon 2002; Gresillon, Amat and Tibaut 2014; Fillon, Hemery and Lanneree 2007; Sheehan 2010).

Following Carl to an abandoned train in the south of Paris and Pascal to a parking lot in La Défense, I will illuminate both how different types of shelter – from open (*abri ouvert*), to covered (*abri couvert*) and closed shelter (*abri fermé*) – are inhabited through what I will describe as a recurring and repeated process of daily shelter-finding and -making. I argue that my informants transform, at least temporarily, non-places into habitable places – what I call *habiter*, following Gaspard Lion. Ultimately, however, their efforts are often thwarted by conflicts within the group or with externals, such as security guards or police; in effect, the process of finding and making a shelter repeatedly continues.

The Processes of Finding Shelter and Making It:
Clothes, Niches, Parking Lots and Trains

When we talk about people being homeless, what we often mean is shelter-less or roofless [*sans abri*]. All of my informants were, at some point, confronted with the problem of not having a place to stay on a daily basis.

While some eventually managed to spend their nights in emergency shelters (*centres d'hébergement d'urgence*) or temporary housing (*Centres d'Hébergement de Stabilisation* (*CHS*); see chapter 6), my informants had all spent months or even years sleeping rough on 'the street'. 'Sleeping on the street', however, is as much of a catch-all term as 'homelessness'. The most extreme practices centred on what Pascale Pichon (2002: 19) calls the *abri ouvert* [open shelter], as in the case of Alex, who slept in an uncovered, unprotected niche opposite the Gare de l'Est, on the vents, which I also describe in a separate paper (Lenhard 2020). In this case, *habiter* is mostly about constructing and ordering a physical space.[4] Others, such as Pascal, Lobo, Carl and Barut, spent more time searching for a solid shelter, *abri couvert* [covered shelter] or *abri fermé* [closed shelter]. The parking lot in La Défense (the banking district in the west of Paris) was a covered shelter, a semi-public space that was temporarily and partly privatized, while I will portray the secluded train cabins Carl and others used as a closed shelter, providing a higher level of intimacy and protection (Pichon 2002: 20). In all three instances, moments of finding and making shelter were part of a process of what can be characterized as *habiter*: 'the action of appropriating one or several spaces and of investing them with meaning by turning them into something familiar with everyday activities' (Lion 2015: 961).[5] Whether they stayed in an open, covered or closed shelter, my informants cyclically went, over time, through the same steps of searching, appropriation and conflict.

The locations my informants were able to appropriate were what Marc Augé calls 'non-places' or what Matthew D. Marr, Geoffrey DeVerteuil and David Snow (2009) call transitional places: grey areas for people (or trains or cars) to pass through at the end of transit and transport. Access has to be negotiated cleverly and tactically ('passing as') and, as regards a homeless person's acceptance in a place, is the exception rather than the rule (see Casey, Goudie and Reeve 2008). As described in the previous chapter, access can be dependent on certain behaviours: people acting quietly, keeping the space clean, not too many people at once, dogs being kept outside, no smoking inside and not disturbing other passengers. Often, if the conditions were not met, surveillance technologies were used to facilitate sanctions (Sharma 2017: 129).

Clothes

The stereotypical image we commonly have of a person on the street is that of a man in run-down clothes, full of holes, wearing multiple layers of fabric, with a big bag in his hand and a sleeping bag on his back (e.g. LePoint 2015;

Huffington Post 2014). I certainly saw people that fit this stereotype, but many of the people I observed and spoke with presented an alternative picture. They regarded the clothes they possessed as valuable and deserving of care and as having the function of protecting the body – in short, as the smallest possible home and as an extension of the self (Dittmar 1992). For instance, Carl, who spent many months living in different outdoor venues all over Paris, had just such a relationship to his clothes:

> The fashion factor doesn't really play a role anymore. ... I don't have to have a certain style of jeans. In winter, the biggest factor is protection from the weather; that it is really warm. ... I get clothes from people on the street; people who come with food, religious organizations, private people. Then I go to the Croix Rouge and I buy from a second-hand shop, Guerissol. They have many shops. ... You get a pair of shoes for €5, trousers for €3. And they have good stuff. Things have to be intact. And a little bit [*sic*], they correspond to my earlier style.

For Carl, it was functionality – warmth, protection – that made clothing valuable; style, which is so important for the average consumer, was only a secondary consideration. Usually, Carl wore a casual outfit based on jeans or a tracksuit: loose-fitting pants, a t-shirt and a cardigan, trainers and a warm jacket (often even in the summer). Most of the time, he also carried his back-pack with him, which contained important documents (his forms from Freedom, his health insurance, the identity papers he had left) and a spare t-shirt, underwear and socks. It was important for him to wash his clothes regularly; he could do this for free once a week or every other week at various institutions around the station. However, it was almost as important for him to change his selection of clothes as well. One way of doing this was to seek help from the Croix Rouge, which supplied garments to people in need free of charge through their Vestiboutique. More often, however, people found clothes, exchanged them or bought them from cheap shops themselves.

Clothing was rarely chosen at random. During a visit to the Vestiboutique with Markus – a German in his late forties who had recently lost his job and spent several weeks on the streets of Paris before moving back over the border – I learnt how important choosing clothing can be. Markus hadn't changed his clothes for several months and was desperate to find new clothes. We went to Vestiboutique on a Thursday in the winter of 2015. Led into the back room where the free clothes are stored – away from other items of clothing that are sold to the general public – Markus was presented with a rack full of items. They had everything he needed: jeans, pullovers, cardigans, big coats, shoes, belts, bags, fresh socks and underwear. Shoes were most important: 'I run around all day; I really need comfortable shoes.' One pair was too small, another was too big; Markus didn't want sneakers. He needed something warmer. After a few minutes of consideration, he finally chose the pair that was slightly too big. Similar issues arose with the coat: 'this doesn't have a hood.' A second coat was too short; a third had too few pockets. He settled on a coat that had a hood and enough pockets, but was slightly too big. After trying four different pairs of jeans, Markus was getting upset: 'they are all too tight and short. I need something else.' It was very important for Markus to find trousers that not only fitted well enough that he would not have to wear a belt (an extra item of clothing to care for), but that were also long enough to keep the cold out effectively. Like Carl, Markus was concerned about the functionality of his clothes: the comfort of his shoes, the warmth his coat would be able to provide. Given the chance at the Vestiboutique, he tried to maximize these parameters along the lines of functionality to make the 'smallest home' as useful as possible in situations in which sleeping on the street meant that his coat would indeed be his outermost protection against the cold.

Pascal's idea of clothing went even further at times. He was not only concerned about functionality; he was also concerned about looks:

> In the beginning I thought about clothes. You had to be dressed decently. When I started sleeping in the train, I lost this sense for a while. ... Clothes become irrelevant in some way, but somehow, today, clothing – yes, it is not so important – but it has to look decent. You never know who you are going to meet on the street. ... The colours have to fit. Even though I am homeless, it has to fit. Don't let yourself loose so much. ... I also have really nice clothes. Like a good leather jacket, a great coat – you couldn't wear that as an SDF. You know why I bought these clothes, really nice? When I am off the street, I am saving them for then. I just bought good stuff which I want to wear sometime soon. When I visit my family. I don't want to look like an SDF.

Pascal saw clothes in terms of belonging to a group; if he looked decent enough, then people would not think he was living on the street. Mirroring his initial reluctance to beg, he wanted to avoid shame through his choice of clothes. The motive of 'normality', which played a role for Pascal in terms of his more general hopes, is also evident in relation to clothing. He was concerned about how other people – people who were not homeless – saw him and particularly how they categorized him. It was important to him that he passed as a 'normal person', as one of 'them' (the 'not homeless'), not only to procure gifts more easily, but also as a matter of self-worth. Pascal's relationship to clothes went even further: he connected his choice of clothing directly to his hope of returning to Germany and to his family. In fact, he was saving some clothes – in a separate bag stored at Freedom – that he would only take out once he made it off the street. He connected his daily home-making practices, his daily hopes, to the long-term goal of leaving the street and rough sleeping behind.

In contradiction to the common saying, 'beggars cannot be choosers', in certain situations, I observed the act of choosing clothing as part of home- and shelter-making activities (Lenhard 2017a). Both when targeting aspects of functionality that are clearly connected to the creation of a more secure, warm, safe space and when thinking about marking membership to a group, clothing is an index of home-making. Focusing on the first aspect, clothing as the first layer of protection is important and demands consideration. For Markus and others, such as Carl and Pascal, clothes were not randomly selected. Like consumers in general, they took the opportunity to maximize utility and looked for the possibility of choice.

In this sense, but also in the sense of being a materialization of Pascal's hopes for the future, clothes can be understood as an extension of the self. As Helga Dittmar argues, psychological research indicates that there is a close link between 'possessions and who somebody is' (Dittmar 1992: 43). William James (1981: 279f) goes as far as to refer directly to clothes when claiming that 'a man's Self is the sum total of what he can call his, not only his body and his psychic powers, but his clothes and his house'. They are particularly important for what Dittmar (1992: 47) calls the evaluative aspects of the self – self-esteem and well-being – aspects that also play an important role as a goal of *habiter*. On the one hand, clothes constituted the first shell of protection and functionality for my informants (Markus, Carl), and, on the other hand, they acted as part of the extended, inhabiting self.

Clothes were an important aspect of rootedness, especially in my inform-ants' constant struggle and *mouvement perpétuel* [perpetual movement] and in the absence of other material belongings (see also Miller 2001). However, even in the most deprived setting, clothes were only one dimension of my informants' shelters; I mainly observed three different types of shelters – open, covered and closed.

Abri Ouvert: *Alex's Shelter Opposite the Gare de l'Est*

Whereas for Pascal, Carl, Lobo and Barut, the choice of a suitable place for a shelter was the most important part of shelter-making work, Alex had a differ-ent approach. For him, shelter-building was more important than shelter-finding. He had picked a seemingly random place, just opposite the eastern exit of the Gare de l'Est, in which to spend his nights and days when he was not at the homeless day centre. The building, owned by the SNCF, was equipped with cosy niches in between massive stone pillars all along its sides. He was on the eastern side, protected by a small roof five storeys above him. Alex's corner – one of about three niches that were inhabited at any given time – was the one closest to the exit of the station. Alex was very careful about the order-liness of his sleeping place. When I approached him there for the first time in early 2015, I immediately noticed how neatly ordered the niche was. The pieces of cardboard serving as floor coverings were ripped so that they fitted perfectly into the 2 square metres of space between the two stone walls. Two layers of cardboard separated Alex from the cold stone underneath him; another layer formed the wall behind him. The whole construction looked like a custom-made built-in wardrobe. He sat on beige cardboard as he showed me the rest of his *trottoir-salon* (Zeneidi-Henry 2002: 207). During the day, his belongings were carefully put away in a backpack and a plastic bag. Whenever he left the niche, he took these two bags with him. He owned a second set of clothes – trousers, a t-shirt, a pullover, underwear and socks – to change into. His dirty laundry was stored in the backpack, wrapped in a plastic bag, kept separate from his other things. His sleeping bag was always attached to the backpack when he left, as Alex considered this to be his most important possession.

Alex's construction of a shelter accords with Lion's (2014: 961) conceptualization of *habiter*:[6]

> Choosing your place to live, clearing the interior space, decorating it, appropriating it, establishing spatial habits … *habiter* could be defined as the act of transforming or trying to transform a space for one's well-being. (Lion 2014: 961)

Like the inhabitants of the Bois de Vincennes (Lion 2014; Gressilon, Amat and Tibaut 2014), Alex divided up his niche according to his needs. While the space was not suitable for a sophisticated arrangement of *chambre* [bedroom], *cuisine* [kitchen], *salon* [living room], *salle de bain* [bathroom] and *débarras* [storage and garbage] (Zeneidi-Henry 2002: 210), Alex managed to separate even the small niche into different zones. Alex had chosen a niche, decorated

Figure 2.1. Alex's cardboard home, east of Gare de l'Est, September 2016. © Johannes Lenhard.

it with cardboard and other belongings and developed spatial habits, such as storing and separating certain categories of things (important/less important, clean/dirty) and closing off his space. In fact, when we left the space, Alex made sure to 'lock it' behind him: he unfolded a third layer of cardboard, which he wrapped around the two main layers and a bag of food in a rectangular shape. Thus, his little niche was perfectly protected against the weather. There was no rubbish or dirt to make it look overly suspicious. He was aware that the security guards at the station opposite didn't like rubbish lying around; consequently, he chose to leave behind what looked like a neatly sealed cardboard box whenever he left his niche.

Extending Lion's very general description, Alex's routines further illustrate what 'appropriation' of a space can look like. For him, the construction of a home out of cardboard, his sleeping bag and a few other personal belongings was an exercise of ordering. He had chosen a small, manageable corner to bring under control, to keep tidy. Home-as-process in the everyday was linked to structuralizing routines in Alex's life, both in terms of the physical structures around him (starting with the cardboard and how it had to be folded and ending with how he separated clean and dirty laundry) and his routine more generally. The space as such – where it was and how well it was covered – was secondary for Alex; the possibility of order, dependent on the small size of the space, among other things, was primary. For Alex, *habiter* consisted of these practices of ordering in the present.

Two important aspects of *habiter* were more complicated or not desired in Alex's cardboard home: what Lion describes as *se cacher* [to hide] and cohabitation or living together with others (Lion 2014: 697, 973). Alex was very exposed to passers-by, which, particularly during the night, could potentially constitute a threat to his personal security. He was also rather solitary in his niche and didn't engage with any of the other people at the Gare de l'Est.[7] At least in part, this lack of togetherness and security (through hiding) was a function of the openness of his shelter, but it also contributed to Alex's success in staying in that place for a long period (more than a year): he was responsible for managing his behaviour so that conflicts with the police could be avoided; no one else was able to intrude on his shelter; and there was no internal hierarchy that could lead to conflict, which is often the reason for the breakdown of a shelter. By taking the risk of being alone and without a proper roof (making his shelter less attractive), Alex was able to change the process of *habiter* from being perpetually cyclical to being at least temporarily stable.

Abri Couvert: *Pascal's and Barut's Parking Lot*

Factors such as the protection and warm offered by a place were key when choosing a location for the night. When a place was well chosen, only a minimal amount of actual construction work for a shelter had to be done; if a location already provided protection against weather and people, it was more a question of making it comfortable. In short, the better the initial choice, the less work necessary in preparing the space. As with choosing a begging spot, Carl followed his logic of thinking about the location first and had very clear criteria for where he would establish his shelter:

Me: How do you find places to sleep?

Carl: I do that systematically. The most important thing is the protection from weather: a roof, a wall, an entrance. The second is not too much human traffic or that there aren't people after a certain time. The third factor is the cleanliness. … And access also plays a role. That the place is within reach at any one point during the day.

The most important category on which Carl's choice of sleeping location was based was functionality, as with his clothing. The shelter had to protect him from the weather. The place should also be quiet and clean and easy to reach. Although Carl was perhaps the most systematic of my informants in the way he made these decisions, I observed similar choices being made in other circumstances: the Polish men had chosen the location for their tent because of its proximity to the Monoprix supermarket and its relative calmness at night; François preferred the playground close to the Saint Vincent de Paul church because of its quietness and the garden shed roof under which he could take shelter. Pascal and Barut went further than all of the above. They slept in a parking lot at La Défense for a long period in 2015 and 2016, but they arrived at this location through a similar process of shelter finding.

The parking garage under the big supermarket in La Défense was a perfect compromise for both Pascal and Barut, who slept there independently from each other at first and eventually with others on the third level down. Although it was only about twenty minutes on the RER from the Gare du Nord, the location was far enough away not to be crowded with other homeless people or passers-by. The first two floors of the parking lot were busy all day with cars driving in and out. When the sun went down, the traffic of people and cars abated. The third level stayed dark the whole day, but, nevertheless, at night, life started to make its way down there. I arrived with Pascal one evening in February 2016 at around 9PM, much earlier than he would usually come 'home', as he called it. We came via the metro and had to walk through about 500 m of the La Défense area above ground. We followed the flow of office workers towards the shopping mall. Pascal led the way into the centre, where we had to pass a security guard to take the elevator down past the first two levels into the parking. The third-floor elevator didn't work anymore, so we took the stairs. I saw the first couple of empty bottles. It seemed as if we were entering a different world; the light already seemed dimmer on this last set of steps:

The first time I came down here, it wasn't so dark. I wouldn't have come down and I definitely wouldn't have slept here. … Now, I know my way around. It's easy but it's still a little bit scary. You see, there are all these people here all the time and you don't know what they are up to. … And not too many people sleep here.

Pascal explained his feelings about the space to me as we turned left at the bottom of the stairs and went through a heavy door onto the parking deck. While the space was easy to reach on the metro and access was straightforward (the security guards rarely checked people entering the parking areas), Pascal was worried, at first, about the number of strangers who spent time on the third floor. Teenagers would go down there in groups to drink, make out or smoke marijuana. As he was on his own a lot of the time or only with Lobo, his Polish friend, the presence of the groups seemed threatening at first. Only later at night, when the youths would start to disappear and after the two had found a more secluded spot in a distant corner of the third floor, did he start to feel more secure.

When we went down to the parking lot in 2016, only the emergency lighting was on. At the end of the wide parking space, a sleeping bag lay on top of several layers of cardboard. A garment hung from a rogue wire in the ceiling ('To dry from the bad weather yesterday'). Pascal had chosen a kind of elevated pavement about 15 centimetres above street level for further protection against animals, such as rats. The abandoned shopping cart served as a place to store things: some pieces of clothing, more cardboard, some food cans.

> This is where I sleep every night. This is my sleeping bag. Lobo sleeps next to me most of the time. I think it is safe down here and it is warm and comfortable and dry. Nobody disturbs us here either. Nobody ever really comes down here during the night.

Lobo's presence made Pascal feel safer in the parking lot. Not only did the two share a daily routine of going to Freedom together; they also shared the shelter together in what Lion describes as cohabitation. Being with Lobo created a feeling of security – both of them would stand up for each other if anything happened (for instance, with the youths). Like decoration – with furniture and material objects – which only played a minor role for most of my informants and the habits they developed,[8] living with somebody, and thereby producing a form of sociality, an 'us', can be central to turn a mere *abri* [shelter] into an *habitation* [abode, dwelling], a 'significant space, which is emotionally charged for the inhabitants' (Lion 2014: 697).

Abri Fermé: *Carl, the Train Man*

'They call me the train man – even though I don't even sleep there anymore. But I found it', Carl explained to me with pride. Carl had found an even more elaborate space than the car park in the form of the train in the south of Paris, where the beds were literally ready-made to jump into once he figured out how to enter. He took me to see the train he was talking about, which stood very close to the Créteil metro stop. It was an old inter-city train waiting to be moved to the place where it would be recycled. It had been down there for several weeks already; previously, a similar train had been parked on the tracks, just a couple of hundred metres away from the overground metro tracks. 'This used to be my job [as part of the German special forces in the army] – intelligence, finding things – and finding this train was easy. I just used Google maps, and a day later I started sleeping here.' About nine months previous, Carl had stopped living on the border of a lake not too far from Créteil (as it was too exposed and easy for others to access) and began searching for a new place. Sitting in the library of the Centre Pompidou, browsing Google maps, his attention was drawn to what looked like a big train graveyard:

> There was the metro stop and right next to it there were another perhaps twenty tracks. Half of them had trains on them. This was perfect – I thought it would be easy to just break into one of them and sleep there.

That is what Carl eventually did. He quickly figured out that parts of the space were only used as an overnight parking area for RER trains, as well as other trains that emerged from the washing area nearby. It wasn't safe to sleep in those trains, as they were often moved. On the tracks farthest away from the metro stop, however, there were trains that were out of use for intervals of up to several months. Luckily, these trains had the most comfortable seats, which could easily be turned into wide beds. The fact that the trains were easy to reach (less than thirty minutes from the Gare du Nord) and were available for stable intervals of time made them perfect medium-term shelters for people like Carl.

When he was showing me around in early 2016, we entered the first train after having crossed the tracks, trying to avoid the security. A strong smell hit me. 'Oh no, they must have been using this as a toilet', Carl explained, pointing at two big piles of what appeared to be human excrement. As we found our way through the train and into the compartments, signs of inhabitation abounded.

Most compartments in this part of the train showed signs of having been lived in recently: leftover food, mouldy patches of liquid on the seats, clothes, ripped-out curtains-turned-blankets, excrement, syringes and needles, methadone ampoules, bottles everywhere. The train's different compartments – one wagon consisted of about ten of them – had been privatized by individuals. Carl explained to me that usually one or two people would sleep together in a compartment and mark their space – consciously and unconsciously. Clothes were left behind during the day, plates and bottles were kept on the 'bed'. Compartments had been turned into personal rooms, as was all too visible through the big window facing the gangway. They constituted what Pichon (2002: 20) calls *abri fermé*, usually a squat or hut that provides an intimate and closed space, far enough away from any other inhabitations and quasi-private. Such spaces were the closest thing to private rooms available on the street – the compartments were about the size of a small double bed and provided enough space for one's belongings – and allowed for moments of isolation and relaxation outside of the usual public spaces, such as the Gare du Nord.[9] Being alone, secure and outside of the public realm was rarely possible for my informants. The train provided a context in which this was possible.

More and more people were attracted by the prospect of the isolated comfort of the trains, as a result of which issues relating to both informal rules of conduct (where to go to the toilet, which possessions to respect) and external security forces arose. Such conflicts lead to the eventual breakdown of shelters and the renewal of the cycle of finding and making homes (*habiter*).

Figure 2.2. Local train with human excrement and drug paraphernalia, Créteil, February 2016. © Johannes Lenhard.

Violence and Rules of Conduct: Make, Fight, Repeat

When more people started to arrive at the train 'graveyard', conflicts arose with the official security forces. As the trains were owned by the SNCF and RATP and were often only waiting to be cleaned or recycled (making them another kind of non-place temporarily turned into a place), security forces patrolled the ground regularly. During the winter months, their attitude was

Figure 2.3. Inter-city train with glass, flip-flops and blanket, Créteil, February 2016. © Johannes Lenhard.

lenient at first. They seemed to accept that people had temporarily claimed the trains as a place to sleep and left them to themselves during the night. Carl explained:

> After midnight, the security guy does his tours. He knows that there are people. ... You shouldn't have lights on then. If he finds you, he can throw you out. The security came every time at 8AM. He was friendly to us but with the others, he was such an asshole, to the Polish people. There was a lot of garbage around after a lot of Romanians arrived; there were many more people, much more noise. You never know when they['ll] come and kick you out. Perhaps after four months, you don't know what is happening when they – Bam! – come at 4AM and throw you out. That's not easy.

In the mornings, the power of the security forces hit particularly hard. 'They come in with the dogs and throw us out. They are so scary. Seven o'clock also on the Saturday. 4AM during the week.' The security forces imposed a certain order on the inhabitants of the train, particularly in cases where informal rules of conduct – coming late and leaving early, keeping the train clean – were not being adhered to. Official RATP guards and their dogs made sure the official non-places of the trains were kept in order and that people moved from one train cart to another.

As in other contexts on the street (Rowe and Wolch 1990; Bourgois 2002; Whyte 1943), violence *within* the group was another means of making sure that certain rules of habitation were respected. Conflicts arose because people were not willing to accept an informal code of conduct. Carl explained to me how he controlled his wagon of the train and would not let people enter:

> When we first arrived, we made sure that our part [of the train] was always locked [using a simple screwdriver]. Usually, that was all fine. There were conflicts – one had to be dealt with [using] a stick. With a Romanian. He wanted [to get] into our train.

***

Similar complications eventually brought an end to the living situation in the La Défense parking lot. Pascal told me, in spring 2016, that Marc and some other Finnish guys had not been respecting him or the rules for some time. Pascal explained how everyone had their own little corner of the spacious underground car park and how they had agreed not to bring drugs and other friends to the sleeping spot. A certain order was established within the group, but Pascal complained that Marc and his friends were not adhering to these rules. He felt ill due to a stomach problem and the others who shared the parking lot corner at La Défense were not allowing him his personal space: 'They were taking drugs and stuff in front of me. And they wouldn't let me alone and I was really in pain.' There were, as he put it, certain *Regeln des Zusammenlebens* [rules of living together], which the Finnish didn't follow. Anger built up over time and culminated in an outburst of at times cathartic violence: 'Marc really is an asshole. He deserves it.' A secondary justification – related to another rule of conduct – related to Marc's income:

> He has so much money. He doesn't need to be on the street. He doesn't work. He doesn't earn his money. He just goes to the cash machine and takes it from his Finnish bank account. He pays a €5 fee and he doesn't care. He buys drugs for everyone and chocolate and always has money. ... And he doesn't share. If we are down at the parking and I don't have water and ask him he would tell me: yes, you can have some, but you have to buy me a new bottle tomorrow. Isn't that horrible? I would give people stuff for free. It's also like that with the drugs. If you get methadone from him you have to pay him back more. He is like that. He is not fair. He really talks at you as if he was someone better. I don't like that.

Not only is there a certain envy in Pascal's speech, but also the explicit suggestion that sharing was part of cohabitation. Moreover, Pascal implies a hierarchy between himself, someone who doesn't use drugs, and people like Marc – as he explained to me on another occasion:

> The Narcos [people consuming hard drugs, such as heroin or crack] are the worst. I don't want to see them. I don't like hanging out with them at all. I am doing my own thing. Not spending any time at the Leader Price anymore. I sleep alone or perhaps with Barut. But with the others, it doesn't work. Already with Barut, I can't share a meal from the same plate as him. You have blood all over your hands, you inject, you rub it everywhere, boah!

Pascal groups the people on the street according to the severity of their addiction and the danger they potentially pose to his own wellbeing. 'Narcos' such as Barut were mostly consumed by their addiction (to crack, heroin substitutes and morphine, in particular). 'Alcoholics', such as the group of Punjabis around Bouti or the Polish group at Place Franz Liszt with which Lobo spent a lot of time, were less active and less aggressive, but similarly consumed by thoughts of how to procure enough alcohol. Pascal neither injected nor drank alcohol and often saw himself as above these two groups. Behaviour associated with addiction – such as with Barut's behaviour – sometimes made Pascal aggressive, particularly when certain rules (not leaving paraphernalia around, not stealing from one another) were broken.

Garnier-Muller (2000: 101) observed similar groupings around substance-abuse problems in her study of French homeless people. She found that the SDF were distinct from both sex workers and *toxicomanes* [people with drug addictions]. She explains how 'ordinary homeless people' and 'people with drug addictions' have different ways of 'claiming and maintaining space'. While I will further explore the specificities of addictions to alcohol and hard drugs in the next chapter, these – at least from Pascal's perspective – perceived classifications had a direct impact on the processes of shelter-making. *Habiter* was not always a lonely and solitary process of hermitic shelter-building, as in the case of Alex. It was often embedded in a sociality that improved the shelter-making by adding security and sociality, but also introduced certain rules of conduct into the process. Good places often attracted more people. The more people there were, the more likely it was that there would be conflict with the security forces. In cases where these informal rules were not respected, violence broke out either internally or with external parties and eventually led to the inhabitants being pushed out of the appropriated place. Over time, this often led to breakdowns in relationships, conflict and a total breakdown of the cohabitation, making it necessary to start the process of *habiter* from scratch at a different site.

Conclusion

For my rough-sleeping informants, the process of shelter-making, or what I have come to call *habiter*, was a multi-faceted process of daily home-making. It involved the finding of a suitable non-place and the transformation of this non-place into a habitable place – at least temporarily. This could include the building of cardboard open shelters (Alex), but also the more sophisticated habituation of intimate practices in parking lots (Pascal, Lobo, Barut) or trains (Carl). This process of *habiter* can be characterized as a kind of productive, materially engaged work, in contrast to the consumption-driven labour of begging. While informal rules of conduct helped, especially in cases of cohabitation – sharing the shelter – conflicts both with external security forces (police, SNCF and RATP; see Lenhard 2020) and within the group were at times unavoidable as more and more people were attracted to the place. These conflicts would often lead to a breakdown of the shelter and restart the cyclical process of finding and transforming a non-place into a liveable place.

Rough sleeping can be seen as a hopeless giving-in, but I want to frame it as part of maintaining the longer-term hope while waiting in the short term, as part of keeping afloat and struggling along (Desjarlais 1994). While constantly moving around, perpetually reinhabiting new spaces, shelter-making was in itself a stabilizing force, beginning with the protecting shell of clothing. Unlike the designated user of the non-place that is the station, the car park or the abandoned train, my informants put effort into creating an identity, into personalizing their surroundings and making them their own (*approprier*). They built relationships in spite of the non-place logic of 'individual anonymity' (Sharma 2009: 131). They worked on making a temporary home where people were never supposed to be at home, according to Augé (2008: 109), despite 'continuous movement and dislocation' (Sharma 2009: 132). In short, they appropriated what was conceived and constructed as a non-place – a space to rush through as comfortably as possible – and turned it into a place. As I highlighted, shelter-making was rarely stable, but was rather based on a cyclical process of shelter-finding, shelter-making (ordering, establishing routines, living in the shelter – what I have been calling *habiter*), conflicts, the breakdown of the shelter and restarting of the process. Again and again, my informants engaged in home-making as 'an active process in which most people are permanently engaged ... a living process and construction' (Moore and Rivlin 2001: 329).

Notes

1. See Declerck 2003 on the medical side of the *Centre d'Accueil et de Soins Hospitaliers* (CASH) at Paris Nanterre; Desjarlais 1997 on mental health as a driving factor in Boston shelters; Benoist 2009 on exclusion and alterity in Nanterre; and Bruneteaux 2010 for a critique of emergency shelters in Paris.

2. See Hall 2003 on UK youth shelters; Grand 2015 as well as Michalot and Simeone 2010 on French temporary shelters.

3. See Dietrich-Ragon 2011 on insecure housing; Bouillon 2009 on squats.

4. I use order here in Douglas's (1991) sense of the word, connected to her notion of home as an order place, following Massey's (2005: 112) instinct to look beyond order as connected to the liberal state.

5. The original French reads: 'l'action de s'approprier un ou des espaces et de les investir de sens en les rendant familiers avec des activités quotidiennes.'

6. Lion builds on Lazarotti (2006); the original French reads: 'Choisir son lieu de résidence, aménager son espace intérieur, le décorer, se l'approprier, instaurer des habitudes spatiales ... [habiter] pourrait être défini comme l'acte de transformer ou chercher à transformer l'espace pour y être bien.'

7. In fact, he spent the better part of his day – between 9.30AM and 12PM and 2PM and 5PM – at Freedom, as I will describe in more detail in the following chapter. Part of the explanation for his particular behaviour might be what the social workers at Freedom described as his 'mental health' issues, which were not investigated or questioned further.

8. *Habitude* [habit] has the same root as *habiter* [inhabit].

9. Lion defines a habitat, in this sense, as 'un espace propre dans lequel ils peuvent s'isoler ... se cacher, de se soustraire à la publicité, possibilité tout à fait essentielle à être humain' [a place of their own where they can be alone ... hide, remove themselves from the public eye, an absolute necessity for being human] (Lion 2014: 697).

3

Drug Time
Cutting through Time with Alcohol and Drugs

The easiest thing in the world is to stop smoking. I did it a thousand times.

—Mark Twain

During the winter months of 2015–16, a group of up to six Polish people made their living on Place Franz Liszt in front of a Monoprix supermarket. There were two big hot-air vents right outside the automatic sliding door. One and a half square metres of ground constantly released a stream of warm air. Pavel and Damian rarely moved away from this spot during the day – they would leave only to urinate right around the corner, in the small side street leading away from the buzz of Place Franz Liszt. The battered white McDonalds cup in front of the men was enough to make people understand: 'Une petite pièce, s'il vous plaît?' [Spare some change, please?]. However, the money they made in front of Monoprix was rarely spent in this up-market supermarket. The beer at Leader Price, less than 150 m from the Gare du Nord, was cheap: under €0.60 for a can of strong, dark beer.

While Damian and Pavel were mostly careful not to make a mess, cleaning up their garbage and making sure they were not seen urinating by potential givers, they didn't always succeed. Consuming between ten and twenty beers a day and often vodka, whiskey or whatever other hard alcohol they could afford, they would both grow increasingly upset and aggressive, as well as tired and passive, as the day unfolded. Pavel often fell asleep while sitting in front of Monoprix. Problems arose when they were too drunk to sit, concentrate and speak nicely to the people coming out of the Monoprix. The hot-air vents on which the men were stationed carried the smell of alcohol right into the noses of people passing by.

Sleeping was at least part of the aim of the alcohol consumption. The men had fled Poland to find jobs, money, a better life – in some cases to avoid prosecution. In Paris, it was hard for them to find work; the manual work they could do was not in high demand and they were not seen as trustworthy and reliable because they lived on the street. Unemployment led to boredom (O'Neill 2017) and collective boredom led to alcohol, which eventually led to sleep. Sleep meant forgetting. When the men were really drunk towards the end of the day, after a good workday begging, during which they made enough money and bought a lot of vodka, they didn't have to think anymore.

Once when I met Carl and the Polish crew, Carl was in such a state that he wouldn't stop talking:

> We made so much money today. This guy, he gave me €20. We bought vodka, that's why Vita is passed out in the tent. [laughs] I spoke to Lisa [his ex-girlfriend] today. The kids and her are fine. [His face becomes more serious.] I want to see them, but I can't go back. ... At night, the dreams come back. Every time. I don't sleep if I don't drink. And usually I need a joint, too. ... All this stuff from the war. I don't want to be in Germany. It was so much worse when I went back to Berlin. I didn't treat Lisa [his girlfriend] well ... was gone for days. ... And now these dreams. I don't have anything to do. Nothing tires me out. I just sit around. That's why I need this [holds up the half-full vodka bottle].

***

Most of my informants – Pascal being perhaps the only exception – were either heavy drinkers or addicted to hard drugs, such as the heroin substitutes methadone and Subutex or different types of morphine pills – the most common being Skenan – and crack. Often, alcohol and drug addictions went hand in hand. In Paris, drugs are consumed by more than a fourth of homeless people, according to a recent Samenta survey (Laporte et al. 2015: 695). In addition, roughly 20 per cent self-reported that they were alcohol-dependent. In contrast, rough sleepers and people who beg – and most of my informants fell into both categories – tend to be more likely to consume alcohol (and drugs), according to statistics from the French Institute of National Statistics (Beck, Legleye and Spilka 2009).

For many of my informants, drugs and alcohol were so much a part of daily life that they dictated the rhythm of it, as I will argue in this chapter. In their attempts to cope with both the uncertainty of the future and the trauma of the past, waiting for something to happen and trying to forget the misery of the present and the past, drugs and alcohol help people, such as the Polish crew described above, as well as Carl, Barut and Moritz, to cut through time. They introduce a different, cyclical kind of time, what I call 'drug time' (see Knight 2015). Alcohol and drugs help users to, at least temporarily, take control over their thoughts – making them subject to the high of the drug rather than the low of the nightmares – while in the longer term resulting in conflict and more pain, which regularly lead to moments of epiphany and a desire to stop 'using'.

I understand addiction in this context, following Jara A. Krivanek (1988), as a process and a 'behavioural pattern involving drug or alcohol consumption that alters the way an individual thinks, feels and behaves, that he or she likes in the short term but dislikes in the medium and long term' (Flanagan 2012:

29). It is my aim in this chapter to describe the inherently ambiguous role of drugs and alcohol alluded to in this definition. I put the notion of drug time at the core of this ambiguity. First, for some of my informants, drugs were part of daily home-making processes in that they produced a cyclical structure – following the rhythm of drug time – that helped my informants to cut themselves out of time, allowing them to forget past traumas and worries about the future, at least temporarily. They were part of (positive and negative) ordering, in Douglas's sense of short-term, immediate and processual home-making.[1] Extending classic ethnographic accounts of homeless addiction,[2] I describe drugs as part of edgework. Both drinking and taking drugs led my informants into a strict, repetitive and cyclical rhythm of begging–buying–using. It is this often stressful rhythm that I call drug time.

However, the imagined control achieved through drugs often collapsed into yet more despair and impotence in relation to taking responsibility for one's life. Hence, in chapter 4, which initiates the second part of this volume, I will demonstrate how short-term home-making does not always add up to a longer-term project. The influence of drugs and alcohol on my informants' lives was often very negative in the longer term, holding them back and preventing them from reflecting and thinking about future plans, about their *projets de vie*. It is in this context that the influence of institutions such as Sun, a bus distributing syringes and medication, and Emo, a day centre for alcoholic homeless people, becomes significant. In proposing different rhythms and ruptures to drug time, they present an alternative way forward. I will illustrate how, in both cases, drug addiction was ordered – this time institutionally – introducing more risk-averse ways of coping and spending one's time and ultimately supporting my informants in focusing on their longer-term hopes and *projets de vie*.

Drug Time and Edgework as a Way of Temporary Ordering

Carl was in his early thirties when I first met him. He was short, only about 170 m, but his frame was solid and heavy. When Carl turned nineteen and had just finished his Abitur in Berlin, he decided to join the army. He acquitted himself well: 'One day after the 100th morning run, one of the officers came up to me and asked me whether I wanted to join this special unit. I didn't even know what that really meant but agreed on the spot.' He was soon sent on his first mission getting hostages out of Kosovo; similar missions in the Congo and other parts of Africa followed. Most of his time was spent in Afghanistan. During a supposedly less dangerous daily patrol there, his jeep came under enemy fire. A grenade killed two of his comrades. Carl and another comrade were heavily wounded, but able to call for support. For weeks, it was not clear whether he would survive.[3]

Back in Berlin, Carl couldn't come to terms with the state he was in. After months in a coma and a lot of medication, he agreed that he was not fit for combat any longer and joined the security forces protecting German embassies around the world. After years of high-adrenaline combat action, Carl grew bored. He had a lot of time to think and started drinking heavily.

> I never liked drugs. My mum was – perhaps still is – a heroin addict. That's why I grew up with my grandparents. I mean, I smoked some stuff when I was in Afghanistan – man, the best you can get in the world – but never got into injecting or anything. Just drinking.

Drinking eventually got him expelled from the army. He was sent back home to Berlin and again referred to a trauma programme. He refused and instead stayed with his long-term girlfriend, Lisa. Nine months later, their son was born. Carl got into trouble more and more frequently. The drinking became worse. He got into fights and came home bloodstained. Before his son was two months old, Lisa threw Carl out of their house. In the end, he had to respect Lisa's decision: 'I didn't want to have anything to do with Germany anymore. I risked my life for them and they wouldn't help me. Yes, they offered me this therapy but I wanted to continue living a normal life.' He went to Paris to work with an ex-comrade driving a truck. After losing this job due to drunk driving, he couldn't afford his apartment anymore. He started sleeping on the street in late 2014. The drinking continued and even increased. It was a means of forgetting for him: 'I don't want to think too much. When I lie down at night, I can't fall asleep because all these pictures are coming back. If I don't drink I can't sleep at all.'

***

The mental pressure, the trauma, the fear of nightmares and flashbacks, boredom (Gardiner 2012: 45) and inactivity – Carl and the Polish group cited various reasons why they drank daily.[4] Drinking was a short-term way of coping with trauma, pain, anxiety and other mostly mental health issues. Rather than focusing on these issues, I want to analyse the effects drinking had on my informants' lives, paradoxically producing what I describe as an ordering function.

The addiction produced a continuous cycle of 'drinking to beg – begging to drink – buying more alcohol – drinking – more begging' as part of the group life of the street.[5] It is this kind of cyclical rhythm that I call 'drug time'. Following Ben Bowles's (2016) analysis of people living on boats in London, I observed that my informants lived according to a different, non-linear 'time map' (Bear 2016). While Bowles's informants' time was produced by 'interactions between humans, the weather, the seasons, animals and the chaos of fate and chance' (Bowles 2016: 102), my informants were subjecting themselves to a cyclical rhythm dominated by the threat of withdrawal symptoms, the availability of begging money at the stations, the opening times of shops and the availability of dealers. While Bowles's informants lived on boats in accordance with the materiality of their river environment, my informants were living in accordance with the materiality of alcohol and drugs. Both rhythms, however, were uncertain and unstable, often involving a lot of movement, which made forward planning complicated. In both cases, time was experienced 'through the prism of the rhythms of the tasks' (ibid.), which, in the case of my informants, was the addiction understood as the procuring and consumption of substances.[6] Drug time was not only a cyclical rhythm involving begging and drinking or taking drugs; it also had an effect on the movement of time, which I call cutting oneself off from time.[7] Norman K. Denzin argues with respect to people dependent on alcohol that, while in drug time, 'the alcoholic will maintain his or her belief in self-control' while in fact 'the drug has taken control of the user's life' (Denzin 1987: 45).

In relation to this last point about control, alcohol and drugs sometimes helped my informants to perform 'edgework'.[8] Edgework, a term borrowed from Carol McNaughton, involves 'actions that people voluntarily engage in ... that carry inherent risk and crucially involve negotiating at the edge of normative, responsible behaviour' (McNaughton 2008: 33). For people like Carl, alcohol and drugs were a means of losing a sense of time and space and falling into drug time instead. Alcohol appears to be a way for Carl to cut himself out of time, out of his worries about the past and an uncertain future in the short term. I describe edgework through alcohol and drugs as cutting through time, cutting oneself off by blotting out past, present and future worries and miseries (Day et al. 1999).

While Carl – and people like Barut – explicitly stated that they drank in order to forget the past, it is implicit that they were also trying to regain a certain kind of control.[9] By engaging in alcohol consumption, Carl chose to subject himself to different thoughts. This produced a kind of freedom. He described at length and repeatedly how, without the influence of alcohol or marijuana, thoughts would take over his mind, particularly in the form of nightmares. The alcohol helped him to disengage from these thoughts. It is in this sense that I call drinking a type of reordering, rather than chaotizing, producing what Douglas (1991) describes as an ordered home, at least temporarily. This type of control was a way of submitting oneself to a different but self-chosen external regime – in this case, the cycle demanded by the alcohol or drugs. Instead of being controlled by thoughts and nightmares of, for instance, a traumatic past event, it was the alcoholic high that controlled the mind.

But control was over the choice of master, rather than the mind. As such, my observations loosely relate to the DSM conception of alcohol as a substance that people attempt to use to govern the realm of freedom (Valverde 1998: 28). People might choose to embrace a substance – handing over control of their thoughts to the substance, as Carl described, for instance – but the substance eventually takes over and forces behaviours onto the people who have become addicted. Empirical philosopher Mariana Valverde explains this paradoxical twist in the exercise of choice and freedom as follows: 'although people begin drinking of their own free will ... the habit of drinking eventually leads to the disappearance of their very willpower' (ibid.: 2). Once it becomes a habit, Valverde argues, alcohol (like drugs) is 'fundamentally conservative, tending to keep us in our place' (ibid.: 35). Life is then structured on the basis of the consumption of the substance: making money, scoring the drugs, consuming them, repeating. It is this cyclical habit that I call drug time. I will now further explore this relationship between the freedom to choose, drug time and the problems that come with a developed habit by extending my analysis to Barut's experience with hard drugs.[10]

Barut between Order, Freedom and Losing Control

Whereas Carl was mainly focused on alcohol – both before and in Paris – Barut was a user of heroin substitutes and crack. On the one hand, this addiction gave rise to very similar considerations – he was also trying to forget past and present worries and wanted to cut himself out of time – but, on the other hand, it also came with a slightly different type of rhythm, a slightly different drug time. The ordering effect the hard drugs had on Barut's life was more apparent than that of alcohol on Carl's life. Crack and methadone made it necessary for Barut to earn more money, move more quickly, haggle and negotiate with dealers – in short, he had to work and care more for the substances. As I describe in an article focused on the care that drugs demand from the user (Lenhard 2017) – in the form of money, time and attention to bodily needs – Barut was subject to a rhythm imposed on him by the drug addiction. The addiction had become a habit, an engrained way of going about things, imposed drug time.

Barut grew up in Bulgaria. His parents had separated early, with his mum moving to Greece and his dad staying in Bulgaria. When he was nineteen, he was studying towards a technical degree, but he stopped to go to Spain to earn money in construction. He worked in Spain for eight years before he got into drugs. After taking heroin for over a year, he decided to join a rehab programme, after which France seemed like a good place to start anew. His older brother lived in France, selling and maintaining property. The two of them tried to work together for a while, but Barut couldn't keep up with his brother's speed and rigour. He got back into heroin. When his brother found out, he kicked him out of his life: 'If you want to die, do it, but not here, not in my arms.' Barut lived on the street for months before he started another rehabilitation programme. He felt left behind by his family. In the programme in Paris, he met Anna, who provided a glimmer of hope for him: 'I thought she was a nurse, she was so beautiful! But then I saw the marks on her arm [from a suicide attempt].' They fell in love and he moved into Anna's flat. 'She helped me feel better. I was like shit but she made me feel good. I had the best moments of my life with her.' After two years, they realized it wouldn't work out; he started taking drugs again. From April 2015, Barut became a regular visitor at the Gare du Nord.

Barut's motivation was extremely low when we met: 'I don't have any ambition. I don't want anything. I wake up in the morning and don't want to do anything. I wake up at night and have nightmares [particularly] if I don't take the methadone before I sleep. I drink during the day and smoke so that I forget.' I ask: 'But you were ambitious before; are drugs the problem?' Barut answers: 'No, I don't have anything, really. My problem is that I don't have anything that I strive for. The drugs come after – they make me forget that.'

As in Carl's case, Barut wanted to forget; he wanted to cut away the past, his isolation, his sorrow in relation to Anna, his poverty, the mistakes that isolated him. He wanted to forget the past and the present – and explicitly pushed away the future; in this sense, he cut through time in a similar way to Carl:

> This [the street] is not for me. I should be somewhere else. I know I can do it. But I am not ready. I did the rehab thing twice [in Spain and in France] so I know I can do it, but not now. (Barut)

The drugs provided a break from the pressure for Barut; he was confident in his ability to eventually work towards a future without drugs, but also believed that he would need more time before he was ready to do so. He was not yet at rock bottom.[11]

When I met him some time later, running around in the Gare du Nord, he seemed very nervous indeed. 'Je suis malade aujourd'hui. C'est la manque' [Today, I am ill. It's the withdrawal]. He needed methadone and was hardly able to concentrate enough to talk to me; he was constantly looking around, seemingly on the lookout for something. He needed to make money quickly as he had missed his chance to get methadone for free from his distribution centre that day.[12] Barut's day was externally dominated and ordered by the struggle to make ends meet so he could get the drugs. His rhythm was subject to drug time and his daily routine was stricter and more pressing than that which alcohol (a much cheaper pursuit) imposed on people like Carl.

Barut would try to have some methadone left to start his day in the mornings, which often began in a parking lot at La Défense. Ideally, he would have enough to allow him to feel stable and ultimately make his way over to the Gare du Nord. Begging there was his main source of income. Like Camilla, he practised spot begging, running through the train station asking people for money. Unlike people such as Carl, who could buy enough beer for the day with €5 to €10, Barut needed somewhere between €40 and €50 to feed his addiction, sometimes considerably more. A dose of crack – which provided the only 'real' high for him as the methadone merely took away the pain and stabilized him – was €15 and lasted the few minutes it took to smoke it. Extra methadone for days when his distribution centre was closed or when he had missed the distribution period would be €5 per hit. Skenan, which could be injected in addition to the other drugs as a small high, was €5 per hit. The need to generate enough money to finance this addiction kept Barut busy and created strong routines. The care the drugs demanded from him (Lenhard

2017; Weinberg 2005) – including both the effect of withdrawal and the threat of it – created a physical urgency that made Barut nervous and unstable. Paradoxically, however, it forced him to order his day to a high degree. It imposed a quick, cyclical drug time that was even stronger than the one associated with alcohol addiction. He had to plan ahead, planning his finances and even the geography of his movements through the city: how much money do I need to make for the next hit? Where will I get it from? When do I need to shoot up so I don't feel too ill to continue making money? If Barut didn't consider these questions every day, he would be in (withdrawal) pain (Bourgois and Schonberg 2009).

I argue that the influence of hard drugs in Barut's life was twofold, both part of and an effect of drug time. On the one hand, the drug cycle is part of daily home-as-process activities, home-making and Barut's daily survival and ordering. While the influence of drugs on the lives of people on the streets is often described in purely negative terms as affecting both mental (Rayburn 2013; Unger et al. 1997) and more general health (Grinman et al. 2010), Bourgois and Schonberg argue, in similar way to me, that users benefit from consuming drugs beyond the high. While Bourgois and Schonberg mainly outlined social benefits connected to group life, for my informants, the group aspect seemed less important than the influence of the substances themselves. Barut's addiction to various substances forced him into routines both in terms of timings and localities. Javier, the manager of the substitute distribution programme of Sun, called it a 'crutch' for people, one 'which helped them to advance in life at first'. On the one hand, the addiction forced Barut to structure his short-term future: getting up as early as possible, taking the train to his workplace, begging at the Gare du Nord to make money for his first shot, buying crack on the platform of the metro line 4, finding a spot above the parking garage behind the station or in the toilet on the drug strip near Lariboisière. Throughout the day, he engaged in a continuous circle of begging/scoring/shooting up/smoking/being high that was only interrupted by brief stints of relaxation when food and alcohol were consumed or the police patrolling the drug strip behind the station made it unusable. This rhythm, the drug time, was initially chosen by Barut (to liberate himself from the trouble with his family, to forget) and allowed him to cope by cutting him out of time, as with Carl. Methadone allowed him to control his pains – both remembered and physically present – while crack or Skenan made him high and gave him pleasure. Javier made a clear distinction here:

> What is forgotten with the substitutes is the pleasure. Why do you take drugs? Because it feels good. You want to feel good. After, the problems arrive, but at first is the pleasure.

Javier – who has worked in drug substitute programmes in Paris for over a decade – is, however, acutely aware of the temporary nature of this effect. His use of the terms 'at first' and 'after' indicates a shift in modes of drug taking.

The user takes control over memory and pleasure, but the addiction often takes control in the end. For my informants, drugs ultimately turned into more of a slippery slope than a crutch that helped them walk farther. Barut was dependent on drugs and at the same time he became unable to exercise responsibility in relation to anyone or anything else, including a possible *projet de vie* and longer-term plan and hopes. Barut was only seemingly and temporarily in control. Engaging in the risky behaviour of drug-taking, he was constantly 'on the edge'. As he himself admits, the drugs demand attention, care and time; control can be taken away from Barut (Rowe 1999: 28). The positive effect drugs might initially have can quickly turn around; one loses control over one's thoughts – dominated by the addiction – and one's emotional state. As Bourgois (2002) argues in his earlier study of people addicted to crack cocaine in the US, drugs ultimately have a negative effect on psychological insecurity and control over oneself. The initial high induced by the drugs and the seemingly ordering drug-using lifestyle eventually disappears. In the ordered short term, drugs and the cyclical quick-time maps they generate create a feeling of being in control that mostly collapses completely in the longer term.

In most cases, the order of the daily drug and alcohol cycle leads down a one-way street in the long run. It disconnects users from their actual desires, as Bea, addictologist at Emo, explained to me. On the one hand, it gives people like Carl and Barut structure in their lives and allows them to feel that they are taking control (at least seemingly, leaving the impact of the substance out of the equation), handing over control to a substance they initially chose. On the other hand, this is done in an explicitly desired time-cutting way, separating users from the past, present and future, and transporting them to a world in which the care for the substance quickly becomes the main source of worry. I regularly found Barut behind the station on Sundays or Mondays in a state of despair, having lost his dog or his backpack. He would tell me this excitedly and angrily, in a voice made high by his not having slept for days on end: 'I haven't slept for more than two days; I was here all day and night yesterday. We made lots of money. Now I can't find my dog anymore.' He looked around nervously, unable to focus. He had smoked crack to keep himself awake; all of his money would have been spent on one pipe after another, shared with one of his friends at the station. Drugs did produce the illusion of taking back control initially; however, the *projet de vie*, with its future orientation, was eventually cut out of their thoughts through heavy alcohol or drug use.

It was in situations such as when Barut was desperate to stop and change that institutions started to come into play. Barut had already done two periods of rehab. Carl had refused to join a medication programme in Germany, but was more and more willing to engage with institutional help now that he was in Paris. Although my informants initially perceived their consumption as a form of taking *back* control, the substance became a stronger force in their life over time – as they drifted further into the addiction – and even more control was lost. When people like Barut and Carl saw that, as well as helping them – to forget, to keep themselves busy, to order their lives – the drugs ultimately created a state of impotence, they were more likely to search for help from organizations such as Sun and Freedom. The latter had just started a special programme for homeless people with alcohol abuse problems called 'Emo' in early 2016. In chapter 4, which marks the transition to the next part of this volume, I will focus on the influence of these institutions, which offer alternatives to drug time to people living with addictions.

In the next three chapters, I will go beyond the short-term focus on immediate hope that we have observed in practices of begging, shelter-making and drug taking and I will describe how my informants started to focus more directly on the longer term, on their *projets de vie*. Moving away from drugs or – at least initially – reducing the harm they were causing constituted the first step in this direction. As drug time was such as a strong ordering mechanism, ruptures were needed, often supported by institutions and *assistants sociaux*. While the body and taking better care of the body are the focus of the harm-reduction practices at Sun, Emo went further. By offering an alternative daily rhythm for people with alcohol addiction issues, the programme tried to replace drug time altogether and as such help people to refocus on the longer term.

Notes

1. See Douglas (1991), chapter 1.
2. See Bourgois and Schonberg 2009; Desjarlais 1997; Weinberg 2005.
3. This is Carl's version of the story, which was later disputed by some of the *assistants sociaux* he worked with. I will address the question of truth in the conclusion of this volume, but generally take what my informants tell me and what I observe at face value.
4. Mental health issues were also clearly one of the reasons, but they were not talked about. Neither my informants themselves nor the institutions they engaged with focused on mental health (neuroses, psychoses); rather, they focused on the addiction directly.
5. See also Snow and Anderson 1993: 210; Denzin 1968: 45.
6. Like Bowles (following Bear 2014), I acknowledge that my informants' environment was not always made up of this kind of time and rhythm. The drug time, however, became the main axis of subjection for informants such as Carl, Barut and Moritz. See also Knight 2015.
7. See Denzin 1987: 112.
8. McNaughton 2008; see also Goffman 1991: 309.
9. McNaughton (2008: 34) ascribes 'exercis[ing] individuality and freedom' to edgework.
10. While there are clear differences in the tempo of the drug time – hard drugs demand more attention and money, the cycle is quicker – I want to begin by stressing the parallels between the two groups of users.
11. Flanagan (2012: 52) calls it 'breaking point'.
12. Most people who had an addiction to heroin substitutes would get a certain part of their intake from a legal distribution centre. I volunteered at one such centre for over a year between 2015 and 2016. Usually, however, additional methadone was traded on the street and supplemented with Skenan – a morphine medication – and crack. This was the mix Barut took.

Part III

Towards the Future, Assisted

4

Ruptures from Drug Time
Institutional Support at Sun and Emo

Drugs and alcohol were a dominant and dominating part of many of my informants' lives, daily struggles and, as I described in chapter 3, the order of their lives. As the example of Barut made clear, such substances were mostly only a very short-term means of home-making; the comfort and order they provided often collapsed into even greater chaos, associated with addiction and the drug time cycle it produced. However, people like Barut or Carl were often engaged with different institutions. While I will focus on the more general support (and challenges) that Freedom's day centre provided in the next chapter, I wish to discuss the institutions that helped them to cope with their drug use in this chapter. The work of these institutions is especially significant in the grand narrative of this volume as it marks a turning point: Sun and Emo begin with that which is often painful and violent – my informants' drug use and the pain associated with them – and provide spaces in which my informants can start to think differently. While the notion of drug time described my informants' strong focus on the short term, Sun and Emo helped to initiate ruptures in this short-term cycle and established starting points for reflecting and thinking about the future, unearthing (again) longer-term hopes and desires for home. I will describe how drug time was counteracted at Sun through the establishment of alternatively ordered daily rhythms and a focus on the body through practices of harm reduction. Emo offered an even more comprehensive alternative daily rhythm and a space for reflection to open up the future and the *projet de vie*.

***

A risk-reduction van and the most prominent methadone distribution van in the north of Paris were run by Sun,[1] which sought to provide understanding, help and advice; a different kind of ordering of time was created in these places to the one searched for in drug consumption. Sun was originally founded more than twenty years ago as a subsidiary of Médecins du Monde, but quickly became an independent organization dedicated to risk and harm reduction among drug users.[2]

Financed by the regional agency for health in Paris, in 2017 it ran both a stationary and a mobile centre for addiction-related support (*Centre de soins d'accueil et de prévention en addictologie*, CSAPA) and one stationary and one mobile centre for risk-reduction issues among drug users (*Centre d'accueil, d'accompagnement et de réduction des risques pour usagers de drogues*, CAARUD). I volunteered with all of these for several months. The main aim of Sun was not to lead people towards abstinence, but rather to help them to take care of their health while they were still taking drugs. This approach is called harm reduction.[3] Herein lies a crucial difference – both in logic and process – between Sun and, for instance, the rehabilitation programme in post-Soviet Russia described by Jarrett Zigon (2011). As in typical Alcoholics Anonymous (AA) programmes, the heroin users undergoing rehabilitation in Zigon's ethnographical work were working towards absolute abstinence, all under a banner of moral obligation. Driven by a Russian Orthodox morality of sin, Zigon's informants were expected to follow a relatively predetermined way of achieving abstinence, engaging in regular activities such as repentance and prayer, processes that focused on the soul (ibid.: 114ff). The activities at Sun were not only more varied, less prescribed and less geared towards abstinence; they were also mainly about the body and reducing the harm done to it.

At Sun, the mobile centres – revamped vans – focused on people who were either sleeping rough or in environments close to the street (*banlieue* high rises, council housing). These centres were a first point of contact for starting a conversation about drugs, the associated health risks and how to deal with them. As Javier, the manager of the CAARUD[4] during my time as a volunteer with Sun, explained to me:

> The [risk-reduction] material [such as syringes], well, that is a means of attracting them, a means of starting conversations about risks with them. ... Somebody who comes and takes one body [of a syringe] and ten needles ... we ask him: why do you only take one body? ... There are bacteria building up and you can contaminate yourself ... It is a means to start discussions about practices.

Hence, unlike Zigon's ethnographical study, the main aim of Sun was not to immediately (and possibly rather forcefully) bring people back to the *projet de vie*, to get them thinking about their hopes for an abstinent future; rather, the goal was to start conversations, to help people to feel safe and stable in the moment and to reduce the (health) risks associated with drug consumption. Only when it was an explicit aim of the user did Sun start a conversation about rehab and abstinence, as Javier explained:

> Our objective ... that's not necessarily to stop with the drugs ... and it will never be us who propose that route ... apart from when we see that the person puts herself in real danger. [If somebody comes and says:] 'Oh là là – now I would like to stop.' – it

is then when we say: 'If you want to get to the bottom of this, we can help you find a place where you can quit [the drugs].'

***

Sun's CAARUD was an adapted white van, the size of two normal cars. Two steps up from street level, people were usually welcomed by at least two or three members of staff and a volunteer. I spent countless hours myself as a volunteer myself. From behind the counter, we would hand over risk-reduction material for free. Eight different types of syringes, fourteen different types of needles and various accompanying materials, such as alcoholic pads, clean water, filters, glass pipes and hydrating cream, were handed over freely and generously. The only requirement was that the person register with a pseudonym and a date of birth.

During an average three-hour period, we would see around fifty to eighty people in the little van, parked right next to Lariboisière Hospital, four times a week, evenings and afternoons. Most of those who came to the van were male, between twenty and thirty, and used methadone, Skenan and crack. The majority were long-term (over one year) users of drugs, with one foot on the street, between sleeping rough, staying in squats and social housing. Most of the interactions in the van were short – not abrupt or unfriendly, but straightforward and goal-oriented. People came in and knew what they wanted. 'I'll take ten 10 ml, five dark brown [needles], five yellow [needles], and water, big cups [little metal cups, in which the mixture could be cooked] and disinfectant. And a crack pipe.' The demands were very similar, only varying in the number of syringes and the types of needles people used. On average, people would come twice or three times a week to stock up; they knew the 'opening times'.

The central hub for Sun was not at the Gare du Nord, but was rather their office in Parmentier, at which doctors held consultations. After an initial interview with a nurse – during which individuals were asked what their addiction was, what their story was and what they thought they needed – a specialized doctor would give the person the right prescription: methadone, Subutex, several types of medication for neuroses and psychoses, Valium. The dosage varied depending on the strength of the addiction. For some people, the *accueil* [reception] at Sun was a place to hang out, like the *Espace Solidarité Insertion* (ESI) of Freedom was for others. Most came and went quickly though. After the initial consultation, the daily or weekly dosage was usually not picked up in Parmentier, instead being collected at the mobile CSAPA,[5] which functioned like the CAARUD. Both vans worked in tandem and could be found in similar spots, but at different times of the day. The main difference was that only registered users were able to obtain medication from the CSAPA, whereas the risk-reduction material at the CAARUD was available to everyone.[6]

***

We were parked next to the Gare de l'Est, looking out at the platforms. It was a rainy winter's day, even snowy at times. People dropped in slowly from when we arrived at 2.30PM. Some finished their cigarettes as they approached the van; others took a moment to recover from the quickly changing weather. Like the CAARUD, the CSAPA van was stocked with risk-reduction material. However, people also came every day for something else: the safe and free distribution of medication. Another door separated the medical cabinet from the rest of the bus. As people stepped in from the queue, which often extended from the bench inside to outside of the van, the door opened and the doctor – Laura, on this occasion – called in the next person. Inside, a little counter cut the room in two. The doctor sat behind a computer screen on the other side of the counter with the nurse, who had the big bottle of methadone. The person gave his or her name and number (identifying him or her in the computer system). Laura found the prescription on the screen and Sarah, a specialized nurse, poured the methadone from the 5-litre bottle into a blue plastic cup. Some also got a pill or two – to combat depression or schizophrenia or to help them deal with an alcohol addiction. The majority came for the methadone. People had to drink the sweet syrup immediately. Most washed it down with a glass of water before leaving through the back door. 'A demain' [see you tomorrow]. Methadone or Subutex were distributed to the same group on a daily basis.

Yana and Jakob, a Finnish couple who were acquaintances of Barut's, came every day. We knew each other from the station and had spoken several times. One day, they arrived almost too late. Yana was not in a good state, just about finding the door to the doctor, while Jakob waited outside, looking after their two big suitcases. At that time, they were sleeping in the train, like Barut. Yana took a while. Jakob got nervous and left the bags sitting next to the public toilet. People walked by. They looked at the bags and looked at the van. Jakob walked towards the Gare de l'Est. Inside the doctor's area, Yana had a hard time explaining her situation. She had not only drunk too much, but had also taken a lot of Skenan. She was unhappy in Paris, pained that she was not at home in Finland and angry with Jakob. She couldn't stop crying and was unable even to stand. The doctors decided not to give Yana her methadone that day. They listened carefully and judged that the risk of the methadone having a negative effect in combination with the morphine and the alcohol was too high. Yana could come back the next day and the situation could be re-evaluated.

***

In dealing with Yana, the Sun staff had a clear aim in mind. The discussion was not about abstinence or forcing her to give up drugs; rather, it was about being safe and stable. The doctors were concerned about Yana's bodily functioning. They tried to give helpful feedback and support her in her difficulty both by withholding the medication and providing caring words. As Adèle, a social worker at Sun for over three years, stated: 'Sun is a place where we give people the feeling that they exist … where they can relax, protect themselves and take a break … We are trying to be authentic and … answer their demands.' At Sun, the aim was to provide a place of refuge, as well as a certain amount of stabilization when people exhibited particularly risky behaviour, as in Yana's case. These harm-reduction practices allowed people to slowly reconnect both with their bodies – avoiding health risks, such as hepatitis and HIV, in particular – and with time.

Harm reduction (Erickson et al. 2012; Campbell and Shaw 2008, Zigon 2019), as it was first conceived in the Netherlands in the 1970s, includes practices that often still have abstinence as their end point, but mainly focus on the intermediate steps. Practices include needle exchanges, HIV and hepatitis testing, educational courses, support groups and the distribution of drug substitutes (or actual drugs), such as methadone. At Sun, harm reduction was also about providing support through self-management practices. Most of these were focused on managing the body *better*, that is, with less risk of contracting diseases and infections. Such practices included providing clean needles to avoid sharing, giving out filters to clean the substance mixture, advising on needle usage, freely distributing clean cups and surfaces for preparing the mixture, giving out heroin substitutes instead of the often very diluted heroin from the street, testing substances to control the quality and offering medical tests for HIV and other communicable diseases. These practices, offered by both the CSAPA and the CAARUD, were geared towards treating the user's body differently, without necessarily changing the pattern of the addiction. Sun aimed to provide free and easily obtainable alternative means of treating the user's body better and reducing the harm done to it. In my view, this is the main support offered by Sun, in addition to the altering of the addiction-time rhythm. When people showed a general willingness – originally attracted by the offer of free paraphernalia – Sun made users adapt their daily rhythms to Sun's opening times. This resulted in people picking up their methadone every day at the same time. The cycle of begging–buying–consuming–getting high was interrupted for people like Yana and Jakob; drug time was, at least for one cycle, replaced by the time dictated by Sun.[7] The influence of institutions on the rhythm and order in my informants' lives was even more apparent at Emo, which was run by Freedom, like the ESI. Emo was focused on homeless people with alcohol addiction and offered a more comprehensive alternative to drug time (and its daily order) by providing a place for reflection and allowing people like Carl to slowly refocus on the past and the future, to switch from being cut out of time and on drug time, focused on the immediate short-term, to re-experiencing time.

**Structuring the Day, Making You Think:
Emo as a Place of Busy-ness**

During my experience of the programme, Emo, established in January 2016, was a space where between five and seven homeless people from all parts of Paris, united by their common alcohol addiction, met every morning at 9AM. Located in a big suite of rooms in the 2nd arrondissement, a volunteer or *stagiaire* (a social work student on an obligatory internship) and a *salarié* (full-time employee) were usually present to engage with the people who came that day. The morning always started with a small communal breakfast; we sat around a big table and shared coffee, some cookies or cake and fruit juice. Everyone spoke freely; people talked about their days, their plans for the weekend, often also their sorrows. After a couple of weeks – the same people tended to come regularly – the atmosphere became familial. This was partly because everyone was in a similar situation and had been referred to Emo by one of the drop-in centres run by Freedom. Annabelle, the manager of Emo, explained: 'They come here and know already that they have a problem with alcohol. ... They want to change something about their relationship with their consumption.' In order to support this existing awareness and willingness to change, Emo was conceived as a space of experimentation, where different practices could be tried throughout the week both by the new institution and by the visitors.

Every day of the week had a different purpose: Monday was supposed to be an easy start to the week, without too much of a programme, a day of games and talking between 9.30AM and 12.30PM. Usually, there was no theme other than the game – which might be anything from Monopoly to Uno, depending on what was chosen by the men.[8] We practised fair play as much as we practised being together in an easy manner. Tuesday was explicitly reserved for planning outings. As at the ESI of Freedom (see chapter 5), money was set aside to provide experiences of rupture, of distraction, which would take the men away from the street and their usual circles. Bea, a psychologist at Emo who ran the Thursday activities, described this as the day when desires and pleasures were planned in an autonomous way. Annabelle, the manager, added: 'The people can really dream up things for the excursions ... We try to give as little guidance as possible.' The activities ranged from evening visits to the cinema to visits to different museums (they went to the Musée de l'air et de l'espace [aerospace museum], for instance) and theme parks (in summer 2016 we went to La Mer de Sable together). These outings were usually planned about a month in advance and would happen on a Friday, instead of the philosophy group. Wednesdays were focused on a more hands-on experience of creativity: an art therapist came to draw and paint with the men. A different topic would be chosen every week. Carl and the others would spend two hours painting and one hour discussing each other's works, connecting the mind back to the body.[9] Thursday was the most similar to the well-known meetings of Alcoholics Anonymous[10] and centred on what Annabelle called a *groupe de parole* (talking group) in which experiences were the main focus.

The men discussed topics related to addiction and alcohol, usually through their personal lens, with Bea or Annabelle and at times another psychologist or addictologist.[11]

On one such Thursday, we discussed abstinence and reduction. The session started with an announcement by the two co-ordinators:

> On the next trip, the next outing, we will have beer. We will also have beer here because we don't want you to be 'in withdrawal' while being here. The idea is to be transparent and to talk to each other and to not have bad feelings about the addiction. We know that you are in different places with your addiction and on your path towards abstinence and we want to help each one of you to deal with these in the way you want.'

Annabelle wanted to create an atmosphere of comfort where the men could feel good, as well as an open space in which everyone could talk. Everyone was supposed to be realistic about their needs – and abstinence was not immediately possible for people like Carl who had just started to think about their addiction as a problem. While the focus on speech and the group setting resembled an AA meeting, the idea of obligations – to be abstinent, to each other, to God – was totally absent at Emo. Step number five of the twelve-step programme reads: 'Admitted to God, to ourselves and to another human being the exact nature of our wrongs.' The AA was geared towards 'immunity from drinking [through] work with other alcoholics' (Antze 1987: 167) and was part of the pressure-making apparatus. Rather than admitting 'powerlessness' (Denzin 1987: 75) in relation to alcohol and the need for surrender, Emo tried to foster reflection and created a space where addicts could figure out their own way to deal with the addiction, a space of comfort rather than pressure. It was, in this sense, a place where the constant cyclical running around of drug time was replaced by a stable structure for each morning and a 'break' for the mind.

The rest of this particular Thursday session centred on the input of a guest – Pierre, who was in his seventies and an alcoholic for over forty-five years, but had been abstinent for almost a decade. He shared some of his experiences and ideas with the group, both about how he got into alcohol and how he felt about it after such a long period of abstinence:

> You start for a reason; you start because things happen and you are depressed and things but alcohol doesn't help. The first time it helps you to forget and to be happy but over time it makes the circle harder to get out of. It pushes you deeper in; you need to drink to feel okay. You are always in pain.

This statement reflected the general spirit of the group. Everyone was there because they had come to a point at which their addiction wasn't helping them anymore; it didn't make them feel better, but rather caused additional pain. For Carl and another one of the regular visitors, for instance, their pain related to failed relationships and leaving their families behind. For others, it was more directly linked to physical violence, the loss of a job and feeling stuck.

At Emo, the men were able to talk about these experiences and encounter people who were dealing with similar problems. Carl explained to me that it was helpful to see that he was not alone in his suffering. This accorded with Annabelle's assertion that 'people come for two reasons: their inactivity and solitude'. The community provided by Emo was different from what the men would have found at AA or in Zigon's rehabilitation facility in Russia: rather than creating an atmosphere of religious and moral pressure, geared towards abstinence through surrender, Emo was about sharing experiences – in the form of pleasure – and alternative routines and time maps.

***

I usually joined the *atelier de philosophie* [philosophy workshop] run by former philosophy professor Paul every Friday. We would sit in the big leather sofas at one end of the room. One Friday, we talked about justice; on another, we talked about freedom. Paul often brought quotations or drawings to start the discussion: 'Which one do you like most? Which associations do you have with the drawing or the quotation?' The discussion about justice centred mainly on injustice: how soldiers misbehave in wars, how corporations are unjust, how people kill each other. Another regular, Tariq, got really upset towards the end of this discussion:

> We always talk about the bad things; we talk about injustice but there are good people as well. Why don't we talk about that? There [are] not only bad things. I want to talk about how we succeed in life!

Interestingly, Tariq's demand that they consider the positive side of things mirrored the general atmosphere and outlook at Emo. People went there when they were still struggling – the addiction was, for most of the regulars, still very much part of their daily lives – but were willing to start thinking about the present and future again. Carl had reached a point at which he was able to face his past and make plans for his future. By the time he started attending Emo regularly (from February 2016), he was drinking less and depended less on alcohol to 'cut the time'. He was no longer caught in drug time, a phase of his life when addiction was all-encompassing. The Friday philosophy work-shops were one way of encouraging thinking and reflexivity. In the programme Zigon describes, the user was similarly encouraged to reflect in a 'laborious and reflexive process of coming to know herself as a sinner', aimed at 'cleansing the soul' (Zigon 2011: 136f). Like the practices of working on oneself and achieving abstinence – praying and repentance – reflection was quintessen-tially moral and religious for Zigon's informants. Alcohol was a sin and recov-ery was a struggle to overcome that evil (ibid.: 143). Despite its religious foundations, Emo did not employ any such language or practices. Reflection was often encouraged on a similarly abstract level, but it was geared towards directly worldly and concrete ideas, such as responsibility and freedom.

At Emo, during the workshop on freedom, the discussion quickly arrived at the question of fragility. Annabelle remarked that 'you need to really know yourself before you can be truly free – including all your shortcomings'. Nico, one of the regular visitors at Emo, wholeheartedly agreed and considered Emo and other associations at least partly responsible for his movement in the right direction:

> I think she is right. It took me some time to uncover [*décacher*], find out about myself and accept where I need help. ... What really helps me are the associations. If I didn't have them I wouldn't be here today ... Others help me to be free; it's not always just because of me that I am free.

***

As with the day centre (ESI) about a kilometre to the north, which will be the focus in the next chapter, Emo was a place of refuge for my informants. They went there after they had realized that they needed to change (by quitting alcohol), but also that they needed help, as Nico made clear.[12] The activities Emo offered contributed to ordering and structuring people's lives (Desjarlais 1997: 93f,175). Having to show up every day at 9.30AM was the first element of structure; it was also expected that group members would notify staff of any appointments that would clash with Emo hours in advance, adding another layer of future planning. The brainstorming on Tuesdays was not only about coming up with interesting ideas for outings; it was also about taking initiative, developing organizational skills and assuming responsibility for small tasks in the group.

The Friday philosophy sessions were similarly ambiguous. As the manager, Annabelle, explained to me, their purpose was to make people think differently, not only about everyday life, but in relation to bigger, more abstract questions. They were also about engaging with each other, building a sociality as a group while always also making members think about themselves. Emo was providing 'tools for working on their recoveries [making] the residents ... the primary caretakers of their own recoveries' (Weinberg 2005: 118). However, the notion of the self fostered at Emo was not primarily that of a responsible individual; I would like to paint this emphasis on recovery in more positive terms as a form of trust, a faith in people to be able to manage. Rather than viewing addiction as a permanent disease, according responsibility to a recovering alcoholic adds something to his or her sense of self-worth. At Emo, the responsibility accorded to those who attended varied, as people were most importantly provided with a space to be and reflect, a home, with a certain order – interrupting the drug time every morning – as well as being provided with considerable freedom to 'misbehave' (drink). Unlike at Sun, the people working at Emo were more directly involved in changing attendees' lives over time, opening up their view of the future again.

***

For Carl, the support at Emo was exactly the right type of push he needed to order his thoughts. While he had gained access to a hotel and, ultimately, medium-term housing (see chapter 6), the conversations I had with Carl at Emo were very clearly linked to a more positive outlook on his future. Not only did he reconnect with his ex-girlfriend and his son in early 2016, he also came clean about the lies he used to tell her and started making hopeful plans again:

> Now she knows kind of where I am. I told her that I don't have an apartment and that I don't have a job and that I am on the street and that things are not good. ... Flights aren't expensive and she didn't say 'no' to not getting back together. I still have hope for this. There is a chance. I am sure. They are the only people in this whole world I care about. I do need to get back closer to them soon. They are my family, you know. They are my people.

Carl came full circle to rethinking his connection to home, now in the sense of what he considers his family, 'his people'. He came to a point at which hope started to play an important role in his thoughts about the future again ('There is a chance. I am sure'). The movement away from using alcohol as an anaesthetic 'painkiller', cutting himself off from time, was very much the result of his own decision. He chose a different type of freedom – not being free of an institutional time structure, as when resorting to drug time, but with a direct anchoring in routines proposed by Emo. It was also a time order in which alcohol did not serve to push away his thoughts – past, present, future – but one that he was plugged into and aware of. He joined Emo because he felt ready for it. He was ready to leave the street behind. However, he was still dependent on the support provided at Emo; he was not able to move towards his longer-term hopes and leave the street behind unsupported. The activities and encounters at Emo supported him, pushed him along further and allowed him to disconnect himself from the street. As he explained to me, this was crucial for him:

> They are all drunkards and if I am with them I drink too. I'd much rather just not go and see them now ... I wasn't here at all yesterday and that helped me not to drink at all. ... It's fine at the moment. I don't have a tremor or anything. I can pretty much just not drink at least for now. When I had this period of hard alcohol last autumn, when I was hanging out with the Polish guys, I really went all the way. We had a lot of vodka and whiskey. Then I had problems getting up in the morning and issues with my hands trembling. Now I am fine, actually. As long as I keep myself busy everything is good. ... I do need to really find something to do. The structure which Emo gives me is good but I still don't really know what to do in the afternoon. I don't really have any place to go to or anything to do really.

While the evaluation was surely a momentary picture – like many people dealing with addiction, Carl engaged in regular episodes of heavy drinking; his development was not linear, but he progressed in waves (Ray 1961) and stages

(Boeri 2019) – Carl evidently had a positive view of his situation. He showed a clear interest in his future again. Emo was a place that kept Carl busy, a place of busy-ness, in a different way to how the painful and stressful drug time kept him busy. Emo gave him something to do and, when he wasn't occupied by its activities, the likelihood of falling back into the habit of spending time on the street with the others brought him closer to drinking. Being at Emo kept him away from the street while also changing his state of mind; it provided a daily structure and a point of departure and it allowed him to discuss his ideas about the future with Annabelle on a regular basis.

As we sat down after a morning at Emo in summer 2016, he explained to me:

> I want to be close to my family again and I want a job. ... I can do software stuff. ... The market here is racist [against foreigners]. No stupid jobs ... but perhaps I need to compromise first to get back into the rhythm. I don't want to have a base here long-term, I think. I want to get back to Germany but then I know it will be so much a harder to cope. When I am on German soil I just can't anymore, it all comes back. ... For now, I need to get my issues under control first. I know that the alcohol will most likely accompany me for the rest of my life but I will have to keep it under control.

Carl's view at this point was more focused on the future than at any point since I first met him in late 2014. He wanted to find a job – to get back into what he described as a 'normal' rhythm – and was thinking of moving back to Germany. While he was aware that his nightmares might become stronger in Germany, he was willing to work on that, as well as the alcoholism, his first means of suppressing the pain. He wanted to get things 'under control' and look towards the future again. But, unlike in Zigon's drug rehabilitation facility, the future was not opened up or pushed onto people at Emo; it wasn't imposed through religious and moral argument and ultimately disciplinary measures, such as public penance, but offered to people through the provision of space in which to reflect and engage, the enhancement of awareness and the creation of opportunities and alternative time maps for people.

Conclusion

Many of my informants' addictions started as a way of self-medicating and forgetting. People like Carl, Barut and the group of Polish men used alcohol and drugs as a way of controlling their nightmares, their trauma and their bad memories, as well as their fears regarding the future. Such addictions helped them not to think about their anxieties and cut them out of time, cut them off. On the flipside, however, they produced stressful drug time, a regime, a routine of begging–scoring–shooting up. As I have observed, drugs and alcohol were part of both coping and response mechanisms and, as such, were part of a better life on the street – in that they allowed people to take control over thoughts and pleasure – but they also mostly led to more pain as the substances took over users' routines and thoughts.

Institutions such as Sun and Emo offered support and, for people like Carl, provided the necessary restructuring and busy-ness – a more reflexive, plugged-in type of institutional busy-ness compared to drug time. While Sun's activities were focused on 'light' restructuring, an interruption of drug time brought about by treating the user's body differently through harm-reduction methods, Emo provided a more radical and comprehensive alternative routine, replacing drug time and creating a space for reflection to open the future again.

In the next chapter, I will further document the institutional support with which my informants engaged and on which they were at least partly dependent. I will turn to the activities and help offered by Freedom's general day centre, just south of the Gare du Nord, where many of the people I have described in the preceding chapters spent a lot of their time. In a similar way to Emo, Freedom enabled many of my informants to re-focus on their hopes about the future and their longer-term desires – though the support provided was based on certain conditionalities.

Notes

1. In this part of the chapter, I will mainly focus on the staff's perspective as access to the users at Sun was limited (encounters were very fleeting). I will point out where this perspective seems to be flawed and add as much detail as possible from the points of view of the users at both Sun and Emo.

2. At Sun, individuals were referred to as *usagers* [users] because they used drugs (not as shorthand for a service user). I will use this term in the same way.

3. On 'harm reduction', see Langendam et al. (2001) and Zigon (2019).

4. *Centres d'accueil et d'accompagnement à la réduction des risques pour usagers de drogues* [Centres for the reception and risk-reduction support of drug users].

5. *Centre de soins, d'accompagnement et de prévention en addictologie* [Centre for care, support and prevention in addictology].

6. Since I finished my fieldwork in autumn 2016, Sun has closed the mobile van for the distribution of substitutes and replaced it with the first stationary shooting gallery in Paris at the Lariboisière Hospital.

7. Bourgois and Schoenberg (2009) argue that substitutes such as methadone only replace one addiction with another. Highly critical of a possibly underlying 'neoliberal agenda', they describe harm reduction as a 'band aid' obscuring the structural forces behind the addiction problem. I follow Teresa Gowan et al.'s (2012) rebuttal that the lives of the users are nevertheless concretely ameliorated; harm reduction has a positive impact on their bodies and in relation to the replacement of drug time.

8. Emo was – at least to my knowledge – a space for men only, in order to avoid the additional complexity of gender conflicts. This is why I write solely of 'men' in this part of the chapter.

9. The men were always alone with the therapist during the Wednesday sessions.

10. For more anthropological perspectives on AA, see Wilcox 1998; Antze 1987; Denzin 1987.

11. As already alluded to above, mental health issues – while surely part of many of my informants' problems – were not discussed at either Emo or Freedom. While I was not able to investigate this further, the lack of resources – psychologists and psychiatrists are expensive – was necessarily a contributing factor.

12. See Weinberg 2005: 196 on the 'pledge'.

5

Between Relationships and the *Projet de Vie*
Social Work at Freedom

And for those who appear to drift through the streets or sit around idly talking, playing draughts or drinking, one hesitates to speak of killing time, of aimlessness or hopelessness, since in the enjoyment of being-with-others a situation of unemployment and lack of opportunities is transformed from futility to fulfilment.
—Michael Jackson, *At Home in the World*

'Why do you come here?' I frequently asked people in the day centre run by the Catholic organization Freedom, where I volunteered for more than a year and a half during my fieldwork. It was about a five-minute walk from the Gare du Nord. Answers differed greatly: it is warm inside; they have free coffee; I like playing chess; I use the toilets; my friends are here; I have been coming for years; they help me with my accommodation; I like the *assistants sociaux* [social workers]; I don't want to queue in the hospital so I visit the nurse here; they give me a razor for free; I just want to sit down; they are my family.

This chapter will deal with the role of an institution in the lives of the people whose dreams, labour of begging and work of shelter-making I have so far presented as home-making activities and short-term ordering activities. I will focus on the role of a day centre run by Freedom that was frequented by many of my informants. I observed two main functions of this centre in relation to home: one more immediate and one directed more at thinking about and establishing a future. The *Espace Solidarité Insertion* (ESI)[1] was what Graham Bowpitt et al. (2014) call a 'place of sanctuary' and, as such, a home. It constituted both an emotional and material refuge, where certain immediate needs for warmth, hygiene, playfulness and togetherness were fulfilled. The second aim at Freedom was to work out the life projects – *les projets de vie* – of the people visiting: what are your goals for the coming year? Where do you want to be and how can you get there? The *assistants sociaux* in the team centred around the manager Pauline and the supervisor Ina helped their *personnes accueillies* [visitors, lit.: received people] to formulate desires and hopes, in a similar way to what happened at Emo. They helped them to face the future, providing a rupture from the street and showing them an immediate way out of boredom and street problems.

I will describe the various activities – *tournées rues* [street tours], the general work at the day centre and the one-to-one social casework encounters – and how they contributed to thinking about the future and constructing a present between responsibility and care (Johnsen, Cloke and May 2005b; Midgley 2016). Differentiating between what I perceived to be four of the core activities at Freedom, I observe these activities in terms of the increasing demand put on the visitors through classical anthropological exchange theory: the street tours resembled a free but unstable gift (Belk 1996; Laidlaw 2002); in the *salle*, the warmth, the coffee and the board games were shared quasi-unconditionally, whereas visitors had to explicitly request to use the showers;[2] lastly, the one-to-one social work encounters followed a much clearer logic of reciprocal gift giving whereby a demonstrated willingness to engage and change was exchanged for social work (Mauss 2001; Sahlins 1977). I use this theoretical lens to describe what other scholars call conditionality (Dobson 2011; Johnsen, Fitzpatrick and Watts 2014) and responsibilization (Whiteford 2010) in social work. Thus, I present an alternative view of social work with homeless people that arises from my fieldwork, avoiding the immediately moralized discourse of neoliberalism. Those measures that demanded more engagement on the part of the homeless people were supposed to safeguard the time of the *assistants sociaux*, but they also imposed an order on my informants. At times, these ordering practices clashed with those I described in the first half of this volume, but the implicit understanding was: if you want to access your future and reflectively plan for the future, you have to be able to follow other people's orders. Freedom, in this sense, oscillated between providing (more or less immediate) support – mostly for free and unconditionally – and fostering longer-term change, always based on the *lien* [relationship].

Freedom: A Matter of Relationship-Building

The organization Freedom[3] was established by a priest in the north of Paris in 1981. Based on the belief that people on the street suffer not only from an economic and psychological injustice, but also from a spiritual one, the organization was first and foremost based on the principles of the *rencontre* [encounter] and the *lien* [relationship]:

> Freedom has as its vocation getting to know the people on the street, particularly the ones who are homeless and sex workers, with the intention of establishing a relationship. Starting from there, we can accompany people in a more global way through the work of our volunteers and employees ... Based on our experience since 1981, we believe that the success of our efforts depends on the capacity of the people

to meet the other person in his or her profound suffering and to accompany him or her on a path towards reconciliation.[4]

This statement, taken from a 2012 brochure published by Freedom entitled *Principes et Fondements* [Principles and Foundations], illustrates the approach I observed over fifteen months as a volunteer in various capacities: be it on *tournées rues* [street outreach tours] or at the day centre, the work of staff is to openly go towards people on the street, to listen and build relationships with them, to accompany them and to build a network around them. Initial encounters happen with *mains nues* [empty hands][5] and are not focused on offering material help. The starting point is the relationship, on the basis of which support, reconciliation and housing help can be built.

Pauline, the manager of the ESI, made this focus on relationships clear to me in an interview: 'the relationship, to know each other, taking the time, generosity, … faithfulness'[6] are the main values in her work. 'We want to be there for discussions with people … share time' and ultimately become 'a place to rest … where the people feel secure … a place of life … where they have their network of friends'. Once a relationship founded on time, safety and trust has been established, everything else can follow: a place in which to reflect on the future, a network of friends and support, positive ruptures from the street, ultimately a place in life. As I experienced it, the first aim at the ESI was to give people the space and the time to settle down and feel into themselves in a place where they did not need to worry in the present and where they were not bored.[7] Unlike at other nominally religious organizations (Scherz 2014), any underlying Catholic economy of salvation was not made explicit at Freedom. While there was a common culture that was likely inspired by Catholic values – the *mains nues*, for instance – the everyday routine could not be traced back to religious principles. The second aim at Freedom was to get people thinking about what was to come, about their *projets de vie* [life projects], their hopes and future ideas of home. I will map the core practices according to the increasing demands made of the homeless people. I will describe how different types of exchange, on the one hand, provided much needed support, but, on the other hand, could lead to disappointment, conflict and tension.

I want to start with a description of how these different principles come to the fore, particularly during the *tournées rues*, which Freedom started running in the early 1980s, before moving on to the ethnography of the ESI as a 'sanctuary' between care, refuge and change.

Street Tours through the 9th: Reaching Out with Empty Hands

Street tours at Freedom – called the *tournées rues* or *maraudes* – always happened in *binômes* (pairs; Cefaï 2015). I met my partner Nina for the first time on a cold autumn day in 2015. We were given the task of covering a large area in the 9th arrondissement, south of the Gare du Nord. The route was predetermined: we would follow Rue d'Hauteville down to the *Grand Boulevards*, occasionally considering the smaller side streets, and find our way back to the starting point at Place Franz Liszt in a big circle. This would take about two hours, we were told. Last year, Nina had done a very similar tour with a different partner, so she knew some of the people on the way. On average, they had encountered between ten and fifteen homeless people during the two hours of the tour. When we first met, we were reminded by Martin, who coordinated the outreach activities for Freedom, to stick to the principles of the *mains nues*:

> These tours are time that you give for free. We are not necessarily searching for a solution during that time, perhaps not even for anything tangible. It is about having *fidelité* [trust, faithfulness] and from there something is created but it is not always something we can see immediately.

To illustrate his point, Martin told us about a woman he had been seeing on the street for years, but to whom he had never really got close enough to convince her to come to the day centre:

> But now she is in hospital and that's only because of us. She didn't want to go to the hospital without us. She knows my name and she was happy to go with me. She is really in a bad state but it might get better. It turned out that she actually has a bank account and we applied for a new card and we got some money out and bought some stuff for her. See, here we reached this point in time where the work – ten minutes every week – pays off. Completely surprisingly.

We were supposed to be confident about the eventual success of what we did. The street tour was the first point of contact, the moment when relationships were established that could eventually lead to positive outcomes for the people we met. It was not about offering immediate help in material form, which was sometimes hard for the people on the street to understand, as we will see, but to create bonds of trust, at times leading people to the ESI.

***

I knew the people at Place Franz Liszt already. When Nina and I first began, the group of Polish people occupied the space in front of the Monop, as well as the park benches on the little roundabout. We approached Darius, Vital, Kola and Carl – who was spending his days with the group at that time – and shook hands. I couldn't help grinning: I knew how the men would react to the young and smiley Nina, how they would want to talk to her and make her laugh, and Nina did indeed receive a warm welcome. The men loved chatting with her, bragging about how long they had been on the street. It was refreshing for them to see a new face, particularly a young female one. They were interested in hearing about her. Everyone was curious why she was doing this with me: 'Are you two dating?' We laughed a lot and the atmosphere was warm.

On that first Wednesday evening, we met a further seven people, none of whom I had seen before. It was challenging – in a way that very much resembled how I had initially approached the field – to walk up to a person sitting on the pavement and introduce ourselves, especially because we didn't have anything to give away; we came empty-handed (*mains nues*). Ali was the most memorable person we met on the tours. He was originally from Mongolia, but had spent time studying in Russia and Germany. I spoke German to him, but we ultimately settled on English for conversations between the three of us. He was very receptive:

> I have been on the street here for years. I moved around a lot but now I have stayed at this spot for a while. People know me and give me things. There is this lady who comes almost every day and brings a little candle from the church. I talk to her. She is nice.

Nina remembered him from the year before, when he had already begun using the spot: 'You were selling Christmas hats here last year, right?' Ali nodded happily: 'Yes, yes. Once last year in December I was. Someone gave me these hats and then I sold them.' A little candle stood next to the hot-air vent he sat on – something we would see again and again during the weeks we visited Ali. If the woman didn't come, he would get a candle from the church nearby. It reminded him of God, he explained: 'God will help me, I believe in that. God will help me find my way.'

We talked about Freedom and what we were doing on the street and he seemed to understand: 'We are not here to give anything away for now. We come to talk to you and see whether you need anything. We can help you find a place to eat and we would very much like you to come to the ESI further up in the 10th arrondissement. You would be very welcome there. But today, we are just here to talk and listen to you.' Ali was open to us over the coming weeks; he smiled when he saw us coming and enjoyed talking to us in different languages. 'I spent time in Germany. For studies. A long time ago. That's where I learnt to speak German.' Ali opened up and told us about his family situation; he missed his brothers and sisters, who were distributed all over the world, in the UK and Pakistan. They didn't know how badly off he was and that he slept on the street, but he was in touch with his sister, whom he wanted to visit sometime soon. Nina and I both thought that our regular visits were working very well for Ali: he was growing more confident and trustful with us; the relationship developed as he told us about his problems, as well as his desires and wishes. He understood that we had come to value him in his own right, as a person, rather than as somebody in need of help – as Ali, a Mongolian man with a story and a life in front of him.

Unfortunately, it turned out that Ali was not always like this. He had bad days and over time became aggressive towards us. When the winter was coming to an end in late February 2016, he refused to speak to us on two occasions:

You don't bring anything. You only come and ask questions. You don't have anything for me. Why would I want to speak to you? You don't help me. I don't want to tell my life story all the time. I need help. It is cold. I don't have anything to eat. At least give me something to eat.

The first time, Nina and I went to buy a little candle for him, the kind we knew he liked. He was very happy afterwards and almost embarrassed by how he had reacted just before: 'I am sorry. I really appreciate that you come. I like you. I am really sorry.' On the following occasion, we didn't know what to do. We proposed – as we had weeks before – to show him the way to the Restaurant du Cœur [soup kitchen], but he wasn't interested in yet another institution he had to go to. He wanted food, right there and then. When he started grabbing Nina's arm, we left. Our quiet and patient explanations and attempts to help had been unsuccessful. We were both baffled.

The situation with Ali is only one example of the values of empty hands and the 'relationship first' causing conflicts – both verbal and physical. On the same street tour in February, Nina and I encountered similar issues with the members of the group of Polish people Carl had spent time with, as well as with Joseph, a middle-aged, psychotic alcoholic man we saw regularly on Rue Lafayette. Joseph sometimes screamed at us and refused to talk or even look at us when he saw us approaching. Usually, he sat in the middle of the pavement on a hot-air vent right next to a restaurant in between Poisonnière and Le Cadet. He was heavily intoxicated every time we saw him, a bottle of cheap rosé next to his backpack. Of course, the alcohol and his mental health problems influenced how he reacted to us. It seems probable that being in winter made him even more nervous about housing and food. Nina and I also discussed how the experience of having all of these different organizations come and talk to you regularly, always asking the same questions, could make you feel upset and frustrated.

In fact, I saw such reactions as signs of an ambiguity at the core of Freedom. Why do you come with empty hands (*mains nues*), Ali asked us. It almost sounded like an accusation. Was he perhaps right to expect help – physical help, as this was what he most needed? Ali did not see the free gift the volunteers were offering as a gift at all; indeed, it was very much conditional in his eyes. This view linked directly to Freedom's project, which seemed to have two pillars, as Nina explained to me:

> I think we are here to look after the person, not after a case. We focus on the human component of the problem of homelessness. And then, we also want to educate the people a little bit. There are a lot of offers around – for food, day centres, showers – and I think we need to make clear to people that they need to move if they want to be helped.

This last point was not only obvious in Ali's case, but also in the case of a Romanian family we encountered towards the end of our tour. Every time we saw the three men – two brothers in their early and late twenties and their father – with their girlfriends and wives, they would ask us:

> How much money do you make? Why don't you ever bring us anything? It is hard for us to make any money. I am begging all day but can't make ends meet. You make a lot of money – look at your coat. Can you bring me trousers next time?

We tried to explain to them how they could get help and tried to convince them to go to the ESI or guided them towards other organizations, such as the Restaurants du Cœur for warm meals or the Vestiboutique of the Red Cross for clothes. However, they expected the support to come to them. When they engaged with associations, one of the Romanian men explained to Nina and me, they expected help: 'They come with food or clothes or at least coffee, but you don't have anything.' This ambiguity – at least from the perspective of the people on the street – is an issue that arose during both Freedom's street tours and day centre activity and was hence at the core of the institutional home-making that Freedom engaged in: why do we have to have a relationship before we are given support? In what way is the relationship part of the support?

***

On the one hand, the street tours were a first point of contact, a way of starting a relationship, of establishing the trust that is central to any homeless outreach activity (Cefaï 2015; Hall 2017; Jost et al. 2010; Rowe et al. 2002). In this sense, they are what Russell W. Belk (1999)[8] calls a perfect gift and Erica Bornstein (2012) terms relational empathy: an act of altruism, still aiming at creating social relations, but often surprising and spontaneous for the recipient. Abstracting from her description of various practices of charity and humanitarianism in India, contrasting relational empathy with the common Western form of liberal, altruistic humanitarianism, Bornstein writes: 'those who practice relational empathy turn strangers into kin' (ibid.: 170). In the case of Freedom, the repeated, free, immaterial gift of the street tour – of time, attention, information, support – brought directly to the person, followed the principle of the *mains nues*. At least from the perspective of Freedom and the volunteers, the street tour was an offering and did not demand anything from the recipient – the homeless person – in return. This initial series of encounters was nevertheless supposed to lead, eventually, to a relationship and also to the ESI, where more advanced care and home-making activities (access to an address, housing, welfare) could be supported and a *projet de vie* created. It was in this sense that a facet of the street tour resembled James Laidlaw's (2002: 58) notion of the unstable gift: 'gifts evoke obligations and create reciprocity, but they can do this because they might not: what creates the obligation is the gesture or moment that alienates the given thing and asks for no reciprocation.' In fact, most of the people we saw during our tours never came to the ESI and never engaged in a reciprocal relationship. As I have described, the first step – slowly building a regular relationship – sometimes went wrong because of a misunderstanding, a frustration linked to the empty-handed principle. The street tours were a free, first gift, in Simmel's (1950: 392) sense, that doubled as a means of probing the possibility of a relationship. In case of failure, street tours turned into nothing more than distractions, sometimes welcome and sometimes not so welcome – a 'free' gift of charity. When Ali – and others – became aggressive, their understanding of the situation became visible: for Ali, we, the volunteers, actually didn't give anything at all; we demanded information, used his time, wanted him to talk to us. Even if it was well intentioned, the immaterial gift we were offering was not always welcome.

People like Ali demanded immediate help, whereas Freedom was careful to establish *liens* [relationships] of the immaterial kind first. The official rationale behind this was slightly different though: Freedom didn't want to replicate the work of other institutions in the neighbourhood – giving out food and clothes, for instance – and was instead focusing on a different kind of poverty, what they called *spiritual* poverty; the work was very much based on the (assumed) lack of relationships on the street. This tension – between reciprocity, conditionality and the demands of the homeless people – also translated into activities facilitated at the day centre, which will be the focus of the remainder of this chapter.

At the ESI

Freedom's ESI is only a five-minute walk from the Gare du Nord.[9] The ESI was a constant in the lives of many homeless people around the station, including many of my informants, which is how it became one of the core locations for my fieldwork. ESI stands for *Espace Solidarité Insertion*, an unusual name for what would simply be called a day centre or drop-in facility for homeless people in the UK. It is a space of solidarity, wherein the reintegration of homeless people is furthered. About fifteen similar centres (Département de Paris 2017) exist all over Paris, run by organizations such as the Armée de Salut [Salvation Army] or Emmaüs. Most of them – including the ESI where I volunteered – are financed by funds from the city of Paris, the region (Ile-de-France) and private funds (foundations, volunteers, gifts). It is at the ESI that the idea of the street tour is extended and the *mains nues* principle translated into what, at Freedom, was perceived as unconditionality: mirroring standard policy at most day centres internationally (Cooper 2001), anyone was welcome to go to the toilet, to have a coffee, to play a game, to meet friends, to simply be inside and warm up, to shave, to talk to someone. At the centre, the regular ten-minute encounters during the street tours turned into something more solid and material; people were given a space in the form of the day centre and a network of people in the form of volunteers and staff. They played in the *salle* as a way of building relationships. Moreover, a network of infrastructure that provided people with the most urgent amenities, like hygiene spaces, the warmth of a heater, chairs, coffee, milk and sugar, was offered quasi-unconditionally to everyone who was willing to obey the rules associated with accessing the ESI (no violence, no drink or food, no aggressive behaviour). Certain elements of this infrastructure – the showers and washing machines – were more conditionally shared, as I will highlight after first describing how people access the ESI. The core of the one-to-one social work at Freedom, however, followed a stricter logic of reciprocal exchange, as I will illustrate in the last part of this chapter.

Accessing the ESI

As I arrive for my weekly three-hour shift as a regular *bénévole* [volunteer] at around 1.55PM on a Thursday, twelve people are already there. Three of the social workers are about to hop over to their offices on the other side of the road, while the leadership team, Pauline and Ina, are having an after-lunch coffee in the kitchen. Four other volunteers, as well as Egon, the 'quiet rock' of a bouncer, and two young men doing their civil service are preparing the space for the arrival of people from the street. We put the chairs in order around the tables, make sure the coffee machine is ready, position the plastic cups in a row in between the hot water and tea bags. The atmosphere is pleasant; people talk to each other about their day, about the people they met last time they were volunteering at the centre. The experience of volunteering as part of the team is like entering into a warm, comfortable place in order to do something helpful once a week. At 2PM, the door opens. Egon walks outside and announces that it's time. Some of the regulars are already waiting to be let in. As soon as the door swings open, they make their way up the couple of steps to the *accueil* [reception]. For the first few minutes, roughly half of the staff stand by the door to the main room – the *salle* – and greet people.

Egon welcomes people as they come in. He stands at the bottom of the stairs leading up to the other rooms, his body filling the whole door. Egon acts as the first point of contact for anyone arriving. He is, on the one hand, the bouncer whose job it is to ensure that people who are too drunk or too violent are not allowed in (or are thrown out), as well as being a constant source of calm, stability and balance. He has had this role for over ten years already. At the top of the stairs, there is a big desk in front of Pauline's office. One member of staff sits behind the desk, counting people as they come in and registering their gender and whether it is their first time at the ESI. No questions are asked, no names are required. Entrance is only conditional on past behaviour, judged mainly by Egon and, in complicated circumstances, by the manager Pauline.

Only violence or aggressive behaviour would lead to people being denied access. In January 2016, for instance, a conflict surrounding two people in my wider network – Moritz and Yosh – initiated a lot of trouble, as Pascal explained while we were sitting in the *salle* of the ESI:

They have been terrorizing everyone for a while. They are beating up people, threatening them, taking money from them. One guy, they almost killed in front of Leader Price. They kicked him in the head several times while he was already lying on the floor. They took money from the old Patrick and even Steph [people who visited the ESI regularly]. They take people's beers.

After having started a violent fight in the ESI, Moritz and Yosh, both part of the injecting drug scene, were not allowed in for several weeks. This protected Pascal and other visitors when there were breaches of the rules of conduct. In this sense, the ESI was what Bowpitt et al. call a 'place of sanctuary' (Bowpitt et al. 2014: 1255; see also Hope 1995), a place of refuge but also of change, a place of what I call softly conditioned but almost limitless sharing to start with and later reciprocal exchange, initiating development in the visitors. In their description of the day centre, Bowpitt et al. refer to the sanctuary of the Judeo-Christian tradition as a place of both 'escape from the demands, injustices and oppression of the outside world' and a place of 'challenge, risk and change' (ibid.). I will unpack this double-sided description of the ESI and examine three closely linked but subtly different practices.

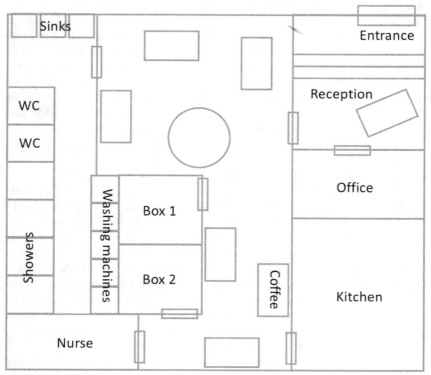

Figure 5.1. Illustration of the ESI, drawn by the author, April 2017.
© Johannes Lenhard.

Playing at the Salle: Sharing Infrastructure

The core of the ESI was the *salle*, a big room of about 50 square metres filled with tables and chairs. There were enough seats for about forty people at a time; six large tables allowed visitors to sit down, relax, rest, play a game, have a chat or quietly enjoy a hot tea or coffee. The chairs in the corners were 'reserved' for the tired ones. One lady from Cameroon named Lise, for instance, came in every day for a long while in winter 2015; at 9.30AM, she was among the first to enter the ESI and immediately found her seat right next to the heater near the back of the room. After having deposited her belongings – normally a significant number of plastic bags – at the door, she sat down, embraced the heater and closed her eyes. Indeed, the *salle* was a resting space for many people. They come to sit down, escaping from the rain or heat and the street more generally. People were invited to relax and left to themselves. One day in March 2016, for instance, an old man from Sudan spent the whole afternoon shift sleeping with his head on the table. Nobody had seen him before; nobody knew anything about him. Nevertheless, the whole team left him alone until closing time approached, when Egon carefully woke him up. Afterwards, Egon explained to me:

> He could barely get up. He slept there all morning – but it's fine. I had to accompany him outside. That's how feeble he was. We leave people stay here to relax and calm down.

The ESI was a space of calmness, relaxation and safety; a space to heat up, a space where there was refreshing water in the summer – in short, a refuge, a space where 'essential maintenance' (Johnsen, Cloke and May 2005b: 805), in the form of warmth, security and sleep, was supported. But it was also a space in which to play and fend off boredom.

***

On my first shift at the ESI in early 2015, I did not know what to do. I had volunteered in similar venues before, but the ESI was different. I wasn't there to solve problems in the narrow sense, but to get to know people – to build the *liens* that were at the core of Freedom's mission. It turned out that one way of doing that in a playful manner was by engaging in a game of chess or another board game. There was a vibrant community of mainly Arab-speaking French men who met at the ESI – most of them formerly homeless and now with an apartment or at least a room in a temporary hostel. They came to play. After having found out what I, the new volunteer, did in life, Yannick asked me to play straight away. I don't remember our first game being particularly long, perhaps fifteen minutes, but it was only the first in a long series of encounters. Every time we were both at the ESI, we played. Luck changed its allegiance regularly; we were both able to beat each other, which made the engagement even more interesting. Yannick explained to me why he went to the ESI:

> I come here every day. I play chess, drink coffee, talk to people, see my social worker. They are my friends here. It's like family.

He was estranged from his core family; his wife had left him, taking their daughter and son, about two years earlier. Over time, the ESI had become akin to a replacement family. Long before I came, he had established a routine that made him feel secure at the ESI.

It wasn't only Yannick I played with; we regularly changed partners, organized little tournaments, challenged each other. The community of chess players consisted of perhaps ten people. During the games, we didn't talk very much. But we learnt other things about each other: how do you deal with stress? Are you a good loser? Do you cheat? We developed favourite partners, learnt each other's preferences for hot beverages, gossiped about each other. We became a group of friends and competitors; these were important, friendly social relationships that many of my informants were missing in their lives.

Chess was not the only game that was played at the ESI. Other board games, cards and Scrabble were commonly played as well. TriX was very popular as it is a game for between four and six people; the players would sit around the big round table at the centre of the room. Guillaume was one of the regular visitors who was always to be found at this table. He never took off his sunglasses as he had a severe eye problem. Although he might not have been able to see very well, he loved to joke and laugh. TriX was exactly the right game for him, particularly when the young women doing their civil service played as well. They joked around, teased, competed and got to know each other. Guillaume explained:

> It is a time off here. Away from the street. I'm not bored here. I play and forget and have all the people. They are my friends. We play together.

Playing TriX was not only a way of dealing with boredom; it was also a way of generating a group feeling, a feeling of being together while at the same time providing an easy battleground on which conflicts could be resolved without violence. Just as in Clifford Geertz's (Geertz 1993) Balinese cockfight, my informants used the safe space of the playful battlefield to resolve little conflicts and make sneaky accusations. Guillaume, for instance, would bring small personal animosities or interests to the TriX board. He loved to cheat. He wanted to win – often to impress the women, sometimes just to stay on top of the (social) game ladder. He loved to mess around, particularly with Lana, a young Norwegian volunteer. After she left Freedom, he talked to me about her regularly:

> I loved playing with Lana. I always won ... and I could joke with her. She was new and I could help her. I explained the rules to her. ... How is she anyway? I liked her.

Newcomers – be they volunteers or homeless people – were offered an easy way in through these games. As with Lana, it was often Guillaume who invited new players to join the group of players. He made people feel welcome, had them participate in the game, which unfolded with a lot of casual conversation and laughter, and used the situation to teasingly play around.

***

Despite the focus on playing and overcoming boredom, people were often drawn to something else at the day centre: minutes after the door opened, the hygiene spaces would already be full. Nina ruled over the showers, the washing machines and the four sinks located on the other side of the big *salle*. She handed out razors, soap and paper towels; took care of the washing for you; and would provide towels and hair-cutting equipment. Many people went to the ESI to go to the toilet, shave, brush their teeth, wash their clothes, shower. All of these services were available for free – though not for everyone at any one time. Men could only come in the morning and ask for a razor or a toothbrush, for instance, and it was necessary to obtain a ticket one week in advance to wash one's clothes. Showers were only permitted to a handful of people, those – as Pauline put it – who were 'the really down-and-out, the ones who can't possibly walk to a public shower, the ones really entrenched on the street'.

In fact, while access to the ESI was only based on adherence to a handful of rules, the infrastructure it provided was not unconditionally shared. Pauline explained to me why certain barriers were helpful in advancing the aims of the ESI:

> When the showers were still open for everyone and we would give out food, we would get all of these people. Quite a few of them were not on the street; they would only come to get some breakfast or take a shower because they didn't have one in their small rooms. They would leave after half an hour without having spoken to anyone, without sitting down. Now, people come to stay much more.

Ultimately, limiting certain parts of the infrastructure[10] – making them available only for people who really don't have an alternative because of their immobility, for instance – helped to put up a barrier against those who would otherwise not come to the ESI and were not interested in its core functionality – relationships and community. This helped to prevent the ESI from becoming a public bath or wash salon and allowed the focus to remain on human interaction. At least, that was the narrative shared among staff.

***

The ESI was firstly 'a safe place, where people can at least meet their survival needs without any further expectations' (Bowpitt et al. 2014: 1259). It was a place where (physical) self-care was enabled and a space of distraction from boredom, a space in which to play. This was one side of its sanctuary character. As at Sun, the primary focus was on the body, from coffee to sugar to razors; thus, the priority was still immediate and short-term survival. The advice, assistance and non-interventionist 'provision of essential resources [not only] aid[ed] people's survival on a day-to-day basis' (Johnsen, Cloke and May 2005a: 327); these were also a starting point for a network of human relationships between staff and visitors, but also between visitors themselves. Relationships were built that were viewed as the basis for any further support and for addressing 'underlying issues' (Midgley 2016: 618). As Pauline put it: 'We do our work well ... if we construct a network of company [social network] for the person with the person.' In all of the above senses, the ESI was a space of home, a space where home-making activities took place and were encouraged.

Analytically, the activities that took place in the *salle* – playing games, talking, drinking coffee – as well as the hygiene spaces – shaving, washing oneself, using the toilets, brushing one's teeth – were part of a sharing infrastructure. John A. Price (1975: 4) defines sharing as an 'integrative or coordinating process ... allocat[ing] ... economic goods and services without calculating returns'. Prototypical acts of sharing can be identified in the 'pooling and allocating of resources within the family'. Not all of the sharing between the ESI, its staff and homeless people involved economic goods; it also – perhaps primarily – involved time and attention. The important aspect of communal ownership (Belk 1984) and the effect of linking people through 'solidarity and bonding' (Belk 2010: 717) were at the core of Freedom's activities in these practices. Giving back was not expected and did not influence entitlement to further participation in the community or use of the infrastructure (see Woodburn 1982; Woodburn 1998). In fact, the sharing of infrastructure and the playing were what Thomas Widlok describes as 'silent' (or indirect demand) sharing, the sharing of something 'for its own sake' (Widlok 2013: 16), that is, for instance, the space or the coffee, but without a demand for such sharing being explicitly uttered. The demand is implicit in the act of entering the ESI.

I have already observed a subtle difference in the logic between the activities in the *salle* and the usage of the infrastructure, particularly the restricted access to the showers. While the *salle* was – beyond the general rules of conduct and the implied rules of exclusion – free and open to use and thus unconditional, usage of certain parts of the infrastructure followed a slightly different logic. To obtain a toothbrush or a razor, you had to ask Nina; to wash your clothes, you had to obtain one of five daily slots at the beginning of the week (free of charge); to access the showers, you had to register your demand, which had to be approved in a general staff meeting (criterion: was he or she able to go anywhere else for a shower?). This second type of sharing – which was more restricted and based on requests – resembles most closely what Widlok calls, in contrast to the silent sharing of the *salle*, explicit demand sharing. Such sharing is clearly 'initiated by the receiver' (ibid.: 21). The desire to use the washing machines, the showers or a toothbrush had to be made explicit; my informants had to voice these demands to staff. Extending Widlok's categorization further, this type of explicit demand sharing was also risky at the ESI: there was a chance of refusal. It was possible that all of the washing machine slots would be taken, while only certain people (the most 'destitute') were allowed to use the showers. This had the potential to make some people feel that they were being unfairly treated.

The activities I have mentioned also explicitly served as a testing ground for the people visiting. How they engaged with these activities would determine whether they would be given access to the care work of the *assistants sociaux*, with whom they would be able to plan their *projets de vie* [life projects] and who would support them in accessing external infrastructure (housing, banks, health insurance). Staff tried to figure out whether the homeless people were 'welfare-ready' (Johnsen, Fitzpatrick and Watts 2014). While relationship-building was at the core of Freedom's work, such relationships were also a means of testing the engagement of the homeless person. The second way in which the ESI served as a sanctuary – a place of challenge and change in the future tense – started thus. The one-to-one social work was challenging people, trying to get them to move and look forward. The aim was to define the *project de vie* as a longer-term hope and come up with activities and steps to reach this goal in the shorter term – often the kind of activities I will describe as techniques of the self below (Foucault 1997). Not everyone was willing or allowed to engage with this kind of support. Access to an *assistant social* followed a much stricter logic of reciprocal exchange than access to the *salle* and the internal infrastructure. As Pauline put it: 'people have to come for some time before they are followed (*suivie*) by a social worker.' Responsibilization[11] was perhaps a necessary part of hope- and future-making from the perspective of the ESI, but it created conflicts, just as the street tours were problematized by the tension between *mains nues* and the provision of services and support. The social work took place 'in a box', a small transparent glass office in the middle of the ESI, where the core of the one-to-one longer-term care and encouragement[12] started – and not everyone had access to this space.

In the Box: Reflecting on the Future with the Projet de Vie

'Quel est ton projet de vie?' [What do you want to do with your life?]. So Carole would start a first session with a new *accueilli* [visitor]. Usually, for these initial encounters, she would sit in the box, one of the two mini social work offices cut off from the *salle* by glass walls. Facing each other over a desk – the only piece of furniture in the room apart from the chairs – Carole would either take notes on a computer or on paper as she listened carefully. It was this kind of help that many people came to Freedom for: individual social work that would lead the way from the street to housing; filling out forms to apply for unemployment benefits, an ID or a health insurance card; support with medical appointments and other administrative necessities. The boxes were used as a space to retreat into in order to have more serious, direct conversations, a space in which to formulate the *projet de vie*.

Many informal conversations preceded this moment of entering the box (or sometimes another office in a different part of the building). During a formal discussion at the weekly staff meeting on a Tuesday, it would be collectively decided that a new person would now be *suivi*[13] by a social worker, such as Carole, Marie or Véronique. One member of staff would bring the suggestion to the group and usually a consensus was quickly reached. The main criteria were simple: has the person clearly asked to be helped? Can we support the person with our resources? Has he or she been around regularly and created a relationship? If the answer to these three questions was 'yes' and if no one felt that things had moved too quickly (Carole: 'la personne accepte de vraiment s'installer' [the person accepts to take his or her place]), one of the *assistants sociaux* would be assigned to take on the person.

The first step would be to listen and facilitate listening. Most social workers, including Carole, told me that their most important task was to encourage the person to listen to themselves honestly and openly. The aim was, in abstract terms, to produce a space of reflective freedom, the 'reflective consciousness [allowing us to] "step back" from and evaluate our own thoughts and desires, and decide reflectively which desires we wish to have and to move us to action' (Laidlaw 2014: 148). Carole described her work in the box as follows:

> We start with talking about the *parcours* [history]. We already have an idea ... what we might be able to do. ... I also observe the needs, the objectives which we devise together because in social work we talk about the person's *projet*, which means the project we have developed together ... which can respond to the situation and the needs associated with his or her *parcours* [past trajectory]. That means that the person speaks out about the desires and needs.

Building on the person's description of the past (*parcours* [personal history]) and, in Véronique's words, his or her *blessures* [injuries], Carole jumps through the present – identifying needs – into the future, towards unfulfilled desires (*projet*). As I described in the 'Frame' chapter, most of my informants had long-term hopes. These hopes were part of their *projets* – from Sabal's longing for his religious and cultural community in India to Carl's desire to return to his family and deal with his trauma; they could also include concrete goals, such as Alex's need for a right to stay (*titre de sejour*) or more abstract objectives associated with home-as-homeland. In every case, the aim of the *assistant social* was to unearth these hopes, give them space, make them accessible and help the people to divide them into manageable chunks that could be worked towards. These hopes would constitute the person's *projet de vie*. Pascal formulated his in the following way:

> I need money and a place to sleep. Immediately if possible. I want to get a European passport so that I can travel back to Germany [where his family was]. I need an

address for that and I need a post office [bank] account to be paid money by the French state. ... I also need a job. I am bored and I want something to do. I mean, I had one in Germany and stuff, but I want to do something else. And they don't know about my life in Germany.

For his social worker, Carole, this translated into the following: he needs a *domiciliation* in order to receive post and to register with the bank and he needed to fill out an SIAO form (*Services Intégrés d'Accueil et d'Orientation* [Integrated Reception and Orientation Services]) to access first temporary and eventually longer-term housing. While there was no standard way to get off the street, Pascal's main demands – the address and housing – would often be part of the *projets de vie* people formulated at Freedom.[14] Neither could be achieved by homeless people alone as they required institutional backing. In both processes, social workers (and the organizations behind them) acted as crucial facilitators. Véronique described this to me in more general terms:

> I would say we try to calm people down. We are mediators ... Often when I take people to appointments, I don't do much. I am just next to the person. I am there to reassure. ... Sometimes I take the role of the mediator, when the person needs me to talk.

Marie added:

> We can have some ideas for the person but it is always necessary that he tells us: 'This is my project.' ... We need to work hand in hand with the person.

The social workers understand themselves as the ones supporting the homeless people in formulating their desires; they are there to support and suggest rather than lead the way, to translate rather than talk. This was at the core of their provision of care.

***

Carole helped Pascal and Carl to formulate their demands; before her, another *assistant social* had laid the groundwork by supporting them as they narrated their histories, in terms of health, housing and work. While Carole only really followed their demands – for instance, the desire for housing – she also helped them to think beyond their own horizons. She extended their wish and translated it into the everyday reality of the administrative structure of the SIAO. She was able to anticipate problems that Carl could not have foreseen – a state agency losing an application, for instance – and so was essential to the success of his striving.

Indeed, a whole group of people was necessary to help Carl, Pascal and others to reach certain goals: people who fill out forms with and for them – Carl's French was passable, but not good enough for administrative tasks; people who accompanied them on visits to potential shelters and hotels;

people who vouched for them in relation to the SIAO and wrote reports on their progress; people who translated verbal explanations and letters for them. Social work at Freedom was a process of constant 'tinkering' (Winance 2010). Volunteers and staff worked together to build a relationship; they built trust together, which allowed the person to more freely think about and ultimately give voice to his desires and dreams of some kind of home-making. The relationship was the platform on which this honesty and confidence to talk openly about the future was constructed. The *assistant social* was then able to nurture these dreams and operationalize them in smaller steps, such as filling out forms, making a phone call, accompanying a person to have passport photos taken – while keeping the big picture, the *projet de vie*, in view.

In the above sense of tinkering, social work is care, according to Annemarie Mol. Mol defines care as an open-ended, needs-based process of support, always with the active involvement of the person receiving the care (Mol 2008: 19). In the context of diabetes care, Mol focuses specifically on the process character of care, as well as its two-sidedness. For a diabetic, for instance, constantly monitoring one's blood sugar level is an important part of the care process (Golightley 2014: 57). The notion of the process of care can again be identified in Myriam Winance's idea of 'tinkering' care, which she describes as a process intended to 'meticulously explore, "quibble", test, touch, adapt, adjust, pay attention to details and change them, until a suitable arrangement (material, emotional, relational) has been reached' (Winance 2010: 111). Hence, the care relationship is one of messy trial and error, of testing different means and measures.

In the setting of the ESI, care began with 'build[ing] a relationship ... [with] assess[ing] the rough sleeper's situation' – with listening and understanding the needs of the person, with understanding their *parcours* (Midgley 2016: 619, 623). The person who was cared for was an essential part of the caring process; the demand had to come from them and the initial information (the narration of the *parcours* [life history]) was provided by them. The process was ongoing – between the social worker and the homeless person through meetings and simple encounters in the *salle* – and two-sided. The person's demand was answered by the social worker. Encouragement, ruptures and directly educational activities sometimes successfully led to further engagement, as in the cases of Carl and Pascal, and at other times they did not. Both parties constantly push, fight and quibble in order for an SIAO request to go through, for instance. Working together is necessary.

In this sense, the activities at the ESI served to create a space of care (Conradson 2003: 508), a 'socio-spatial field disclosed through practices of care that take place between individuals', providing welfare that goes beyond the merely bodily, encompassing the social and emotional (Johnsen, Cloke and May 2005a: 326). This space included freely shared resources (coffee and tea, hygiene spaces), as well as advice and assistance (provided at the reception of the ESI), usually with an open-door or no-questions-asked policy. It also focused on the *projet de vie* – in which bodily maintenance was complemented by mental stretching that helped the person to open up to the future and the hope of a future home.

***

As helpful and crucial as this kind of care proved to be for many visitors at the ESI – including Pascal and Carl, among others – I also observed complications (ibid.). Through analysing the process of following (*suivre*) a new person more closely and understanding this using the analytic of exchange – the most reciprocal one – these complications become apparent.

I have already alluded to the fact that not everyone was helped immediately in the same way at the ESI. Just like access to the shower, access to *assistants sociaux* was restricted. Access to such services was restricted as not everyone was deemed 'service-deserving', to use a term used in the English-speaking context (Meanwell 2013). Marie described it in the following way in an interview in late 2016:

> We don't answer [demands] immediately. ... It is necessary to take the time to get to know each other. ... Sometimes they don't even stay for five minutes and they want something. ... We need to understand whether we can help and who is best [which social worker]. ... [We want to avoid] that the person is excluded from the centre [for housing] immediately because there is a big [drug] addiction or perhaps a mental health problem or just because the person is violent.

Time – time spent at the ESI, time shared with staff and other visitors, and the passing of time more generally – was an important part of the initial investment expected from the homeless person. Relationships – initiated and freely offered at first by a volunteer or an *assistant social* – had to develop over time before the person could be 'followed'. While the types of sharing at the ESI were centred on building relationships (Belk 2010: 717), the relationship was itself a prerequisite for the social work encounter. Time was a condition that differentiated the one-to-one social work as gift exchange from other kinds of exchange at the ESI.

The example of a Tunisian woman, Bela, whom I first encountered on a street tour in late 2015, demonstrates these principles at work. Although I was able to convince Bela to come to the ESI, she caused immediate confusion there. In addition to arriving with a shopping cart full of things and requesting immediate storage for some of her luggage, she tried to see a social worker on the spot. She made a lot of health requests – she suffered from several visible skin diseases and a thyroid problem – to which staff at the ESI were unable to respond. Bela came back a couple of times, but grew more and more frustrated because her demands for help were not being answered. I lost track of Bela after having accompanied her to the hospital on my own initiative once, several months after first meeting.

As the example of Bela illustrates, only people who came regularly, spent time at the ESI – people who established a relationship in the *salle* – and were known to be non-violent and responsible, with a manageable set of needs, would be taken on by an *assistant social*.[15] The manager Pauline made it clear that this was mainly a self-protective mechanism on the part of the ESI; it was supposed to prevent people from having several *assistants sociaux* in different institutions. Staff at Freedom also wanted to make sure that only people who *could* be helped were supported; refugees, for instance, usually had a different set of problems, for which the staff at Freedom were not well trained. This second point was crucial: if the aim of the social work, of care, was ultimately to support people to formulate a *projet de vie* and then to work towards it – to change their way of living – it was important to ensure that one's resources, experience and knowledge were suitable for tackling the individual set of problems each person had. In other words, intense care was going to be provided where change was possible. Building a relationship was one way of figuring whether such change was possible; thus, the relationship was a testing ground.

Consequently, care was only provided for people who were willing to give something first. Following the logic of Marshall Sahlins's (2004: 195ff) balanced reciprocity – a direct exchange in precise balance that does not tolerate one-way flows – (social work) care was only offered to people who had spent considerable amounts of time at the ESI. Only people who 'engaged', who came regularly and were known to everyone, who were open to talking and interested in the community and relationship-building, would be taken on. People had to demonstrate their willingness to engage and ultimately to change before they would be given access to the expertise of an *assistant social*. The gift of their engagement, their time, would be reciprocated with care in the form of an address and support with housing and benefit applications and so on. The relationship-building in the *salle* was both an aim in itself and a testing ground for the provision of this kind of care. This type of exchange most closely resembled the archetype Marcel Mauss described as gift exchange: a *reciprocal* exchange unfolding over *time* based on *relational* bonds. In contrast to the sharing (of space, described above), the exchange surrounding social work was based on an existing relationship and was part of its continuation into the future (Mauss 2001).

An important question was how the judgement was made: how were people deemed service-deserving? As on the street tours, when people became angry because we didn't offer any immediate (material) help, visitors like Bela could not comprehend the reluctance to support them. Why were some people getting appointments? Pauline only had a vague response to this: 'It is a question of *feeling* – it is for this reason that that some might at times have the idea that certain people have certain privileges.' There were no clear checklists – how much time was enough? – just subjective judgements on the suitability and readiness of candidates to be 'followed' (Dobson 2011: 553f). While this subjective decision-making might sometimes lead to conflict, I didn't witness systematic or conscious exclusion at the ESI. Sometimes initial judgements might not have been accurate, but judgements would usually be revised and, for most people, the process ultimately worked out. Both Pascal and Carl were willing to wait, to engage further and were finally housed. However, did the most structurally disengaged people – people suffering from several mental and physical health problems, such as Bela – fall through the cracks systematically? Would the ESI have been able to support them properly?

A second issue followed immediately from the logic of reciprocal exchange as a condition to accessing one-to-one social work: it could be necessary to *perform* an identity to fulfil the exchange conditions. As I described in chapter 1 in relation to the work of begging, people figured out what they needed to say and do in order to get what they wanted (Desjarlais 1997: 215). Informants would switch discourses to position themselves adequately according to what they thought the situation demanded; they jumped between multiple self-representations, mostly in order to maximize outcomes in the form of access to support.

Did the social workers at Freedom need to expect such a tactical façade? Help was based on the relationship, but what happened when the relationship was faked? I discussed this with Pauline during a casual conversation in early 2016. She explained how difficult it is for people working at the ESI to see everything transparently: 'We only really see one part of people's lives; only the life they have when they come here. I know this is sometimes not enough. But what can we do?' Moritz and Yosh had just left the *salle* when Pauline and I started talking. They were the reason I had thought of this question of the façade in relation to the ESI. I explained my worries to Pauline: 'I know them from the street. I see them in a different space, where they behave differently. They beat people up. They threaten people and take their stuff. They have beaten up some of the people here before and taken their money. I don't like that they come in here and invade this space. They want to profit from your help.' She was aware of the issue but maintained the principle of the unconditional space: 'This is shocking, in fact. It's horrible what happens on the street. I know that these things happen all the time – but like I just said: I can't do anything. I only know them in here. I only know so little about the people who come in here. I only see them here where they present a particular part of themselves.'[16]

Moritz, in particular, was capable of producing a performance of the self that led to his deserved outcomes: towards the end of 2016, he managed to secure a space in a hostel through the ESI. Despite being aggressive and violent on the street – to secure material benefits – he was well spoken, nice, polite and, most importantly, a regular at the ESI in order to build the necessary relationship to access his desired form of support. The fact that people used different masks in different situations was not necessarily an issue for Marie; she felt that such masks were part of the protection necessary on the street:

> We are happy when the person comes out from their little space on the pavement ... When they come here from the street ... you can feel that the masks fall down ... They might play Dr Jekyll and Mr Hyde on the street, but here...

The problem of 'flipping the script' was potentially less of an issue at the ESI due to the position adopted by the *assistants sociaux*. During my interviews, staff at the ESI ultimately rejected the categorization of people into bad and good SDF or deserving and undeserving poor (Rullac 2008: 157). While a certain reciprocity was part of everyday practice, almost everyone – as long as their needs were not too complex – would ultimately be taken on by one of Freedom's *assistants sociaux* if they explicitly asked for help. While the soft rules of the ESI had to be met and the condition of 'regular engagement' had to be fulfilled, the Freedom approach to what is often termed 'responsible citizenship' seemed tamer, with less demanding exchange conditions, than what can be found, for instance, in the UK context (Johnsen, Cloke and May 2005; Whiteford 2010). At the ESI, there was an explicit negation of the notion of making the homeless people responsible for behaving in certain ways (paying rent regularly, for instance). There was very little control and surveillance at the ESI beyond preventing violence. Also, what happened on the street stayed on the street and did not necessarily influence people's treatment at the ESI. I observed this as a conscious effort to focus on care rather than responsibilization at the ESI. In this regard, the ESI stands in stark contrast to the kind of welfare conditionality Clara Han (2012: 67) analysed in Chile: she described the 'system of punishments and rewards' in place there, pushing people to 'learn responsibility'. In order to obtain support – mainly financial, in this case – the people dealing with the social workers in the Chilean government office in which Han carried out her fieldwork had to define and reach personal goals: 'You're in a program that has goals. Have to reach those goals. So, if you don't reach them, we do not give you the things' (ibid.: 66). At the ESI, I did not observe this kind of exclusionary and inflexible conditionality of support. It is crucial to achieve a balance between a rule-driven setup and the provision of care; this should never tip in favour of the former and should focus on supporting people directly, as unconditionally as possible (Midgley 2016: 625). Most of the basic care at the ESI – health, a place to rest, hygiene, coffee, play – was shared almost unconditionally and only more complex parts of the social work were based on a logic of reciprocal exchange. Partly to avoid doing work that another social worker might be doing for a person at another institution, the one-to-one social work demanded longer-term engagement, the investment of time and the demonstration of a certain kind of responsibility from the homeless person, often judged subjectively but usually in favour of the person.

Conclusion

The ESI, in the form of its space, its infrastructure and, most importantly, the people there and the activities facilitated by the ESI, provided a variety of (home-like) facilities of care. Freedom provided support in the more material short term, first and foremost. Basic goods – a conversation with an outreach volunteer, access to the warm space in the day centre, coffee, sugar, the toilets and a space to play board games – were shared (almost completely) freely. Certain parts of the infrastructure – showers and washing machines – were slightly more conditional. However, all of these activities were part of building a relationship (*lien*) from the perspective of the *assistants sociaux*. They were necessary starting points for the second, more future-oriented and less immediate aspect of the support the ESI offered. This analysis of the day centre on the basis of a logic of different forms of exchange not only provides a complementary view of social work, but also helps us to think about issues of what is called welfare conditionality or neoliberalist responsibilization in other research. In providing a more directly ethnographical description of the activities at the ESI, I am trying to avoid whitewashed societal narratives of neoliberalism, for instance, and am focusing instead on the core ambiguity relating to the desires and demands of homeless people and the expectations and demands of care providers.

Seen critically, many of these relationship-focused activities were also a way of testing the people taking part. The space for reflection, planning and changing, with the support of the *assistant social*, was only accessible after having 'proved oneself'. The *assistants sociaux* had a gate-keeping function and access to them ('in the box') was dependent on a strong commitment from the homeless person (time, engagement, willingness to change). Once 'followed' by an *assistant social*, care went beyond materiality to the formulation of longer-term hopes, which were translated into manageable chunks to be worked on. It was at this point that the focus shifted towards the longer-term hopes, which often involved leaving the street and returning home.

Overall, by providing a secure space and by helping people to make boredom more productive and create relationships based on trust, the ESI made many of my informants feel more comfortable planning and talking about their hopes. In this sense, the ESI is a space in which reflective freedom (Laidlaw 2014) is fostered, as in the case of Emo. Through its variety of activities, the ESI provided alternative ways of looking at the world, of playing and learning, and ultimately of thinking about one's future.

Notes

1. I will use this short form of *Espace Solidarité Insertion* [space for solidarity and insertion] interchangeably with 'day centre' from now on.
2. Widlok 2012; in his literature review of the concept, Belk (2010: 715) calls this 'open sharing' or a 'commons to be shared by all', following Stephen Gudeman (2001).
3. Freedom has operations all over Paris: six day centres, several dozen regular street tours, almost fifty full-time staff members, as well as over 250 volunteers (Freedom's Annual Report 2015).
4. Freedom Brochure 2012: 4; my own translation.
5. Freedom was, indeed, founded on Catholic principles – the *mains nues* [empty hands] was only one such principle – and certain activities also led directly to the church (the

celebration of an inclusive mass open to all denominations), but overall Freedom was explicitly a) not missionary and b) not communicating particular religious values, adhering to the French principles of *laïcité* [separation of state and church]. I was not able to conduct interviews with members of the highest level of management of the organization; such interviews might have revealed a more religious agenda. During my interviews with staff, religious values were not in the foreground. Hence, I will not dwell on the religious background of the organization further, beyond the direct influence it had on my informants' lives and the everyday running of the day centre.

6. In the original French: 'la relation, se connaître, prendre le temps, la graduité, … la fidelité.'

7. This is what Bowpitt et al. (2014: 1258) call a place of refuge and Johnsen, Cloke and May (2005a) term a space of care.

8. In Sahlins's (2004) classical terminology, this end of the exchange spectrum is called generalized reciprocity, a category he uses for 'goods [that] move one way in favor of the have-not, for a very long period' (194). Following Widlock (2013), I refrain from linking this form of exchange – even only through its name – with reciprocity to differentiate it more clearly from the following forms.

9. I heard about Freedom from one of the volunteers who worked there in a conversation with Natasha in late 2014. The week after, I did my first shift at the ESI. I would continue to volunteer with Freedom until the end of my fieldwork. I met other informants here, like Carl and Werner; yet others – the group of Punjabs around Sabal, for instance – frequented the ESI regularly. I took others, such as Bela, there for the first time.

10. Additional infrastructure at the ESI included a nurse, who came in twice a week for the morning period to treat minor medical ailments. In her 2 x 4 m corner room, which – besides a stretcher – contained only a big cupboard with the most important medical supplies, she mostly looked after infections, ingrown nails, rashes and wounds.

11. A concept that resonates with Martin Whiteford's (2010) study of homelessness in Dorset.

12. See Mol 2008; Winance 2010; Lenhard 2014.

13. While *suivi* literally translates as 'being followed', it does not mean that the social worker actually follows the person; rather, it indicates that a social worker is working with and supporting the person on an ongoing basis.

14. It is important to note that these needs are not universal. Housing, for instance, was not within reach for or desired by everyone. There was no ideal case; hopes differed widely. At the ESI, hopes usually involved leaving the environment of the street.

15. Unlike in Amir B. Marvasti's (2002) study of an emergency shelter in the US, the construction of the homeless people at the ESI as service-deserving did not primarily happen through narrative construction, but rather occurred as a result of certain behaviours.

16. This conversation was the only instance in which I talked to an institution about my informants. One of the reasons for this was concern for my personal safety as I felt threatened by Moritz, who had previously approached me in a violent manner. The conflict was resolved soon after.

6

Towards a Room of One's Own
Living in 'Ruly' Temporary Accommodation

In this chapter, I will follow the development of Carl, who, in 2016, managed to find temporary accommodation in a hotel and eventually moved into a *centre d'hébergement de stabilisation* [shelter for stabilization] in the 12th arrondissement. Looking closely at his time in emergency winter accommodation in the hotel, which was not too different from Patrick Declerck's (2003)[1] famous study of Nanterre – a classic *centre d'urgence* (CHU) – I argue that, despite its short-term nature, the hotel created an important rupture in Carl's life on the street. Located in the far west of Paris, his small room not only provided him with a relatively stable space, privacy and autonomy; it also led to the restructuring of his daily routines. Both in terms of geography and activities, Carl was able (and willing) to focus less on begging, drinking and addiction time and instead focus on thinking about how to leave the street behind and working towards his longer-term hopes.

In the second part of this chapter, I will move on to observations from my time as a volunteer at Valley of Hope (VoH), a *centre d'hébergement de stabilisation* (CHS) run by Freedom in the 15th arrondissement. In France, institutional housing for homeless people is mainly provided in so-called *centres d'hébergement et de réinsertion sociale* (CHRS), which made up about half of the 80,000 places available in 2010 (Rullac, Noalhyt and Neffati 2014). The other half take the form of either hotel rooms or CHSs/CHUs. I lived for three months in a CHS that I call Valley of Hope (VoH) with men such as Franck, Jean and Patrice, during which time I observed how these men were, on the one hand, adapting their single rooms as material homes (see Zulyte 2012; Miller 2001), while struggling, on the other hand, with rules and routines. The structure proposed by staff and *bénévoles* – no drinking in the centre, instructions on how to clean the bathroom, how to use the bins, when and where to shop, when to eat together – constituted what Morgan Clarke (2010: 249, 251, 253)[2] calls a 'ruly' environment. By following rules and repeating practices and routines, people *may* advance towards the good life (leaving the street context behind, to begin with) through internalization and entrenchment. Rules become part of the person by being learnt or relearnt. At VoH, however, conflicts occurred as a result of the tension between 'being a good shelter resident' and other desires, such as the desires to drink and socialize (Schielke 2009). For some inhabitants, learning the rules of *habiter ensemble* [living together] was not easy; this often led the project to collapse. Ultimately, this approach had ambiguous results: the rules helped some people, such as Franck, to relearn and practise routines of living together and managing their lives, while they created obstacles for others, such as Jean, who chose to return to the street rather than following the pathway to more independent living.

Overall, temporary accommodation – be it the emergency shelter of a winter hotel or the three to four years my informants were able to spend in centres such as VoH – involved a struggle between enough or too much of freedom and 'ruly' order, which worked for some but not all of the people I met. I will unravel this struggle and demonstrate how the imagined *parcours* out of homelessness often leads to a semi-permanent cycle (Bruneteaux 2005: 108).

Living in a Hotel Room: A Rupture from Life on the Street

As part of a winter initiative of the city and the mayor of Paris,[3] Carl was offered three months in a private hotel in the west of Paris (Le Méner 2013). Organized by Carole, Carl's social worker at Freedom at the time, Carl moved in before Christmas 2015. I visited him on a cold afternoon in mid-January 2016. The train took me to a bourgeois suburb of the city. I climbed up the stairs from the metro and stepped out onto the street at around 4.30PM. The only other people around were elderly women. The house was right on the corner, impossible to miss with its big sign and its brightly lit restaurant on the ground floor. Two people were sitting at the bar talking to the patron as I walked past the windows and through the black door with the sign 'hotel'. Nobody greeted me as I entered and climbed up the three storeys that led me past rooms with erratic numbers – 1, 157, 2, 269, 3, 389.

As I knocked on Carl's door, hoping that he hadn't forgotten our rendezvous, I wondered: 'Can this ever be [his] home?' He opened the door and invited me into his room with a smile. The window was wide open. The room was small, but it had everything a person needs: the bed, built into a niche, took up most of the space; black duvet covers and sheets made the room appear dark. A large, open shower right next to the toilet was separated from the main area by a curtain. The floor was laminated and the bathroom, which was a centimetre higher, was tiled. The walls were covered in white, unassuming wallpaper. The closet was walled off and, again, separated with a curtain. During my stay, Carl didn't turn on the light. The room smelled of cigarettes.

I brought some things to eat – a baguette, cheese, some sweets. We started talking about 'stuff':

> I don't have anything from my Berlin days anymore. Everything was in my backpack which was stolen. All my pictures – of [family], the cats – my knives and flashlights. The only thing that is left is my belt. I got it from my grandfather once. I think I must have it for over fifteen years. I was wearing baggy pants to school and one day my belt just ripped. I went up to him and asked him whether he had a belt for me. That's the one that he gave me.

In fact, Carl didn't have a lot of things: the clothes he was wearing, another pair of shoes, another t-shirt, some underwear, a brand new Adidas jacket ('I got it yesterday'), some magazines and lighters, a fork and a set of scissors, a pocket knife and a spoon. There was no food other than what I had brought. There wasn't even a bottle of water; there were only plastic cups he had taken from the day centre. It seemed that he wasn't all that interested in things and he was only a little upset about the loss of his precious (and expensive) army backpack containing all the different items he had brought from Berlin.

His deceased grandfather's belt was associated with an important memory from earlier days. His recounting of this memory was one of the first times Carl spoke positively about the past; I think the hotel – and the rupture it effected – opened up a space for this type of longing for an idealized past, translated into and connected to a possible future home. I argue that this relates to the change in rhythm the move to the hotel signified for Carl – it constituted a rupture from his routines around the Gare du Nord and the people there.

***

From January 2016, Carl's daily rhythm changed drastically. Unlike in many other emergency shelters in Paris, where, for instance, opening times and eating times were strictly fixed (Declerck 2003; Bruneteaux 2005), Carl was able to enter or leave the hotel and eat meals as and when he wanted. As I described in the previous chapter, Emo had just opened and Carl went there every morning at 9AM. Importantly, Carl claimed that he didn't drink during or even before the Emo sessions. 'That would totally take away the whole point. I smoke a joint in the morning so that I don't drink. But I don't wanna touch alcohol before I go there.'

He detached himself from the Gare du Nord, not only by going to Emo, but also by changing his working habits. Although he found it harder to beg in the west of Paris because people seemed less inclined to give, he spent most of his time outside the city centre. As for his food consumption, after having moved to the hotel, Carl stole most of his food. He no longer went to food places for homeless people (*Armée du Salut, Restaurants du Cœur, Trinité*). 'I did that when I was on the street. Not anymore. It's far away and you must queue and it's just a nuisance. I can just as well walk into a shop and take what I want. Here, they don't even have security.' The part of the city where Carl's hotel room was located was not particularly affected by the homelessness problem. Perhaps the consequent lack of awareness explains why Carl didn't have any problems with security guards, even though he often went back to the same shops.

Most importantly, Carl's social group changed dramatically after he started living in the hotel and going to Emo. He no longer spent time with the Polish guys.

> Whenever I am with them, I will drink. It's just like that. They don't do anything else all day. They don't have any ambitions or goals. It's a shame. Darius [one of the group of Polish men] is my age but he just doesn't get himself together.

Carl had goals; he had ideas about what he wanted to do with his life. He wanted to leave his social group of homeless people behind and seemed dedicated to making a different kind of living for himself:

> I need housing, then I will find a job. I want to somehow be there for my son. That's the most important thing. And like this here [on the street] I can't.

The hotel constituted an important starting point, providing closure and distance from the street. It allowed Carl to spend time away from the Gare du Nord and offered him a space in which he could build his own alternative routines. While these routines were still partly illegal or marginalized (stealing food, begging), many of them were no longer tied to his former social group. As Carl stated, it was often the sociality of the group of Polish people that led to his heavy drinking. Additionally, through the support that Emo's structure gave to his life, Carl was able to focus on future goals again by detaching himself from the home he had previously made on the street: these goals included a proper place to live, a job and reconnecting with his family.

***

Carl knew that the comfort of having his own room was only a temporary benefit that the Mairie de Paris offered during the winter months. He didn't want to go back to living on the street. He and his social worker at Freedom, Carole, had been working on a solution to this problem for months. The necessary form[4] had been sent out in late January. In fact, Freedom managed one centre of its own – Valley of Hope (VoH) – in the south-west of Paris. Carl and I visited this centre in late January 2016.

I picked him up from Emo. He drank the first beer of the day on the train, partly because he was worried about visiting and moving in, as he did not feel confident speaking French. The first thing we talked about after lunch, which Carl barely touched ('Too much red wine yesterday. I am feeling sick'), was the availability of language courses at VoH. The centre had a lot to offer, from personal training to regular classes, as long as Carl made his needs and demands clear. In general, this was how VoH seemed to work: like a general 'housing first' approach (Houard 2011; Joubert 2015) – practised with great success in some US states (Padgett, Henwood and Tsemberis 2016) – it was framed as the first step out of homelessness and into society.

> We are a community and want to help people follow their projects. We help people to live together again by just doing so. Eight people share a flat, each with his or her own room, with the kitchen and bathroom and living room facilities being shared. The shopping and cooking and cleaning are done communally. Everyone finds and then follows their own path; ideally, your flat becomes a constant in your life at least for a couple of years.

This was how Victoria, the centre manager at the time, explained VoH to Carl after lunch. Carl seemed to really like the place: 'I would have my own room and could just be there. And within a couple of months I would be able to find work. I need this kind of structure and stabilization. In February, I will start with my [psycho]therapy and I will continue going to Emo to think about my addiction. So, I hope I can really use this chance properly.'

Carl started to look further into the future during the time at the hotel. As I stated, it provided a break from the street, both geographically and in terms of routines. It was a space of temporary stability and security that allowed Carl to focus anew on his desires (seeing his family) and hopes (finding a proper place to stay, finding a job) and the path towards achieving these goals – working with Carole, filling out forms, going to Emo, drinking less. While Carl was left very much to himself during the four months he spent at the hotel – he saw Carole and the Emo staff regularly, of his own accord – the next step out of emergency and into longer-term accommodation would alter this autonomy, with both beneficial and challenging consequences for the homeless individual, as I will describe in the remainder of this chapter, mainly through my observations at VoH.

The most important question became how much of an emphasis would be on alleviating Carl's struggles (trauma therapy, drug rehabilitation) and how much would be on what Morgan Clarke describes as techniques of the self in the process of successfully moving into the housing system (or the staircase system (Busch-Geertsema and Sahlin 2007: 68f), from the street to the emergency shelter to a transitional shelter)? What influence does a 'ruly' environment have on a shelter inhabitant? When his stint at the hotel came to an end, the most important thing for Carl was continuity – paradoxically a continuity of the rupture from the street. Carole was very aware of this and regularly pushed the administrative body responsible for the SIAO forms to consider Carl's demand for temporary housing, which was ultimately granted just before his time at the hotel came to an end in late spring 2016.

Moving In and Moving On: Carl's Arrival at His Centre

Carl was offered a place in the all-male *centre d'hébergement de stabilization*, which I call BdR, in the 12ᵗʰ arrondissement. This seemed to be a better match than VoH as the people living there were slightly younger and less in need of support. Almost by accident, I accompanied Carl on his moving-in day. I hadn't seen him for some weeks when I went to a Friday morning session at Emo and he told me excitedly that he had left the hotel that morning to move into BdR. We spent the morning with the others, discussing the question of 'sharing', before leaving the centre early to take the metro to Carl's new home.

> The hotel was nice and everything. I had my own room with stuff, but there was really only one chair and not enough space and it didn't feel like a home. Now this is definitely at least one level better.

He was excited; after spending days worrying about what his future would be like after he left the hotel, he was happy. I also saw signs of this in his appearance: he seemed bronzed from the sun that had been blessing Paris recently. The relative security that he was expecting seemed to give him confidence, a certain halo.

> I left the hotel with all my stuff just two weeks ago. It was raining horribly and I had all these bags with me. I arrived at Emo with them and didn't know what to do. Fortunately, Carole had just received the news that my hotel would be prolonged for another month and that, by the end of that period at the latest, I would be able to move. It's so important. I couldn't sleep for days.

Not knowing where to sleep at night was perhaps the most serious worry Carl had. Having a place to stay for the night is about more than just sleeping. It is about having space in which to rest and relax; a space to which one can go after a hard day of begging on the street to make ends meet; a space for hoping and thinking about the future. Carl had already found this in the hotel, where his mind was able to look forward, towards a different future. But in the centre, Carl was offered longer-term stability – stability to plan, a secure place to start from – for over three years. Line 14 took us to the 12ᵗʰ in no time. Five minutes' walk from the station, a modern, clean, 5-storey building awaited us. Carl had already visited the previous week to see whether he could imagine living here. He did have doubts. After all, the offer was for a double room, a room that he would share with somebody else. Could Carl really imagine moving in with another person? What about privacy? What if the other person was messy or a snorer? He was willing to take the risk and agreed to accept the offer. As his stint in the hotel was coming to an end, he didn't really have another option.

It took a moment before the door was answered. Upstairs, we met the two social workers responsible for the centre: Elena and Camillo were welcoming, friendly, with open faces and the patience to explain the rules of the house more than once for Carl, who still had some trouble understanding French. Camillo made sure that Carl knew what to expect:

> We do as little as we can. The people here are adults and they can do most things themselves. We are here for them if problems arise, but overall they are responsible. This is the difference between the *centre d'urgence* and the *centre d'hébergement.* Here people do their own washing, they buy their own cleaning products and their toilet paper. They can stay away if they tell us beforehand. They are free to do whatever they want.

Carl nodded. Freedom and responsibility sounded good to him; he was very much able and willing to take his life into his own hands. He didn't have any questions and was ready to see his room and, almost more importantly, meet his roommate. We climbed the stairs to the third floor. There were forty rooms in the centre. Seventy per cent of them were single rooms. All of them were inhabited by men. Carl's roommate turned out to be a nice, quiet Italian man. Carl was confident that the two would get along. Camillo and Elena took us downstairs into the canteen to introduce Carl to the kitchen staff ('Just so that they know your face') before leaving us to it:

> Bienvenue. Vous êtes chez vous maintenant. Voilà.
> [Welcome. You are at home now.]

***

Moving into the centre meant a continuation of Carl's housing stability, a continuation of the rupture from the street, as well as moving up the ladder of the 'continuum of care' – the ladder that could eventually lead to *logement* [long-term housing]. But, in comparison to his stay at the hotel, where this rupture began, Carl's move to the centre differed in several ways.

As at Freedom's ESI and Emo, the environment at BdR – and VoH, as we will see – was geared towards changing the residents' behaviour (Hoch 2000: 868). As illustrated by Camillo's opening statement vis-à-vis Carl, people were usually not 'free to do whatever they want'. More freedom – in comparison to CHUs, in particular – was linked to more responsibility (Bruneteaux 2005; Grand 2015). Responsibility usually translated into rules – rules relating to individual behaviour at and outside of the centre, as well as rules governing collective behaviour, for instance, around dinner times and cleaning schedules. Hence, the environment at BdR might also be called 'ruly': Carl was supposed to assume responsibility for various tasks (cleaning, shopping) in the context of an environment of support (cooking and general administration at BdR was taken care of, for instance). He was given the autonomy to create his own routines within a structure provided by a loose set of rules, including rules related to interactions with others (his roommate, most importantly). In this sense, BdR does not, from the outside, seem too different from what I observed at VoH.

Vivre Ensemble at Valley of Hope

In the summers of 2015 and 2016, I spent a total of almost ten weeks in a *centre d'hébergement de stabilisation* run by Freedom that I refer to as Valley of Hope (VoH), This centre is part of a new wave (Busch-Geertsema and Sahlin 2007: 72) of smaller and longer-term hostels providing single rooms, replacing large communal shelters such as Nanterre (Declerck 2003). It is conceptualized as a communal living space where people from the street – *résidents* [inhabitants] – and *bénévoles* [volunteers] live together. Twenty-four people – eight women and sixteen men – occupy three shared apartments and two small flats for couples, across three floors under one roof. Fifteen of these people were sleeping rough during the period prior to moving into Valley of Hope. Most of the *résidents* were older (fifty-five years or more), had come out of long-term unemployment and were able to live on state benefits while unable to work due to physical and mental health issues. Having applied through SIAO, they eventually moved into VoH, with the prospect of staying for up to four years. The volunteers, on the other hand, were mostly students, young professionals and people in between jobs. The explicit idea of VoH is that the two groups live together (*vivre ensemble*) on a daily basis, sharing spaces such as the kitchen, the bathrooms and the toilets on each floor, as well as a living room, a computer room and a garden for everyone on the ground floor. Shared facilities come with shared responsibilities, such as the weekly shopping and communal cooking, as well as maintaining the garden and cleaning. VoH is a hostel built for the special purpose of stabilization.[5] VoH, which is financed by both public and private means, aims to:

> give people who have lived on the street previously the necessary time and the space to find themselves and a new autonomy again – this is achieved through a shared living arrangement between 'volunteers' and people in precarious situations. (From the organization's website, translation author's own)

The explicit aim is to offer a space of stability in which they can relearn longer-term decision-making skills in the context of being with other people; although individual goals are not specified, VoH is a training ground (McNaughton 2008). This training is supervised by three permanent members of staff – a *responsable* [manager], an *assistant social* and an *educatrice spe-cialisée* (both different types of social workers) – as well as a varying number of temporary staff – people doing civil service or a social work internship. While the manager and sometimes the *assistant social* take care of many of the administrative burdens, like budgeting and organizing the maintenance of the house, the temporary staff is responsible for organizing specific activities, like those at Freedom. Certain activities, such as gardening, are carried out by volunteers who do not live at VoH. Before I consider the role played by staff at VoH, I will focus on the two groups of people who were living there permanently, starting with the residents.

A Room of One's Own: Material Home-Making

VoH is located not far outside of the centre of Paris, in the 15th arrondissement; the neighbourhood is comfortably middle class. The street is dominated by large and, by Parisian standards, tall apartment blocks. The former convent that houses VoH was given to Freedom (which still rents it for a symbolic sum) by a Catholic order in 2010. It is hidden in the second row of houses.

I enter the premises through a heavy metal door, stepping into a courtyard the length of the building on the right. There is a garden on the left, as well as a shed (used for activities such as painting workshops). When I ring the bell, Paul, the director of VoH until summer 2015 and himself a former monk, welcomes me into the ground-floor area. The spacious garden where people go to smoke borders a big open-plan eating, sitting and cooking area. We briefly sit down in a media room with two computers that doubles as the library. This room is tucked away between the two offices for staff and the living area. Paul is in a good mood, excited to move on after four years of running VoH. We already had a briefing when I first visited several months ago, so today he leads me quickly to the second floor, where I will have a room for the coming weeks. Three apartments are stacked on top of each other: the first two floors are for men, the top floor for women. All three floors have eight rooms, situated on either side of a long, windowless corridor. At one end of the corridor, there is the kitchen (and a set of stairs leading up and down); at the other end, there are two toilets and three showers, as well as the washing machine and cleaning utensils. Despite there being many posters on the walls, the apartment feels empty outside of the private rooms.

Paul unlocks the door to my room. My gaze is immediately drawn to the window opposite the door: it takes up the whole back wall. The shutters are down to keep the hot July air out. A single bed by the window occupies most of the space in the room. There is also a small desk, a chair and a cupboard against the opposite wall. Right behind the door, there is a built-in wardrobe and a dustbin. The initial setup is the same for everyone, volunteers and *résidents* alike.

***

Unfortunately, I was not able to observe anyone moving in. What kinds of routines did people engage in to make the place their own? I could only look at rooms that had already been decorated and were crowded with things after years of being lived in. I did not see all of the rooms on my floor. Three months was not enough time to build up strong enough relationships to secure access to everyone's private rooms. Franck, however, was very open with me and showed me around his room when I arrived for my second summer in 2016. He is a diminutive but charming man in his sixties with a lot of grey hair hanging around his face. He was born and raised in Belgium, lived in

Luxembourg and eventually moved to France several decades ago. He is interested in music and technology, which immediately became apparent upon
entering his room.

Franck's room was full of things. Some of them were ordered – notably his
laptops stacked on top of each other by the window – but most of his things
were distributed all over the room in a disorderly fashion, some loosely, some
in bags. As Franck walked me through his room, he pointed out the things that
were most important to him: his electrical equipment. He was proud of his
17-inch monitor, which he often connected to the only laptop in his

Figure 6.1. Franck's room at VoH, August 2016. © Johannes Lenhard.

possession that still worked, and his collection of tablets, pocket PCs and phones. There were cables everywhere. Most of the bags contained clothes, bed linen and towels; some were filled with documents. His walls were totally empty and there were no visible personal items, such as photos or family memorabilia.

Franck listened to loud rock music most of the day, loved to wear leather clothing and owned about five different mobile phones and tablets, in addition to his non-functioning laptops. As he told me, he had found most of these things in bins in wealthy neighbourhoods of Paris prior to moving into VoH in January 2015: 'You find a lot if you do the bins and know where. I found everything there.' He was very proud of what he perceived as his material affluence.

***

Private space is very often lacking on the street and many hostels only offered shared accommodation, as in Carl's hostel. At VoH, the residents all had their own rooms. As Ginte Zulyte found in her study of a shelter for homeless mothers in Lithuania, material objects – and the memories connected to them – played an important role in people's home-making activities. She describes how decorating with objects and the sense of refurbishment associated with this activity can 'mark the beginning of a new period in one's life' (Zulyte 2012: 24).

Zulyte identifies these more general patterns in the shelter, where people enjoy changing around furniture, finding and buying new pieces as 'one of the ways of recreating one's room in the shelter' (ibid.: 36). For Franck, the arranging of pieces was not as important as the collection of them; he seemed to enjoy both the acquisition (striking a good deal or finding them for free) and the hoarding of what would once have been expensive technological equipment. The items in his collection were an expression of his self-esteem and persona – he was somebody who was able to 'get things' and take part in a modern lifestyle involving phones and technology – as well as being an expression of his tastes (his guitar symbolized his interest in rock music). The material environment of the one-room home that Franck constructed around him was, as Alison Clarke theorizes, a home-in-process 'in which past and future trajectories … are negotiated through fantasy and action, projection and interiorization' (Clarke 2001: 25). Through objects like the computers, Franck was still connected to his past on the street (where the objects came from), while allowing him to imagine and fashion himself as a tech-savvy individual; his mobile phone(s) helped him to connect to friends from his time on the street, as well as family in Belgium and Luxembourg. The objects gave him something to do (Garvey 2001: 55), allowed him to construct a history and a narrative of how he had found his way off the street and ultimately also allowed him to progress further by enabling him to build (new) personal connections. In this sense, they were a bridge between the past and the future that grounded him in a material present.

The freedom to decorate one's room, to use it in one's own way, was also viewed as highly beneficial by staff, such as the first director, Paul. He explained to me, with reference to Franck:

> It is really good for him here. He has enough space and is really making the most out of it. He is also able to live together in the group here unlike many others.

He referenced space and what Franck makes of it, explicitly linking the 'good use' of one's room to the good life more generally. But he also highlighted a second dimension of life at the shelter, one that is more contested and contestable, even though it is more in focus: living with others. The emphasis at VoH was not solitary material life in one's room, but sociality, the *vivre ensemble* [living together] that was connected to 'moving on' in various ways, as I will describe in the following sections.

Vivre Ensemble

I arrive in the kitchen, where a lot of people are already sitting around the table, cooking or stretched out on the sofa and chairs. It is sweltering. Jan looks over his shoulder from his position at the oven, sweating, and smiles at me: 'Bonsoir. Good to see you. It's hot.' Niceties are exchanged. I shake hands with everyone. Hanna, the *assistante sociale* who is responsible for our *étage*, is present too. It is Monday, which means the communal dinner doubles up as the *reunion* [meeting].

Every Monday, all the inhabitants of every flat meet over dinner with one of the staff to discuss the week ahead and questions that may have arisen during the previous week. This week, all seven inhabitants – five *résidents* and two *bénévoles* – are in the kitchen by around 8.10PM, when Hanna starts talking about cooking and deliveries: 'We should have two more dinners this week. When do you want to eat together again? Who wants to cook?' We decide on Wednesday and Thursday, and two people volunteer to prepare the meals. Everyone fills out their schedules – when they will be around for dinner and lunch – for the whole week to make planning and cooking easier. Fewer people will be there at the weekend, as usual, because people visit friends or want to keep their evenings free. This week, there will be a delivery of food, which is ordered centrally for the whole house. Franck and I will pick it up from the storage space on the fourth floor on Wednesday after checking what we are lacking in the kitchen. Lastly, the cleaning tasks are distributed. A list with all our names on it is handed out; everyone chooses a part of the communal spaces to clean. 'Oh, I don't know. I did the kitchen last week. I'll do the entrance this week.' Nobody likes to clean the bathrooms or the toilets, which are usually cleaned by the volunteers. But everyone is expected to do their share.

Jan is in the mood to talk today. He observes that people steal the water bottles he puts in the fridge and don't clean up their plates and also that glasses, cutlery and cups are missing. 'It is not the right way of living together. Everyone is supposed to do their share. We are all in a *cohabitation* [shared house] together.' He seems really angry. He is still sweating after having prepared dinner at the hot oven. Food is distributed onto our plates and the reunion comes to an end for the week. Hanna puts the sheets up on the fridge – a visible reminder – and lighter dinner conversation ensues.

***

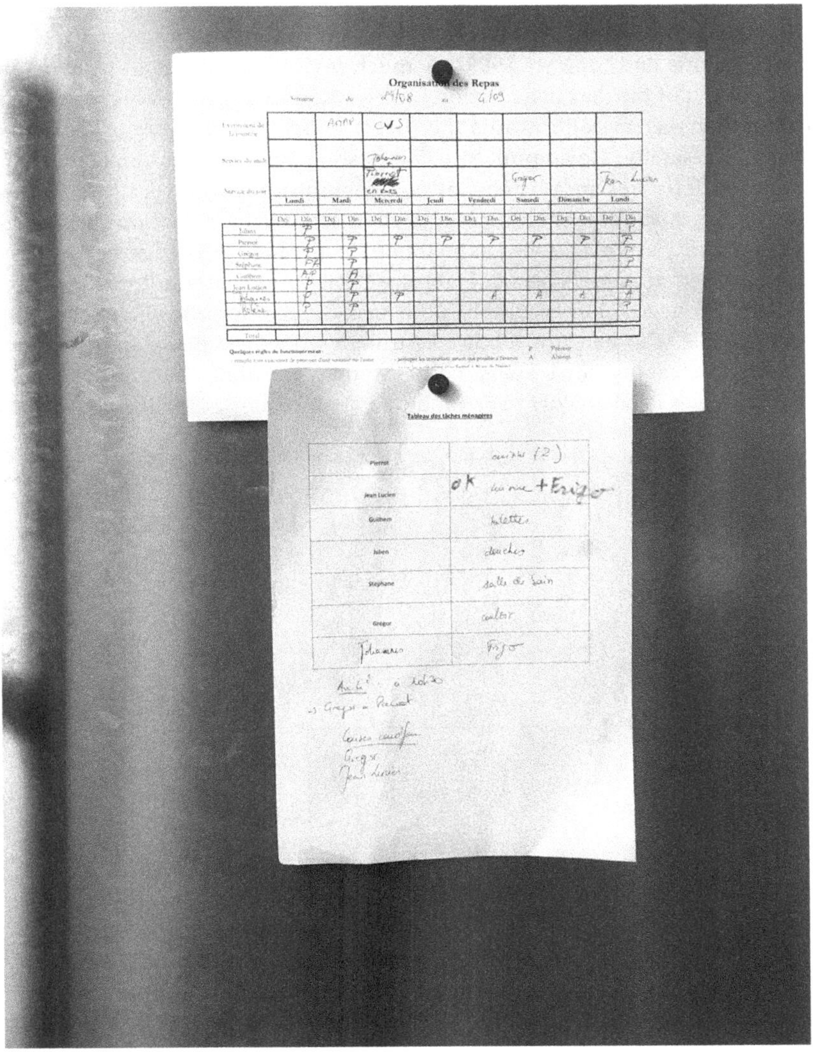

Figure 6.2. The planning lists on the fridge; meal plan above, cleaning below; August 2016. © Johannes Lenhard.

Many of the Monday reunions unfolded in a similar way, although they often occurred after the dinner. Three important elements were always on the agenda: the timetable for the week's lunches and dinners, distributing responsibilities for cleaning the communal spaces and lastly questions and complaints. As Hanna explained to me:

> The planning sheets, I know they have difficulties reading and using them but symbolically it represents something very important in terms of spatial and temporal order. It is a symbolic structure in terms of the time and the days.

Planning the week ahead was not usually done on the street (Day, Papataxiarchis and Stewart 1999). A much less mediated idea of time – or being cut out of time, as in addiction time – was exchanged at VoH for an idea of time that was geared towards the (near) future. People were asked – not always successfully – to commit to accomplishing certain tasks and taking part in certain activities in advance, at the beginning of the week. As Hanna observed, this was essential to an important structuring effort on the part of the community at VoH, as well as enabling the people to live together without friction. Written and visible timetables were used as material techniques (of the self; Clarke 2015) to accomplish this task of planning ahead and checking up on people who had not followed through with their plans and promises (relating to cleaning, for instance). The Monday meeting was another one of the techniques used at VoH to remind people of certain rules and routines of

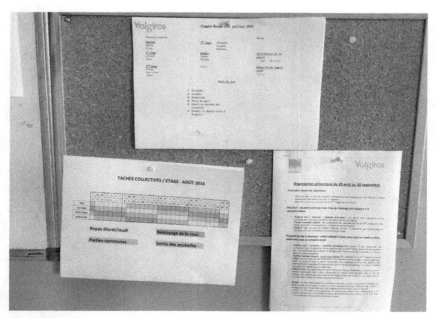

Figure 6.3. The noticeboard with different announcements and collective tasks. © Johannes Lenhard.

communal life, but also to highlight breaches of such rules, as highlighted by Hanna's distribution of tasks and Jan's complaints regarding people stealing his water bottles and missing cups and cutlery.

The residents were reintegrated into a weekly calendar, into what E.P. Thompson (1967) calls 'work time', which distanced them from street or addiction time (Desjarlais 1997: 77, 90). Schedules and timetables at VoH were a means of encouraging residents to lead more active lives and helping them to make and commit to plans. Timetables and planning sheets were material manifestations of the 'ruly' environment at VoH, with time being structured in a partly self-determined way (inhabitants were allowed to choose activities or make it known when they wouldn't be there). Ultimately, this 'ruly' environment of technologies of the self was geared towards a transition out of homelessness, not necessarily through imposed and sanctioned discipline, transparency and omniscience, but rather through the encouragement of slow change and the development of embodied new routines (Desjarlais 1997: 102).

Other sheets ordered different aspects of life at VoH. The ordering regime extended quite literally to the cleaning of the toilet seat.

Esther, the latest *directrice* at VoH, who started in early 2016, explained the origin of these sheets to me: they were often the result of the reactions of *bénévoles* to residents' complaints. To resolve issues such as messy bins or unclean toilet facilities, a written prescription often seemed to be best and easiest solution. The fact that most of the *résidents* were unaccustomed or

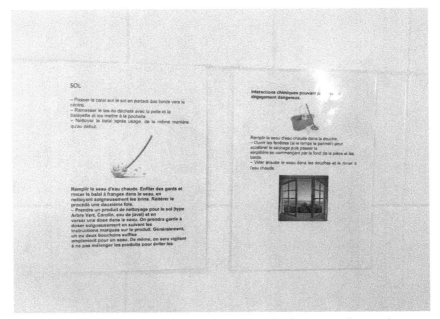

Figure 6.4. Laminated sheet in the second-floor bathroom explaining how to clean the showers. © Johannes Lenhard.

unwilling to read and then follow pages of written rules on how to use a sponge rarely changed these patterns of printing and making such prescriptions visible. The many sheets I encountered in 2016 were the result of months of being short-staffed and the resulting complaints from the *résidents*. However, the underlying principles were watered down as the ubiquity of the sheets often led people to stop paying them any attention.

The sheets devoted to cleaning and the garbage were only the visible tip of the iceberg. Living together at VoH involved more general restrictions. On the entrance doors on each floor were A4 pages full of rules. Alcohol and smoking, in particular, were sensitive subjects at VoH, as in many institutions for homeless people. The patterns of alcohol and substance usage, for instance, often posed problems when an *hébergement* was offered. As Fabian, another volunteer, explained to me in an interview, most of the residents at VoH were alcohol dependent. On paper, VoH was a dry hostel: it was not permissible to consume any substances inside, reflecting standard practice in many comparable institutions (Flanagan 2012: 64; Michalot and Simeone 2010). In theory, VoH was, in its statutes, completely opposed to inhabitants consuming alcohol. In practice, however, the *résidents* either smuggled alcohol inside or went outside the front door to sit on a bench and drink. If bottles were found in the rooms, the consequences were minimal;[6] a verbal warning was considered a harsh way of dealing with such a transgression. In practice, VoH was already almost a wet hostel, though it clung to certain more traditional rules that were slowly changing.[7]

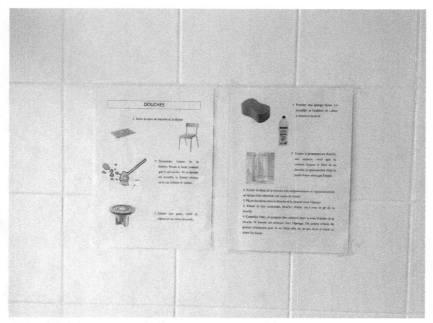

Figure 6.5. Laminated sheet in the second-floor bathroom explaining how to clean the floor. © Johannes Lenhard.

***

In general, Esther and her staff did still believe in the positive effect that the order sheets, food and shopping routines, consumption rules and budgets could have on the residents. 'So, when a guy is ready to move on, he will order his stuff, voilà.' The work starts with small and concrete things, like the cleaning or the shopping, fixing certain meeting times with the idea that 'if you start taking care of little things in terms of your cleaning or your hygiene ... that will help you after when you are alone to live normally.' Esther cites Georg – one of the newer residents on my floor, a Polish man in his mid-fifties, ex-military, very friendly, albeit not too talkative – as a positive example of this:

> Georg, he does the whole floor and even more but he would never say anything if the others don't do their work ... he understands that one needs to work together, live together, work on living together.

Hanna added to this analysis:

> I believe that says a lot about oneself – if you see how certain people just clean their rooms, make food, do their tasks. If everyone did that, VoH would already be a better place. ... Georg, for instance, he manages to deal with rules because he is good at integrating a new habit.

Georg was seen by both Esther and Hanna as somebody who followed the rules and was making progress on his path out of homelessness. He was able to pass the various tests of *vivre ensemble*: not drinking inside, fulfilling communal cleaning tasks, taking part in meetings, volunteering to cook. As Hanna and Esther both argue, this experience would, in due time, qualify him for the next step, a different kind of (often more independent) living arrangement. Parallels can be drawn with Zulyte's study of a Lithuanian shelter. Zulyte observed similar rules relating to cleaning and timetables and the absence of substances (and visitors): 'they have to adapt to the rules of the shelter and to get on with the other inhabitants here' (Zulyte 2012: 34). Complaints about the rules were frequent and so were certain breaches of rules. Zulyte concludes that ultimately the shelter was a testing and training ground both for the institution (is the resident able to move on?) and the inhabitant (what do I really need and want?): 'While interacting with the "potential environment" of the shelter, most of the homeless mothers are able to feel and to perceive who and what is not included in their most intimate space and their personal life. Thus, a shelter definitely can help homeless people to build up their self-awareness' (ibid.: 44).

At VoH, rules were even more fixed in the form of an initial – again more or less symbolic – contract that new residents had to sign when they started living there. Hanna explained:

> They all sign a contract, yes. ... They set themselves goals in five areas: health, work, housing, rights and everything which has to do with pleasure. For some, it is just 'I need to see a doctor regularly', 'I need to take care of my addiction', 'I need to check

with the unemployment agency'. ... I try to identify the principal problem of the person and after that to construct different steps to deal with it.

The contract – beyond the general rules of *vivre ensemble* – was focused on more personal development goals. Defined in an initial discussion with Esther or Hanna and refined on a regular basis, it was the ultimate personal goal sheet. How am I developing? Thus, constant self-reflection was written into the inhabitants' routines, in a similar way to how it was encouraged by Emo. The contract can be seen as another technique of the self in Clarke's sense: geared towards continuous development of and reflection on a personal future, it constituted a constantly adapted, but again usually sanction-less technique, a measuring tool (how much have I progressed?) and a self-defined catalogue of goals. For my informants and the *assistants sociaux*, it was both a way of imposing certain daily routines and a way of thinking of a better future beyond these routines. But what role do the different personifications of the institution – staff and volunteers – play in these techniques of the self?

'Working' at Valley of Hope: Mimetic Education and Restoration

One day during my first summer at VoH, I was preparing food in the kitchen when Jean stormed in: 'Did you clear the table yesterday after dinner?' he asked. 'Yes,' I said, 'isn't that what we do? You weren't there by about 8.45PM so rather than leaving it out, I thought it would be best to just put it away.' 'We are not in prison here. I can come and eat when I want and you can't just clear the table like that.' Jean was one of the long-term *résidents*. His stay in VoH would end about twelve months later. He was in his fifties, relatively short but bulky, with a drinker's belly; his arms were covered with amateur tattoos. He was very friendly to begin with, as he spoke good German thanks to his time on exchange in Germany with the French military, but he became unpredictable when he drank, such that people avoided him and were afraid of his erratic behaviour.

Suddenly, the discussion shifted to another level: 'You have only been here for a month; you can't just change everything and make your own rules.' Jean became very aggressive, stormed through the kitchen, violently opened and closed the door of the fridge, as he had done with the kitchen door. He turned around, shook his fist at me and threatened me: 'It will be hot tonight' (at the reunion).

Jean arrived last for dinner that night. He was still aggressive. He wouldn't look at me as he screamed: 'Do you want me to tell everyone now? Do you wanna eat first?' However, nobody asked Jean what he meant and the dinner went relatively smoothly. After dinner, though, Jean voiced his complaints about me taking away the plates, as well as taking the table from the kitchen to my room (as Paul had advised me to do). 'This is not to be excused', he argued, 'these two mistakes, there is really nothing that can take them away. I will stay angry with him. It's fine for everyone, but really this doesn't work for me.' He then shifted to a more general complaint: 'Something on this *étage* needs to change and it is up to you [looking at Fabian and Christophe, the two other *bénévoles*] to do this.' Fabian answered very clearly: 'We are not in a forest; this is a shared living arrangement. We are living together.' He explained that the volunteers were not responsible for looking after, ruling or deciding about the *résidents*: 'Staff tell us: you live together. There is no hierarchy. There are a couple of rules that everyone follows and if needs be there is the *directeur* but on the *étage*, there is no hierarchy.' Fabian wanted to establish that he had no more responsibility than the *résidents* – we were supposed to figure out problems together. This togetherness also meant sharing responsibility: 'Everyone gives as much as he can and wants to. At times, people give more, at others they take more.' He was careful to explain this to Jean, reflecting on other situations in which similar conflicts had arisen and calming Jean down by complimenting him: 'Often, you give a lot [contribute a lot]. Some people can't do it the same way, though. They might be giving back other things.'

When cleaning up after the reunion – no one else had said much during the discussion between Fabian, Jean and me – we came to a point at which Jean and I embraced, exchanged a couple of words in German and could look each other in the eye again.

***

One of the *bénévoles* in my second summer at VoH described the role of the *assistant social* as follows:

> The social workers need to define the frame [*cadre*], propose activities and take care of everything related to reintegration and health. … They have the right to put pressure onto people; it is them who make sure the limits are guarded.

In contrast, the role of the *bénévoles* – permanent occupants of rooms, like the *résidents* – is, according to Fabian, another *bénévole* from 2015, much more complicated:

> [We are playing] a kind of double game, as [we] are the 'long arm' of the social worker in the apartment while at the same time trying to integrate into a life with the habitants on an equal level. … We need to be visible and respect the order of things. … But the turnover of us is so high; we don't really provide any kind of stabilization.

Both of these statements taken together recall the conflict with Jean: it is unclear who is responsible for dealing with disputes; the hierarchical positions of permanent staff and *bénévoles* vis-à-vis the inhabitants are not obvious and, as a consequence, there are unresolved questions about who is able to communicate and enforce rules of *vivre ensemble*. In relation to Jean, he was, additionally, testing his own limits: how far can I push the newcomer (me) and impose my own ideas on him – educate him, in a way? Who is going to stop me? The conflict is resolved not through the demonstration of authority – Fabian is very clear about the *bénévoles'* lack of authority – but appreciation. As soon as Jean realizes that we are not trying to blame him for anything but rather value his contributions to communal living – his cleaning, washing, ordering – he retreats. This kind of treatment mirrors what Hanna describes as the most important element of the *bénévoles'* box of tools:

> The volunteers are there to live at VoH and press their rhythm on their flat. Their main instrument is mimesis.

By appreciating Jean's action in more general terms – as opposed to producing a (false) hierarchical order – Fabian demonstrates the kind of behaviour he would expect of the other *résidents* in similar situations. On the one hand, Jean's aggressive behaviour had no material consequences; no sanctions were put in place. On the other hand, the volunteers had a certain level of responsibility; people like Fabian were expected to 'manage well', foresee how much pressure they could put on people like Jean, how much space was necessary. Ultimately, the volunteers were part of a process of collective education and training (McNaughton 2008: 113): resolving conflicts together, shopping together, cooking together, cleaning the flat collectively. The idea is to serve as an example and thereby practise a light kind of pedagogy (Humphrey 1997).

The conflict with Jean brings to the fore an issue that is at the core of Volker Busch-Geertsema and Ingrid Sahlin's (2007) critical reflections on the use of homeless hostel accommodation in Europe: a hostel is not the best place to prepare inhabitants for the independence of living alone or outside of an institution. They argue that 'staying in a hostel requires a special competence which is quite different from living independently. Whether or not people behave well in hostels has very little to do with their capacity and capability to manage in a self-contained dwelling.'[8] Was Jean's issue dealing with certain social situations the result of the artificial social setting, which was so very unlike other settings outside of the hostel? Busch-Geertsema and Sahlin continue: 'Instead of learning how to cope in society outside inmates have to struggle to defend their identity and adapt to their role as, in this case, shelter residents' (ibid.: 78). According to their critique, in most shelters it is much more important to control the residents than it is to service and support them. At VoH, I did observe a 'ruly' environment where certain techniques of the self – in the form of timetables, planning and prescriptive sheets, contracts – were put in place. But control in the sense of surveillance, room checks and sanctions was more or less absent. While this lack of disciplinary power could be seen as negative, the environment seems to be different to those Busch-Geertsema and Sahlin observed in the homeless shelters they studied.

However, was something else missing? I saw how unlikely it was that people passing through VoH would live independently again in the near future, even if only because they couldn't find work. Most of the residents that had left VoH since 2010 either went into other collective housing projects, some of which were slightly less supportive, or back into a street environment. Perhaps the utopic notion of climbing up the ladder of different hostels to 'ultimately exiting from homelessness through acquiring a flat' should be questioned. Was the possibility of relearning 'how to have control over his choices, ... to manage his "freedom" and the pressure this "freedom" brought' (McNaughton 2008: 113) more important than any kind of preparation for what is often called independent living? Was it only at a later stage of the ladder that the focus should have shifted to preparing people for living alone as opposed to supporting them in learning or relearning rules of collective togetherness? A first step – and VoH was very much seen as a first point of stabilization – might have to be restoration of the person, as Hanna explains below.

***

In contrast to the *bénévole*, the role of the social work staff – in particular, the *assistante sociale* Hanna, the *educateur specialisé* Bernard and the varying directors – is more explicitly geared towards enabling change. As Hanna explains:

> The social workers are there to press for change and to apply the catalogue of rules. Their main instrument is the contract.

She goes on to explain that her main goal is restoration:

> I often think of a façade or a nice picture which was somehow damaged. My role is to repaint the parts which have been damaged and to see which material is the best to restore it. This takes a while and if something goes wrong – the paint doesn't work or something – I need to make sure it doesn't further damage the person.

On the one hand, Hanna sees herself as a restorer of people; she wants to protect the inhabitants from outside forces and from falling down, accompanying them on their chosen path, proposing activities and projects (materials). On the other hand, she follows a stricter set of practices in her role as a change-maker. She is responsible for imposing the rules when necessary and softly enforcing the contract and the goals the *résidents* defined for themselves. Ultimately, as in the conflict with Jean, the practices relating to holding people responsible were rather weak, supportive rather than sanctioning. During my three months at VoH, not a single sanction – a house arrest or a fine, for instance – was enforced. The culture was one of restoration (Huston 1999). While VoH is a place of training – 'training to take responsibility, to behave in the right way, to make the right choices and to be able to reintegrate into society' (McNaughton 2008: 113) – it was also a place where poor decisions, slips and mistakes were not sanctioned; both staff and volunteers had to accommodate the *résidents*. In this sense, VoH was perhaps not 'real life', not a testing ground, really, for being independent.[9]

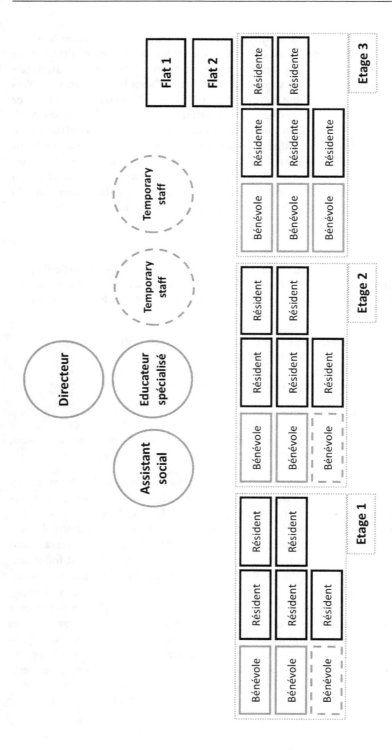

Figure 6.6. Organigram of the order of people at VoH. © Johannes Lenhard.

I have tried to capture the ideal and imagined situation of living and defining life together at VoH in figure 6.6. As we have seen in descriptions of situations of conflict, in particular, this picture is indeed an ideal scenario: volunteers – such as Fabian – have to step up at times and take the roles of staff; at other times, volunteers are absent.[10] Inhabitants push against other residents and staff and volunteers. The structure can collapse into a rather unhierarchical organisation even when things go well, such as during outings and celebrations, like the five-year anniversary of VoH in 2015. Most importantly, however, the structure is always a temporary one – a testing ground – for the *résidents* as the ultimate aim is to move on and out.

Moving On: Towards Home?

It is kind of like the cocoon (which the caterpillar spins for itself) where the office [staff] and the 'house' [material environment] protects you from the outside ... and allows you to be and become yourself. The interior is really soft and you can develop until you are ready to become the butterfly.

This is how Fabian, a *bénévole* during my first summer, described VoH to me in an interview. He saw the place as a kind of cocoon, a material and personified structure of protection, that gave the *résidents* the chance to develop themselves. This view seems rather fitting in light of the ethnographic descriptions in the last section; VoH is not only a place of protection but also a place of change, a place where *résidents* are (gently) pushing along the (imagined) continuum of progress out of homelessness, like a cocoon protecting the caterpillar's transformation into a butterfly. It is important to note one significant difference: inhabitants are not necessarily protected until they are ready; rather, they are only protected until their three to four years are over (four years being the maximum amount of time at VoH). Despite this limit on the *résidents'* time at VoH, I did not observe the kind of paradox that Desjarlais (1997: 37) noted in the Boston shelters, where staff had trouble making it clear that the accommodation should *not* become a home. VoH really did become a home for many residents and finding ways to move towards the goal of moving on was perhaps left a little bit too late.

The time limit at VoH was looming for Jean just before I arrived in the summer of 2016. I learnt about his plans to move to the much more independent living/working environment at the Bretagne only retrospectively. He had already spent a week there and decided it would be the right place for him. As Fabian told me, however, his last weeks at VoH were complicated: he engaged in a lot of drinking and violence, he feared leaving and he missed meetings with staff. Ultimately he didn't take the train to the new place, but instead disappeared in Paris. He returned to VoH a week later pretending that he had passed a week at the Bretagne, though he had been spotted by members of

Freedom in his old neighbourhood in the east of Paris. As his room was already reserved for somebody else, he was not able to return to VoH and left more or less unaccompanied, starting another complex cycle on the street and in homeless institutions (McNaughton 2008: 87ff). We cannot say for certain, but it seems likely that he returned to the street community he had come from.

***

Jean's situation is extreme, but it is not unique,[11] whereas other inhabitants of VoH do indeed go on to live in different hostels and more independent living situations, following the pathway (Marr 2012) off the streets. Having spoken to directors, members of staff and volunteers, however, the general opinion seems to be that moving on from VoH is complicated.

Another volunteer explained this to me with reference to other problems that the inhabitants often bring with them to VoH. Commenting on Jean's situation, he said: 'This [VoH] isn't working for him. It's sad to say, but I think he isn't really able to live in a shared living situation or even society.' Jean, like many of the other inhabitants at VoH, suffered from severe alcohol addiction, as well as varying degrees of mental health issues.[12] A one-year intern had her own explanation, related to people's motivations:

> A lot of them are not easy to motivate, they are sitting in their rooms all day long watching DVDs, playing games, drinking and being bored; but they also don't want to be engaged very often.

Both explanations blame the people themselves and their (lack of) capacities for their failure to move on successfully: they are ill; they don't want to change; they resist. However, Paul, the first director of VoH, seemed more realistic and self-accusatory in his judgement of the place:

> It is complicated. There are people here who simply manage to reconnect to life. They find projects, friends, little things to do. But there are others who don't. We invest time and effort but it only works for some people.

I would propose a slightly different view on things, starting with the explicit aim of the work at VoH, following Esther, its most recent director:

> You see, passing from a 'now' – because on the street 'where do I sleep tonight, what do I eat now' ... creating a time that is a little bit longer and ultimately ... a future [is a great success].

VoH was neither a home necessarily nor a step towards a more independent home on the next level, the next stage of the 'continuum of care'. It was a testing and experimenting ground that provided relative (temporary) stability, a space in which to use technologies of the self to define oneself in relation to (imposed) rules and structure and timetables (Zulyte 2012: 44). Some (social) mechanisms had to be restored or relearnt (Hanna); others were taken up naturally (material home-making). The ruliness of the space was really focused on technologies of the self, on self-government rather than the external disciplining. Rules – including their material manifestations, such as timetables, planning sheets and contracts – were in place, but they were negotiated with the inhabitants; they were neither strictly enforced nor – possibly even more importantly – sanctioned, opening up the space for reflection and ultimately allowing *residents* to think about the future on their own terms.

Franck was doing exactly that when I last spoke with him in the summer of 2016. He explained proudly that he had recently visited his mother in Belgium: 'I am not at home here. I need my people.' He was thinking about moving back – back to where his family was, both his mother and his ex-wife. He was trying to reconnect to his past and his home country. His hoped-for and desired home was never going to take the form of a shelter – or, for that matter, an apartment in Paris. It was deeply linked to his past, his memories and his family, as it was for Sabal and Carl. I learnt in late 2017 that Franck actually made this move back to his family, leaving VoH behind.

Notes

1. See also Pichon 1996; Gaboriau and Terrolle 2003; Bruneteaux 2005.
2. In using this notion, Clarke is expanding on Foucault's analysis (1997).
3. Paris 2017; this plan already holds that when temperatures fall below -5°C at night, additional efforts by the Samu Social and other organizations are put in place (increased number of street tours, additional resources for hotel rooms).
4. SIAO – which is the 'integrated system of reception and orientation' used by the service providers.
5. VoH corresponds closely to the definition of a homeless shelter provided by Busch-Geertsema and Sahlin (2007), who explain that hostels tend to involve shared spaces, limited (or no) private space and some kind of supervision.
6. The practical non-existence of sanctions – at least sanctions imposed by staff – was an interesting difference to the environment experienced by Clarke's Muslim informants. In many contexts in which Shariah law was applied, he argues that the transgression of rules and the correction of the mistake was 'where the presence of a rule becomes apparent' (ibid.: 233). The 'danger of error' (ibid.) at VoH was also present, but errors were rarely corrected in a strict fashion; rather, there was a certain leniency in treating breaches and conflicts, as illustrated by the episode with Jean below.
7. Particularly in 2016, after the opening of Emo, discussions within the organization Freedom were much more geared towards allowing people to continue their consumption at VoH too. The paradigm of risk reduction was taking over from the paradigm of abstinence. By the time of my departure, however, no changes had been introduced in daily life at VoH.
8. While the togetherness practised at a hostel might indeed be a good preparation for (wage) work – something Busch-Geertsema and Sahlin underestimate – this aspect is not overly important for my informants as most of them were not able to work or were long-term (and entrenched) unemployed.

9. However, unlike Vincent Lyon-Callo (2004) in his devastating critique of the homeless shelter industry in the US, I cannot make any substantial critique of places such as VoH being a 'governmental intervention designed to reform poor people' (ibid.: 109), a 'liberal effort [as part of the] neoliberal and conservative policy makers['] interventions'. Rather, my observations were on a 'lower', more everyday, practical level, focusing on practices of support, restoration and proposed change.

10. When I arrived in 2016, a shortage of volunteers (four, rather than six, male volunteer positions were filled) was resulting in significant complaints from residents. I convey this in the graph through the broken line around two of the volunteer boxes. Normally, even live-in volunteers have occupations outside of VoH during the day and are present mainly in the evenings and at weekends.

11. Another woman had just left VoH before I arrived in the summer of 2015 and had been seen living on the street again.

12. Other inhabitants, Momo and Jan, were diagnosed with even more severe mental health issues, such as hallucinating depression. They went to outpatient facilities in the *quartier* on a regular basis to deal with these issues, which – as at Emo and Freedom – were not discussed within VoH as the necessary resources (psychological or psychiatric care) were consciously acquired from the outside.

Conclusion

Better Lives on the Street

There is no panacea for the suffering and self-destruction of the protagonists in these pages ... I hope my presentation of the experience of social marginalization in El Barrio, as seen through the struggles for dignity and survival of Ray's crack dealers and their families, contributes on a concrete practical level to calling attention to the tragedy of persistent poverty and racial segregation in the urban United States.

—Philippe Bourgois, *In Search of Respect*

On these sidewalks, the vendors, scavengers and panhandlers have developed economic roles, complex work and mentors who have given them encouragement to try and live 'better' lives. This is the story of the largely invisible social structure of the sidewalk.

—Mitchell Duneier, *Sidewalk*

Comparing Bourgois's and Duneier's concluding remarks from their studies of two different types of American urban economies both heavily centred on the street, the sidewalk and drugs, it strikes me that while Bourgois explicitly refers to the suffering of his informants and his attempt to make people aware of the tragedy surrounding this suffering, Duneier closes his study by drawing the reader's attention to his informants' attempts to construct *better* lives. This is also what is most remarkable to me after my two years of fieldwork with homeless people in Paris. Structural inequality, housing shortages, unemployment, drug use and mental health problems – all of these factors contribute to Pascal's, Carl's, Natasha's and Barut's situations, as in the cases of most of the people I encountered during my fieldwork on the streets of Paris and, before that, London. However, in my analysis of my informants' hopes of home, (ordering) techniques of the self and their link to the future, I have gone beyond the conception of homeless people as marginalized, entrapped, passive and suffering, and instead observed how such individuals actively struggle to survive and make a better life on the street.[1]

To conclude, I want to conceptualize this better life more abstractly as based on the creation of spaces of freedom – from the freedom from fear and the freedom facilitated by the relative safety and stability that a home provides, to the reflective freedom fostered by the *assistants sociaux* at Freedom, Sun and Emo. My informants were striving – in their own ways – to become better selves. I understand the self in Foucault's sense as 'not given to us [but] as a work of art' (Foucault 1997: 262), defined through a *rapport à soi* 'which [he] call[s] ethics, and which determines how the individual is supposed to constitute himself as a moral subject of his own actions' (ibid.: 263). The means that enable the self to become an ethical subject are conceptualized by Foucault as the 'self-forming activity (*pratique de soi*)' (ibid.: 265). Foucault further defines these practices of the self as practices of freedom, understood always in 'relationships with others' rather than being liberated from any form of domination or isolation in autonomy. In this sense, I want to describe the activities, processes and routines my informants engaged in – the labour of begging (chapter 1), the work of making a shelter (chapter 2), engaging in drug time (chapter 3), working with institutions such as Sun, Emo and Freedom (chapters 4 and 5) and accessing temporary housing (chapter 6) – not as activities of resistance or liberation but as practices of the self, processes of home-making and ordering and, as such, of freedom. These are split, like this monograph, on the basis of temporality and immediacy; in Part II, the focus is on the short-term hopes and home-making processes, while Part III describes longer-term planning and working towards more distant hopes – mostly supported by *assistants sociaux*.

Thus far, in the field of anthropology, ethical studies of freedom have often looked at religious contexts (Robbins 2004; Laidlaw 2014), where techniques of the self are deliberate, often very disciplined religious practices of monks or believers, for instance. They typically involve prayer, religious devotion and repentance for sins (e.g. Cook 2010; Mahmood 2012; Elisha 2011). Although much of the other strand of the anthropology of ethics – the ordinary ethics debate (Das 2012; Lambek 2010) – is concerned with lost or random moments of deliberation and reflection, my study is nevertheless best situated within this context and Robbins's (2013) anthropology of the good. In particular, Mattingly's (2014) observations, in relation to poverty-stricken African-American families caring for children with chronic illnesses, prove constructive in relation to my own fieldwork. Some of her informants were, in fact, homeless before they had a family and care provision for children became one of the main goals to work towards. Minor moments – a visit to the clinic, coaching the drill team – served as 'moral laboratories' in which 'the moral work of transformation' took place (ibid.: 76). The everyday moments she describes – like many of the everyday struggles I have observed – 'feed an ongoing practical and dogged hope to create something morally better' (ibid.: 78). The context of homelessness is obviously rather different from the specific institutional settings of most of the anthropology of ethics studies focused on religious settings, but I believe similar processes are at work on an abstract level. Looking back at the daily home-making processes on which chapters 1, 2 and 3 are centred – begging, shelter-making and drug-taking – I focused on the different kinds of reflection and deliberate action involved. Different conscious choices – how to dress, how to address people, where to stand, which narratives to use with whom – are at the core of the different activities I describe as short-term home-as-process, including the labour of begging in chapter 1. In a similar way, finding and making a shelter is often highly reflective, as I describe in chapter 2. Carl described the ideal shelter place for him: protection from weather, not too much traffic, cleanliness, easy access to amenities. Pascal added another important dimension: the safety provided by sleeping with friends. These reflective considerations, although relating to daily survival rather than spiritual well-being and purification, are techniques of the self in the Foucauldian sense. According to Foucault, such techniques are practices that 'permit individuals to effect, by their own means, a certain number of operations on their own bodies, their own souls, their own thoughts, their own conduct, and this in a manner so as to transform themselves, modify themselves, and to attain a certain state of perfection, happiness, purity, supernatural power' (Foucault 1997b: 177, cited in Laidlaw 2014: 101).

It would not be appropriate to speak of a state of perfection or purity in the context of my informants; it is for this reason that I describe them as striving for a *better* rather than a good life. Most importantly, however, I want to argue that many of my informants often used what Laidlaw describes as reflective consciousness: reflection requires that 'we "step back" from and evaluate our own thoughts and desires, and decide reflectively which desires we wish to have and to move us to action' (Laidlaw 2014: 148). The self of my informants was also 'to a significant degree self-constituting and self-responsible [and] to that extent free' (ibid.: 149). Having said that, it is very important to keep in mind the external limitations of this freedom, which I have addressed throughout this monograph. Not only did the general condition of poverty and living on the street exclude my informants from many spaces – think, for instance, of the policing of the Gare du Nord that I describe in chapter 1 – it also made it necessary for them to be supported by *assistants sociaux*, for instance, to access temporary housing through the SIAO system (see chapter 6). Hence, I am not trying to describe my informants as being free from restraints or free from power relations. In fact, Foucault does not think that such freedom could ever exist. As he argues:

> I do not think that a society can exist without power relations, if by that one means the strategies by which individuals try to direct and control the conduct of others. The problem, then, is not to try to dissolve them ... but to acquire the rules of law, the management techniques, and also the morality, the ethos, the practice of the self, that will allow us to play these games of power with as little domination as possible. (Foucault 1997b: 298)

For my informants, drugs firstly served as a technique for pushing away power (often the influence of trauma and other mental health issues, as well as the anxiety evoked by the past and the future more generally). They were a means of – in the short term – taking back control, a feeling that eventually collapsed in what I call the rhythm of addiction time. Perceived freedom quickly turned into increased dependency, this time on the substance.

Thus, I can summarize what I describe in Part III of the volume – chapters 4, 5 and 6 – as follows. How did my informants put themselves in situations of dependency – in the day centre and Emo, the alcohol centre, with the *assistants sociaux*, in the homeless shelter VoH – and how did they try to manage these relationships? In chapter 4, I describe a first instance of depending on *assistants sociaux* and institutions; in order to refocus on the health of their bodies, they engage in harm-reduction techniques at Sun; to be able to live according to a rhythm different to the one dictated by addiction time, people like Carl went to Emo. Through various activities – rupturing outings to theme parks, bonding over playing games together, thinking abstractly during the philosophy *atelier* – the visitors at Emo are presented with a strong alternative to drug time. In addition, reflective thinking about the future is made possible for them. In chapter 5, which focuses on the day centre run by the Catholic organization Freedom, the same narrative of chosen dependency continues. Many of my informants were willing to invest time, effort and trust in order to access *assistants sociaux*. While the day centre was a place of home – of warmth, security, hygiene, coffee – it was also a place where change was initiated and the *projet de vie* was formulated. This *projet* was future-oriented, a description of my informants' longer-term hopes for better lives, often connected to home-as-idealized homeland. In the offices of the *assistants sociaux*, informants such as Carl and Pascal were provided with both a space to reflect and think about the future and support in the form of a *lien* [relationship]. They were able to think ahead and hope for a return to their homeland, their families, their culture.

What we saw in Freedom's day centre, at Emo and, to a certain extent, at Sun was even more pronounced at VoH, the homeless shelter where I lived for three months. Building on a voluntary desire expressed by the *résidents* of VoH, living with volunteers – often students or people in between jobs – could act as a kind of exemplary practice of the self. The volunteers were supposed to be exemplars (Humphrey 1997), who, by sharing responsibilities and space, provided an anchor for the homeless people, an example of how to act. As we have seen, in reality, the 'ruly' environment of the hostel caused many problems too. While posters with prescriptive rules in the bathroom and kitchen, contracts and disciplinary punishments were intended to ready *résidents*, such as Jean, to move towards a better life, they often stifled the inhabitants. The problem my informants ultimately encountered was described by Foucault, who argued that 'the final goal of all the practices of the self still belongs to an ethics of control. ... one exercises over oneself an authority that nothing limits or threatens' (Foucault 1988: 65).

Once again, we see that there is a very clear and understandable limitation on my informants' striving for a better life and engagement in techniques of the self to achieve this end. Throughout this monograph, but particularly in my discussion of drug time in chapters 3 and 4, it becomes clear that my informants were not always able to 'control [their] desires, rather than being a slave to them' (Laidlaw 2014: 120, 124). What I call short-term hope could take over my informants' imagination, especially when this took the form of drugs, though (other) mental health issues also had an impact; this short-term hope could make reflective thinking impossible, which is why so many people follow an up-and-down, rather than a continuous, trajectory away from the street. For my informants, the conflict of values described by Laidlaw manifests in this tension between long- and short-term hopes and techniques. Laidlaw argues in general terms that 'living a life requires doing so with reference to values that make conflicting demands'. The aim can then only be the 'cultivation of an open responsiveness to the sheer contingency of what might come into view' (Laidlaw 2014: 176).

***

I didn't meet Carl again after I left Paris in September 2016. On various visits during the year that followed, I was unable to trace him, even through institutions such as Emo. Only when I bumped into Pascal on my way home late one night in spring 2017 did I receive news of Carl, who had left Paris and had apparently gone to London. From the *assistant social* they shared at Freedom, Pascal had learnt that Carl had not only left his secure housing in the southeast of Paris, but also that he had made up all kinds of things about his past. He had lied to his *assistants sociaux*, his friends on the streets and me.

Does this jeopardize my description of Carl, who was one of my main protagonists? Any doubt about the 'validity' of my data in this sense – people lying to me about their pasts – only has a limited effect on the validity of my descriptions. Unlike many other studies of homelessness, my focus has not been the reasons that people end up on the street; rather, I have sought to understand how my informants creatively engaged in making better lives with, on and eventually off the street. My focus has been home-making techniques, ranging from begging and shelter-making to taking drugs and accessing temporary accommodation, and how these can be considered techniques of the self that ultimately lead to certain types of (still limited) freedom. Lying was part of the repertoire of techniques of the self. It was part of the way Carl used his freedom to reinvent himself, between resident, soldier, beggar and 'drinker'. While not always successful or reflective and consumed by short-term hope, such as obtaining drugs, for instance, my informants engaged in many efforts aimed at freedom, defined as 'the always qualified and provisional outcome of ongoing efforts and reactions; it therefore stands not in opposition but requires self-discipline' (Laidlaw 2014: 108). While self-discipline is not commonly attributed to homeless people – nor is agency – I witnessed it repeatedly, be it in begging, shelter-making or defining their *projets de vie*. We should value this in homeless people. Without minimizing their suffering, the tragedies that unfold on the streets, I hope that I portrayed my informants as actively struggling and striving, albeit often invisibly so. While they oscillated between their short- and the long-term hopes, they were always working towards 'better lives', on and off the streets.

Note

1. I am very consciously choosing 'better' rather than 'good' as a descriptor for my informants' lives to avoid the critique of romanticization; here, I am referring explicitly to
   Robbins's call for an 'anthropology of the good' (see Introduction), but as a strongly
   empirically driven rather than theoretical connection. Thus, it is particularly important
   to understand the 'better life' as intrinsically connected to the movement and striving I
   so often observed, which is the opposite of passive suffering. This is also encapsulated in
   the notion of home-as-process.

References

Ahmed, S. 1999. 'Home and Away: Narratives of Migration and Estrangement'. *International Journal of Cultural Studies* 2(3): 329–47.

Albert-Bireau, P. 1983. *Les amusements naturels*. Paris: Rougerie.

Antze, P. 1987. 'Symbolic Action in Alcoholics Anonymous'. In M. Douglas (ed.), *Constructive Drinking*. Cambridge: Cambridge University Press, pp. 149–82.

Appiah, K.A. 2008. *Experiments in Ethics*. Cambridge, MA: Harvard University Press.

APUR. 2011. 'Sans-abri à Paris: la présence des sans-abri sur le territoire parisien et l'action de la collectivité pour aider à leur réinsertion'. Paris.

Arendt, H. 1998. *The Human Condition*. Chicago: University of Chicago Press.

Augé, M. 2008. *Non-Places: An Introduction to Supermodernity*. London: Verso.

Bear, L. 2014. 'Doubt, Conflict, Mediation: The Anthropology of Modern Time'. *Journal of the Royal Anthropological Institute* (April): 3–30.

Beck, F., S. Legleye and S. Spilka. 2009. *Alcohol Consumption among Homeless Adults: Challenging a Stereotype*. Paris.

Belk, R.W. 1984. 'Cultural and Historical Differences in Concepts of Self and Their Effects on Attitudes toward Having and Giving'. In T. Kinnear (ed.), *Advances in Consumer Research*. Provo, UT: Association for Consumer Research, pp. 753–60.

_____. 1996. 'The Perfect Gift'. In C. Otnes and R.F. Beltramini (eds), *Gift-Giving: A Research Anthology*. Bowling Green, OH: Bowling Green State University Popular Press, pp. 59–84.

Benoist, Y. 2009. *Sans-logics de Paris à Nanterre: ethnographie d'une domination ordinaire*. Paris: L'Harmattan.

Bergamaschi, M., and C. Francesconi. 2008. 'Urban Homelessness: The Negotiation of Public Spaces'. *Visual Sociology* 11(2): 35–44.

Berlant, L. 2011. *Cruel Optimism*. Durham, NC: Duke University Press.

Biehl, J. 2005. *Vita: Life in a Zone of Social Abandonment*. Berkeley: University of California Press.

Bloch, E. 1995. *The Principle of Hope*. Boston, MA: MIT Press.

Boeri, M. 2018. *Hurt: Chronicles of the Drug War Generation*. Oakland: University of California Press.

Bornstein, E. 2012. *Disquieting Gifts: Humanitarianism in New Delhi*. Palo Alto, CA: Stanford University Press.

Botticello, J. 2007. 'Lagos in London: Finding the Space of Home'. *Home Cultures* 4(1): 7–23.

Bouillon, F. 2009. *Les mondes du squat. Anthropologie d'un habitat précaire*. Paris: Presses Universitaires de France.

Bourdieu, P. 1977. *Outline of a Theory of Practice*. Cambridge: Cambridge University Press.

———. 2002. *In Search of Respect: Selling Crack in El Barrio*. Cambridge: Cambridge University Press.

Bourgois, P, and J. Schonberg. 2009. *Righteous Dopefiend*. Berkeley: University of California Press.

Bowles, B. 2016. '"Time Is like a Soup": Boat Time and the Temporal Experience of London's Liveaboard Boaters'. *The Cambridge Journal of Anthropology* 34(1): 100–12.

Bowpitt, G., P. Dwyer and E. Sundin. 2014. 'Places of Sanctuary for "the Undeserving"? Homeless People's Day Centres and the Problem of Conditionality'. *British Journal of Social Work* 44(5): 1251–67.

Breman, J. 2013. *At Work in the Informal Economy of India*. Oxford: Oxford University Press.

Brousse, C., B. de la Rochère and E. Mass. 2002. *Hébergement et distribution de repas chauds: le cas des sans-domicile*. Paris: INSEE.

Brun, C. 2015. 'Home as a Critical Value: From Shelter to Home in Georgia'. *Refuge* 31(1): 43–54.

Brun, C., and A. Fábos. 2015. 'Making Homes in Limbo? A Conceptual Framework'. *Refuge* 31(1): 5–17.

Bruneteaux, P. 2005. 'L'hébergement d'urgence à Paris ou l'accueil en souffrance'. *CAIRN*: 105–25.

Busch-Geertsema, V., and I. Sahlin. 2007. 'The Role of Hostels and Temporary Accommodation'. *European Journal of Homelessness* 1: 67–93.

Campbell, N.D., and S.J. Shaw. 2008. 'Incitements to Discourse: Illicit Drugs, Harm Reduction, and the Production of Ethnographic Subjects'. *Cultural Anthropology* 23(4): 688–717.

Casey, R., R. Goudie and K. Reeve. 2008. 'Homeless Women in Public Spaces: Strategies of Resistance'. *Housing Studies* 23: 899–916.

Cefaï, D. 2015. 'Outreach Work in Paris: a Moral Ethnography of Social Work and Nursing with Homeless People'. *Human Studies* 38(1): 137–56.

Chaput-Le Bars, C., and A. Morange. 2014. 'Le Housing-first. L'experimentation à la française'. in J. Fraisse (ed.), *Nouvelle gestion sociale des SDF*. Paris: Champ social éditions, pp. 67–79.

Cieraad, I. 2006. *At Home: An Anthropology of Domestic Space*. Syracuse, NY: Syracuse University Press.

———. 2010. 'Homes from Home: Memories and Projections'. *Home Cultures* 7(1): 85–102.

Clapham, D. 2003. 'Pathways Approaches to Homelessness Research'. *Journal of Community and Applied Social Psychology* 13(2): 119–27.

Clapham, D., P. Mackie, S. Orfod, I. Thomas and K. Buckley. 2014. 'The Housing Pathways of Young People in the UK'. *Environment and Planning A* 46(8): 2016–31.

Clarke, A.J. 2001. 'The Aesthetics of Social Aspiration.' In D. Miller (ed.), *Home Possessions: Material Culture Behind Closed Doors*, Oxford: Berg, pp. 23–47.

Clarke, C. 1997. *Misery and Company: Sympathy in Everyday Life*. Chicago: University of Chicago Press.

Clarke, M. 2015. 'Legalism and the Care of the Self: Shari'ah Discourse in Contemporary Lebanon'. In P. Dresch and J. Scheele (eds), *Legalism: Rules and Categories*. Oxford: Oxford University Press, pp. 231–59.

Conradson, D. 2003. 'Spaces of Care in the City: The Place of a Community Drop-in Center'. *Social and Cultural Geography* 4: 507–25.

Cook, J. 2010. *Meditation in Modern Buddhism: Renunciation and Change in Thai Monastic Life*. Cambridge: Cambridge University Press.

Cooper, A. 2001. 'Working with People Who Are Homeless, Vulnerably or Insecurely Housed'. In C. Clark (ed.), *Adult Day Services and Social Inclusion: Better Days*. London: Jessica Kingsley.

Courtenay, T. 2017. 'What I Learned about Our Attitude to Homeless People When I Was on the Streets'. *The Guardian*. Retrieved 27 March 2021 from https://www.theguardian.com/commentisfree/2017/jul/24/beaten-urinated-homeless-people-abused-coffee-shop-london.

Crapanzano, V. 2003. 'Reflections on Hope as a Category of Social and Psychological Analysis'. *Cultural Anthropology* 18(1): 3–32.

Cresswell, T. 2004. *Place*. London: Blackwell.

Crisis. 2017. 'Rough Sleepers Being Targeted by Legal Powers Designed for Antisocial Behaviour'. London.

Dambuyant-Wargny, G. 2004. '"Sans toit ni loi": les exclus'. *Ethnologie française* 34(3): 499–508.

Das, V. 2012. 'Ordinary Ethics'. In D. Fassin (ed.), *A Companion to Moral Anthropology*. Oxford: Wiley-Blackwell, pp. 133–50.

Day, S., E. Papataxiarchis and M. Stewart. 1999. *Lillies of the Field: Marginal People Who Live for the Moment*. Oxford: Westview Press.

Declerck, P. 2003. *Les naufragés: avec les clochards de Paris*. Paris: Pocket.

Denzin, N. 1968. 'Communications: On the Ethics of Disguised Observation'. *Social Problems* 15: 502–4.

———. 1987. *The Alcoholic Self*. Newbury Park, CA: Sage.

Département de Paris. 2017. 'ESI: les espaces solidarité insertion'. Paris.

Desjarlais, R. 1994. 'Struggling Along: The Possibilities for Experience among the Homeless Mentally Ill'. *American Anthropologist* 96(4): 886–901.

———. 1997. *Shelter Blues: Sanity and Selfhood Among the Homeless*. Philadelphia: University of Pennsylvania Press.

Dietrich-Ragon, P. 2011. *Le logement intolerable. Habitants et pouvoirs publics face à l'insalubrité*. Paris: Presses Universitaires de France.

Dietz, M.L., R. Prus and W. Shaffir. 1994. 'Introduction: The Study of Everyday Life'. In *Doing Everyday Life: Ethnography as Human Lived Experience*. Mississauga, Canada: Copp Clark Longman, pp. 1–6.

Dittmar, H. 1992. *The Social Psychology of Material Possessions: To Have Is to Be*. New York: St Martin's Press.

Dobson, R. 2011. 'Conditionality and Homelessness Services; "Practice Realities" in a Drop-in Center'. *Social Policy and Society* 10(4): 547–57.

Donley, A., and E. Jackson. 2014. 'Blending in the Presentation of Self among Homeless Men in a Gentrifying Environment'. *Theory in Action* 7(1): 46–64.

Douglas, M. 1991. 'The Idea of a Home: A Kind of Space'. *Social Research* 58(1): 287–307.

Dovey, K. 1985. 'Home and Homelessness'. In I. Altman and C.M. Werner (eds), *Home Environments*. New York: Plenum Press.

Duneier, M. 2000. *Sidewalk*. New York: Farrar Straus Giroux.

Easthope, H. 2004. 'A Place Called Home'. *Housing, Theory and Society* 21(3): 128–38.

Edgar, B., M. Harrison, P. Watson and V. Busch-Geertsema. 2007. *Measurement of Homelessness at European Union Level*. Brussels: European Communities.

Edgar, W., J. Doherty and H. Meert. 2004. *Third Review of Statistics on Homelessness in Europe. Developing an Operational Definition of Homelessness*. Brussels: FEANTSA.

Edwards, J., and J.-P. Revauger. 2018. *Discourse on Inequality in France and Britain*. London: Routledge.

Elisha, O. 2011. *Moral Ambition: Mobilization and Social Outreach in Evangelical Megachurches*. Berkeley: University of California Press.

Emmanuelli, M.X., and B. Landrieu. 2006. *Des travailleurs en situation de précarité en Ile-de-France et à Paris*. Paris: Samu Social.

Englund, H. 2006. *Prisoners of Freedom: Human Rights and the African Poor*. Berkeley: University of California Press.

Erickson, P.G., D.M. Riley, Y.W. Cheung and P. O'Hare. 1997. *Harm Reduction: A New Direction for Drug Policy and Programs*. Toronto: University of Toronto Press.

Erickson, R. 1995. 'The Importance of Authenticity for Self and Society'. *Symbolic Interaction* 18: 121–44.

Farmer, P. 2004. 'An Anthropology of Structural Violence'. *Current Anthropology* 45(3): 305–25.

———. 2005. *Pathologies of Power: Health, Human Rights, and the New War on the Poor*. Berkeley: University of California Press.

FEANTSA. 2006. 'ETHOS: Taking stock'. Brussels.

———. 2007. 'Criminalisation of People Who Are Homeless'. Brussels.

Ferguson, J. 2015. *Give a Man a Fish*. Durham, NC: Duke University Press.

Fillon, E., C. Hemery and C. Lanneree. 2007. 'Les sans-abri des quais d'Austerlitz'. *EchoGeo* 1. Retrieved 11 August 2021 from https://journals.openedition.org/echogeo//1013?lang=fr.

Fitzpatrick, S. 2005. 'Explaining Homelessness: A Critical Realist Perspective'. *Housing, Theory and Society* 22(1): 1–17.

Fitzpatrick, S., H. Pawson, G. Bramley, S. Wilcox, B. Watts and J. Wood. 2018. *The Homelessness Monitor: England 2018*. London: Crisis.

Flanagan, M.W. 2012. '"Where There Is No Love, Put Love": Homeless Addiction Recovery Perspectives and Ways to Enhance Healing'. PhD dissertation. Georgia State University.

Foucault, M. 1997. 'Technologies of the Self'. In P. Rabinow (ed.), *Essential Work of Foucault 1954-1984: Volume 1: Ethics*. London: Penguin, pp. 223–53.

Fournier, S. 2017. 'Itinéraire d'un jeune en errance'. *Empan*, 106(2): 124.

Freedman, J. 2017. *Immigration and Insecurity in France*. London: Routledge.

Gaboriau, P., and D. Terrolle. 2003. *Ethnologie des sans-logis. Etude d'une forme de domination sociale*. Paris: L'Harmattan.

Gaetz, S., and B. O'Grady. 2002. 'Making Money: Exploring the Economy of Young Homeless Workers'. *Work, Employment and Society* 16(3): 433–56.

Gardella, E. 2014. 'L'urgence comme chronopolitique: Le cas de l'hébergement des sans-abri'. *Temporalites* 1.

Gardiner, M.E. 2012. 'Henri Lefebvre and the "Sociology of Boredom"'. *Theory, Culture & Society* 29(2): 37–62.

Garnier-Muller, A. 2000. *Les 'Inutiles': survivre au quotidien en banlieue et dans la rue*. Paris: Les Editions Ouvrières.

Garvey, P. 2001. 'Organized Disorder: Moving Furniture in Norwegian Homes'. In D. Miller (ed.), *Home Possessions: Material Culture Behind Closed Doors*. Oxford: Berg, pp. 47–69.

Geertz, C. 1993. 'Deep Play: Notes on the Balinese Cockfight'. In *The Interpretation of Cultures*. New York: Fontana Press, pp. 412–53.

Girard, V., P. Estecahandy and P. Chauvin. 2009. *La santé des personnes sans chez soi*. Paris: L'Harmattan.

Goffman, E. 1959. 'Presentation of Self in Everyday Life'. In *The Presentation of Self in Everyday Life*. New York: Anchor Books.

_____. 1991. *Asylums: Essays on the Social Situation of Mental Patients and Other Inmates*. London: Penguin Books.

Golightley, M. 2014. *Social Work and Mental Health*. London: Sage.

Gonyea, J.G., and K. Melekis. 2016. 'Older Homeless Women's Identity Negotiation: Agency, Resistance, and the Construction of a Valued Self'. *Sociological Review* 65(1): 67–82.

Goode, S. 2000. 'Researching a Hard-to-Access and Vulnerable Population: Some Considerations on Researching Drug and Alcohol-Using Mothers'. *Sociological Research Online* 5(1). Retrieved 11 August 2021 from http://www.socresonline.org.uk/5/1/goode.html.

Gowan, T., S. Whetstone and T. Andic. 2012. 'Social Science & Medicine Addiction, Agency, and the Politics of Self-Control: Doing Harm Reduction in a Heroin Users' Group'. *Social Science & Medicine* 74(8): 1251–60.

Grand, D. 2015. 'Etre chez soi en hébergement? Les paradoxes de l'hébergement pour les personnes sans domicile'. *Vie sociale et traitements* 4(128): 67–72.

Green, S. 2012. 'Reciting the Future Border Relocations and Everyday'. *Hau* 2(1): 111–29.

Gregory, C.A. 1982. *Gifts and Commodities*. New York: Academic Press.

Gresillon, E., J.-P. Amat and A. Tibaut. 2014. 'Les SDF du bois de Vincennes: une précarité dans des espaces de durabilité'. *Géocarrefour* 89: 1–15.

Grinman, M.N., S. Chiu and D.A. Redelmeier. 2010. 'Drug Problems among Homeless Individuals in Toronto, Canada: Prevalence, Drugs of Choice, and Relation to Health Status'. *BMC Public Health* 10(1): 94.

Grint, K., and D. Nixon. 2015. *The Sociology of Work*. Cambridge: Polity.

Gudeman, S. 2001. 'Postmodern Gifts'. In S. Cullenberg, J. Amariglia, and D.F. Ruccio (eds), *Postmodernism, Economics and Knowledge*. New York: Routledge, pp. 459–74.

Gueslin, A. 2013. *D'ailleurs et de nulle part: mendiants vagabonds, clochards, SDF en France depuis le Moyen Age*. Paris: Fayard.

Hage, G. 2003. *Against Paranoid Nationalism: Searching for Hope in a Shrinking Society*. Sydney: Pluto Press.

Hall, T. 2003. *Better Times than This: Youth Homelessness in Britain*. London: Pluto Press.

_____. 2017. *Footwork: Urban Outreach and Hidden Lives*. London: Pluto Press.

Han, C. 2012. *Life in Debt: Times of Care and Violence in Neoliberal Chile*. London: University of California Press.

Hart, K. 1973. 'Informal Income: Opportunities and Urban Employment in Ghana'. *Journal of Modern African Studies* 11(1): 61–89.

Heathcote, E. 2012. *The Meaning of Home*. London: Frances Lincoln.

Herring, C. 2014. 'The New Logics of Homeless Seclusion: Homeless Encampments in America's West Coast Cities'. *City and Community* 13(4): 285–309.

Herschkorn-Barnu, P. 2014. 'Femmes enceintes et bébé SDF'. *Enfances & Psy* 3(64): 6–8.

Hill, R.P. 2003. 'Homelessness in the US: An Ethnographic Look at Consumption Strategies'. *Community and Applied Social Psychology* 13(2): 128–37.

Hill, R.P., and M. Stamey. 1990. 'The Homeless in America: An Examination of Possessions and Consumption Behaviours'. *Journal of Consumer Research* 17(3): 303–21.

Hoang, K.K. 2010. 'Economies of Emotion, Familiarity, Fantasy, and Desire: Emotional Labor in Ho Chi Minh City's Sex Industry Historical Context: Prostitution during the French and American Colonial Periods'. *Sexualities* 13(2): 255–72.

Hobsbawm, E. 1991. 'Exile'. *Social Research* 58(1): 65–68.

Hochschild, A.R. 1983. *The Managed Heart: Commercialization of Human Feeling.* Berkeley: University of California Press.

Hodder, T., M. Teesson and N. Buhrich. 1998. *Down and Out in Sydney: Prevalence of Mental Disorders, Disability and Health Service Use among Homeless People in Inner Sydney.* Sydney.

Hodgetts, D.J., O. Stolte and K. Chamberlain. 2010. 'The Mobile Hermit and the City: Considering Links between Places, Objects, and Identities in Social Psychological Research on Homelessness'. *Journal of Social Psychology* 49: 285–303.

Hope, S. 1995. 'Sanctuary'. In P. Sedgwick (ed.), *God in the City: Essays and Reflections from the Archbishop of Canterbury's Urban Theology Group.* London: Mowbray.

Houard, N. 2011. 'The French Homelessness Strategy Reforming Temporary Accomodation and Access to Housing to Deliver "Housing First": Continuum or Clean Break?'. *European Journal of Homelessness* 5(2): 83–98.

Human Rights Council. 2015. 'Report of the Special Rapporteur on Adequate Housing as a Component of the Right to an Adequate Standard of Living, and on the Right to Non-Discrimination in this Context'. New York.

Humphrey, C. 1997. 'Exemplars and Rules: Aspects of the Discourse of Moralities in Mongolia'. In S. Howell (ed.), *The Ethnography of Moralities.* London: Routledge, pp. 25–47.

Hutson, S. 1999. 'The Experience of Homeless Accommodation and Support'. In S. Hutson and and D. Clapham (eds), *Homelessness: Public Policies and Private Troubles.* London: Cassell, pp. 208–25.

Israel, M., and I. Hay. 2006. *Research Ethics in the Social Sciences.* London: Sage.

Jackson, M. 2005. *At Home in the World.* Durham, NC and London: Duke University Press.

James, W. 1981. 'The Consciousness of Self'. In *Principles of Psychology, Vol. 1.* Cambridge, MA: Harvard University Press, pp. 279–379.

Jeffrey, C. 2010. *Timepass: Youth, Class, and the Politics of Waiting in India.* Stanford, CA: Stanford University Press.

Jencks, C. 1995. *The Homeless.* Cambridge, MA: Harvard University Press.

Jérôme, L. 2002. 'Les itinéraires de l'exclusion pour un groupe de sans-abri'. *Espace* 24(1): 101–17.

Johnsen, S., P. Cloke and J. May. 2005a. 'Transitory Spaces of Care: Serving Homeless People on the Street'. *Health and Place* 11(4): 323–336.

———. 2005b. 'Day Centres for Homeless People: Spaces of Care or Fear'. *Social and Cultural Geography* 6(6), 787–811.

Johnsen, S., S. Fitzpatrick and B. Watts. 2014. *Conditionality Briefing: Homelessness and 'Street Culture'.* London.

Jones, A., and S. Johnsen. 2009. 'Street Homelessness'. In S. Fitzpatrick, D. Quilgars and N. Pleace (eds), *Homelessness in the UK: Probems and Solutions.* Coventry: Chartered Institute of Housing, pp. 38–53.

Jones, G. 1995. *Leaving Home.* Buckingham: Open University Press.

Jost, J.J., A.J. Levitt and L. Porcu. 2010. 'Street to Home: The Experiences of Long-term Unsheltered Homeless Individuals in an Outreach and Housing Placement Program'. *Qualitative Social Work* 10(2): 244–63.

Joubert, A. 2015. 'Loger les SDF, au-delà de l'urgence: inventer des modes d'habiter'. *Apres-demain* 1(33): 34–36.

Kassah, A. 2008. 'Begging as Work: A Study of People with Mobility Difficulties in Accra, Ghana'. *Disability & Society* 23(2): 163–70.

Kellett, P., and J. Moore. 2003. 'Routes to Home: Homelessness and Home-Making in Contrasting Societies'. *Habitat International* 27(1): 123–41.

Kleinman, A., V. Das and M. Lock. 1997. *Social Suffering*. Berkeley: University of California Press.

Kleinman, J. 2012. 'The Gare du Nord: Parisian Topographies of Exchange'. *Ethnologie française* 42(3): 567–76.

———. 2019. *Adventure Capital: Migration and the Making of an African Hub in Paris*. Oakland: University of California Press.

Knight, K.R. 2015. *Addicted. Pregnant. Poor*. Durham, NC: Duke University Press.

Kovess, V., and C. Lazarus. 2001. 'Use of Mental Health Services by Homeless People in Paris'. *International Journal of Mental Health* 30(3): 26–39.

Krivanek, J.A. 1988. *Addiction*. Sydney: Allen and Unwin.

Laidlaw, J. 2002. 'A Free Gift Makes No Friends'. In M. Osteen (ed.), *The Question of the Gift: Essays across Disciplines*. London: Routledge, pp. 45–66.

———. 2014. *The Subject of Virtue: An Anthropology of Ethics and Freedom*. Cambridge: Cambridge University Press.

Lambek, M. 2010. *Ordinary Ethics*. New York: Fordham University Press.

Langegger, S., and S. Koester. 2016. 'Invisible Homelessness: Anonymity, Exposure, and the Right to the City'. *Urban Geography* 37(7): 1030–48.

Lankenau, S.E. 1999. 'Stronger than Dirt: Public Humiliation and Status Enhancement among Panhandlers'. *Journal of Contemporary Ethnography* 28(3): 288–318.

Laporte, A., and P. Chauvin. 2010. 'La santé mentale et les addictions chez les personnes sans logement personnel d'Ile-de-France (Samenta)'. *Rhizome* 38: 11.

Laporte, A., E. Le Mener and M.-A. Detrez. 2015. 'La santé mentale et les addictions chez les personnes sans logement personnel en Île-de-France: l'enquête Samenta de 2009'. *Bull Epidémiol Hebd* 36: 693–97.

Lazzarotti, O. 2006. *Habiter, la condition géographique*. Paris: Belin.

Lear, J. 2006. *Radical Hope: Ethics in the Face of Cultural Devastation*. Boston, MA: Harvard University Press.

Lee, R.M. 1993. *Doing Research on Sensitive Topics*. London: Sage.

Le Méner, E. 2013. 'Quel toit pour les familles à la rue? L'hébergement d'urgence en hôtel social'. *Métropolitiques*: 1–8.

Lenhard, J. 2014. 'Austere Kindness of Mindless Austerity: The Effects of Gift-Giving to Beggars in East London'. *Antipoda* April(18): 85–105.

———. 2017. 'You Care More for the Gear than the Geezer? Care Relationships of Homeless Substance Users in London'. *City and Society* 29(2): 305–28.

———. 2017a. 'Beggars and Choosers: On Dressing while Homeless'. *Vestoj*. Retrieved 11 August 2021 from http://vestoj.com/beggars-and-choosers/.

———. 2020. 'The Economy of Hot Air: Habiter, Warmth and Security among Homeless People at the Gare du Nord in Paris'. *Housing Studies*.

Lenhard, J., and F. Samanani, eds. 2019. *Home: Ethnographic Encounters*. Abingdon: Routledge.

LePoint. 2015. 'Logement: le nombre de SDF a augmenté de 50% en dix ans'. Retrieved 11 August 2021 from https://www.lepoint.fr/societe/logement-le-nombre-de-sdf-a-augmente-de-50-en-dix-ans-03-02-2015-1901872_23.php.

Lévy-Vroelant, C. 2015. 'The Right to Housing in France: Still a Long Way to Go from Intention to Implementation'. *Journal of Law and Social Policy* 24: 88–108.

Lion, G. 2015. 'En quête de chez-soi. Le bois de Vincennes, un espace habitable?'. *Annales de Geographie* 697: 956–81.

Loison-Leruste, M. 2014. *Habiter à côté des SDF: Représentations et attitudes face à la pauvreté*. Paris: L'Harmattan.

Loison-Leruste, M., and D. Quilgars. 2009. 'Increasing Access to Housing: Implementing the Right to Housing in England and France'. *European Journal of Homelessness* 3: 75–100.

Lyon-Callo, V. 2004. *Inequality, Poverty, and Neoliberal Governance*. Toronto: Toronto University Press.

Mahmood, S. 2012. *Politics of Piety: The Islamic Revival and the Feminist Subject*. 2nd edn. Princeton, NJ: Princeton University Press.

Mallett, S. 2004. 'Understanding Home: a Critical Review of the Literature'. *The Sociological Review* 52(1): 62–89.

Malmauret, L., J.C. Leblanc, I. Cuvelier and P.H. Verger. 2002. 'Dietary Intakes and Vitamin Status of a Sample of Homeless People in Paris'. *European Journal of Clinical Nutrition* 56(4): 313–20.

Marpsat, M. 2007. *Services for the Homeless in France*. Paris: INED.

Marpsat, M., and J.-M. Firdion. 2000. *La rue et le foyer*. Paris: Presses Universitaires de France.

Marvasti, A.B. 2002. 'Constructing the Service-worthy Homeless through Narrative Editing'. *Journal of Contemporary Ethnography* 31: 615–51.

Massey, D. 1992. 'A Place Called Home?'. In *The Question of Home*. London: Lawrence and Wishart.

_____. 2005. *For Space*. London: Sage.

Mattingly, C. 2010. *The Paradox of Hope*. Berkeley: University of California Press.

_____. 2014. *Moral Laboratories: Family Peril and the Struggle for A Good Life*. Oakland: University of California Press.

Mauss, M. 2001. *The Gift*. London: Routledge.

McIntosh, I., and A. Erskine. 2000. '"Money for Nothing"?: Understanding Giving to Beggars'. *Sociological Research Online* 5(1): 1–13.

McNaughton, C. 2008. *Transitions through Homelessness: Lives on the Edge*. London: Macmillan.

McNicoll, A. 2013. *How to Make Personalisation 'Core Business' in Mental Health*. London: Community and Care.

Meanwell, E. 2013. 'Profaning the Past to Salvage the Present: The Symbolically Reconstructed Pasts of Homeless Shelter Residents'. *Symbolic Interaction* 36(4): 439–56.

Messing, V. 2014. 'Methodological Puzzles of Surveying Roma/Gypsy Populations'. *Ethnicities* 14(6): 811–29.

Michalot, T., and A. Simeone. 2010. 'L'alcoolisation apparente: un critère d'exclusion pour l'admission en C.H.R.S. d'insertion?'. *Pensée plurielle* 23(1): 109.

Midgley, J. 2016. 'Perspectives on Responsibility in Practice as Revealed through Food Provisioning Offers for Rough Sleepers'. *Critical Social Policy* 36(4): 1–20.

Millar, K.M. 2008. 'The Precarious Present: Wageless Labor and Disrupted Life in Rio de Janeiro, Brazil'. *Cultural Anthropology* 29(1): 32–53.

Miller, D. 2001. *Home Possessions: Material Culture Behind Closed Doors*. London: Berg Publishers.

Minnery, J., and E. Greenhalgh. 2007. 'Approaches to Homelessness Policy in Europe, the United States, and Australia'. *Journal of Social Issues* 63(3): 641–56.

Miyazaki, H. 2006. 'Economy of Dreams: Hope in Global Capitalism and Its Critiques'. *Cultural Anthropology* 21(2): 147–72.

Moeschen, S. 2008. 'A Crippling Deceit: Mendicancy and the Performance of Disability in Progressive America'. *Text and Performance Quarterly* 28(1): 81–97.

Mol, A. 2008. *The Logic of Care: Health and the Problem of Patient Choice*. London: Routledge.

Moore, J. 2000. 'Placing Home in Context'. *Journal of Environmental Psychology* 20(3): 207–17.

Moore, J., and L.G. Rivlin. 2001. 'Home-Making : Supports and Barriers to the Process of Home'. *Journal of Social Distress and the Homeless* 10(1): 323–36.

Murray, C. 1990. *The Emerging British Underclass*. London: IEA.

Neale, J. 1997. 'Homelessness and theory reconsidered'. *Housing Studies* 12(1): 47–61.

Noblet, P. 2014. 'Les Enfants de Don Quichotte: de la stabilisation au logement d'abord'. In J. Fraisse (ed.), *Nouvelle Gestion Social des SDF*, Paris: Champ social éditions, pp. 11–20.

OHCHR. 2008. *Number of Homeless Persons Per 100,000*. Geneva.

O'Mahony, L.F. 2013. 'The Meaning of Home: From Theory to Practice'. *International Journal of Law in the Built Environment* 5(2): 156–71.

O'Neill, B. 2017. *The Space of Boredom: Homelessness in the Slowing Global Order*. Durham, NC: Duke University Press.

Orwell, G. 2001. *Down and Out in Paris and London*. London: Penguin Classics.

Padgett, D.K., B.F. Henwood and S.J. Tsemberis. 2016. *Housing First: Ending Homelessness, Transforming Systems, and Changing Lives*. New York: Oxford University Press.

Paris.fr. 2017. *Le plan Grand froid à Paris: comment ça marche*. Paris.

_____. 2019. *Nuit de la Solidarité: 3 622 sans-abris recensés*. Paris.

Parry, J., and M. Bloch. 1989. *Money and the Morality of Exchange*. Cambridge: Cambridge University Press.

Passaro, J. 1996. *The Unequal Homeless: Men in the Streets. Women in Their Place*. New York and London: Routledge.

Pedersen, M.A. 2012. 'A Day in the Cadillac: The Work of Hope in Urban Mongolia'. *Social Analysis* 56(2): 1–16.

Peressini, T. 2009. 'Pathways into Homelessness: Testing the Heterogeneity Hypothesis'. In J.D. Hulchanski, P. Campsie and S. Chau (eds), *Finding Home: Policy Options for Addressing Homelessness in Canada*. Toronto: University of Toronto Press. Retrieved 11 August 2021 from https://yorkspace.library.yorku.ca/xmlui/bitstream/handle/10315/29366/FindingHome_Full.pdf?sequence=1&isAllowed=y.

Pichon, P. 1996. 'Survivre la nuit et le jour. La préservation de soi face au circuit d'assistance'. *Politix* 34: 164–179.

_____. 2002. 'Vivre sans domicile fixe: l'épreuve de l'habitat précaire'. *Communications* 73(1): 11–29.

_____. 2014. 'Sortir de la rue. Question de recherche et enjeu d'action'. In J. Fraisse (ed.), *Nouvelle gestion sociale des SDF*. Paris: Champ social éditions, pp. 79–91.

Pierre-Marie, E., S. Roger and M.-L. Chausse. 2014. *Les sans-domicile dans l'agglomération parisienne: une population en très forte croissance*. Paris.

Pimor, T. 2014. 'Du jeune en errance aux zonards'. *Les Sciences de l'Education* 1(47): 67–93.

Power, R. 2002. 'Participatory Research amongst Marginal Groups: Drug Users, Homeless People and Gay Men'. *Drugs: Education, Prevention, and Policy* 9(2): 125–31.

Price, J.A. 1975. 'Sharing: The Integration of Intimate Economies'. *Anthropologica* 17(1): 3–27.

Prolongeau, H. 1993. *Sans domicile fixe*. Paris: Hachette.

Ray, M.B. 1961. 'The Cycle of Abstinence and Relapse among Heroin Addicts'. *Social Problems* 132–40.

Rayburn, R.L. 2013. 'Understanding Homelessness, Mental Health and Substance Abuse through a Mixed-Methods Longitudinal Approach'. *Health Sociology Review* 22(4): 389–99.

Ricœur, P. 1992. *Oneself as Another*. Chicago: Chicago University Press.

Robbins, J. 2004. *Becoming Sinners: Christianity and Moral Torment in a Papua New Guinea Society*. Berkeley: University of California Press.

———. 2007. 'Between Reproduction and Freedom: Morality, Value, and Radical Cultural Change'. *Ethnos* 72(3): 293–314.

———. 2013. 'Beyond the Suffering Subject: Toward an Anthropology of the Good'. *Journal of the Royal Anthropological Institute* 19: 447–62.

———. 2015. 'On Happiness, Values, and Time: The Long and the Short of It'. *Hau* 5(3): 215–33.

Rowe, M., D. Fisk, J. Frey and L. Davidson. 2002. 'Engaging Persons with Substance Use Disorders: Lessons from Homeless Outreach'. *Administration and Policy in Mental Health* 29(3): 263–73.

Rowe, S., and J. Wolch. 1990. 'Social Networks in Time and Space: Homeless Women'. *Annals of the Association of American Geographers* 80(2): 184–204.

Rullac, S. 2005. *Et si les SDF n'étaient pas des exclus?* Paris: L'Harmattan.

———. 2008. *Le péril SDF: assister et punir*. Paris: L'Harmattan.

Rullac, S., M. Noalhyt and N. Neffati. 2014. *Les enjeux de l'accompagnement dans le cadre de l'accès au logement pour tous*. Paris: L'Harmattan.

Russell, B.G. 2011. *Silent Sisters: A Study of Homeless Women*. New York: Routledge.

Sahlins, M. 2004. *Stone Age Economics*. Oxford: Routledge.

Sanyal, D. 2017. 'Calais's Jungle: Refugees, Biopolitics and the Arts of Resistance'. *Representations* 139(1): 1–33.

Schak, D.C. 1988. *A Chinese Beggars' Den: Poverty and Mobility in an Underclass Community*. Pittsburgh, PA: University of Pittsburgh Press.

Scheper-Hughes, N., and P. Bourgois. 2003. *Violence in War and Peace*. Malden, MA: Blackwell.

Scherz, C. 2014. *Having People, Having Heart: Charity, Sustainable Development, and Problems of Dependence in Central Uganda*. Chicago: University of Chicago Press.

Schielke, S. 2009. 'Being Good in Ramadan: Ambivalence, Fragmentation, and the Moral Self in the Lives of Young Egyptians'. *Journal of the Royal Anthropological Institute* 15(1): 24–40.

———. 2015. *Egypt in the Future Tense: Hope, Frustruation, and Ambivalence before and after 2011*. Bloomington: Indiana University Press.

SCIE. 2010. 'Personalisation: A Rough Guide'. London.

Seele, G. 2011. *Die Eigenen Vier Wände*. Berlin: Form und Zweck.

Seuret, F. 2016. 'Femmes SDF: les invisibles'. *Alternatives Economiques* 4(356). Retrieved 11 August 2021 from https://www.alternatives-economiques.fr/femmes-sdf-invisibles/00003758.

Sharma, S. 2017. 'Baring Life and Lifestyle in the Non-Place'. *Cultural Studies* 12(1): 129–48.

Sheehan, R. 2010. '"I'm Protective of this Yard": Long-Term Homeless Persons' Construction of Home Place and Workplace in a Historical Public Space'. *Social & Cultural Geography* 11(6): 539–58.

Simmel, G. 1908. 'The Poor'. In D.N. Levine (ed.), *On Individuality and Social Forms: Selected Writings of Georg Simmel*. London: University of Chicago Press, pp. 150–79.

———. 1950. 'Faithfulness and Gratitude'. In K.H. Wolff (ed.), *The Sociology of Georg Simmel*. London: Collier-Macmillan, pp. 379–95.

Singer, M. 2006. *Something Dangerous: Emergent and Changing Illicit Drug Use and Community Health*. Long Grove, IL: Waveland Press.

Smiley, C.J., and K.M. Middlemass. 2016. 'Clothing Makes the Man: Impression Management and Prisoner Reentry'. *Punishment & Society* 18(2): 220–43.

Snow, D.A., and L. Anderson. 1993. *Down on Their Luck: A Study of Homeless Street People*. Berkeley: University of California Press.

Sprake, E.F., J.M. Russell and M.E. Barker. 2013. 'Food Choice and Nutrient Intake Amongst Homeless People'. *Journal of Human Nutrition and Dietetics* 27(3): 242–50.

Stettinger, V. 2003. *Funambules de la précarité*. Paris: Presses Universitaires de France.

Stewart, M. 1997. *The Time of the Gypsies*. Oxford: Westview Press.

Strangleman, T., and T. Warren. 2008. *Work and Society: Sociological Approaches, Themes and Methods*. London: Routledge.

Summerson Carr, E. 2006. '"Secrets Keep You Sick": Metalinguistic Labor in a Drug Treatment Program for Homeless Women'. *Language in Society* 35(5): 631–53.

———. 2011. *Scripting Addiction: The Politics of Therapeutic Talk and American Sobriety*. Princeton, NJ: Princeton University Press.

Sykes, K. 2007. *Arguing with Anthropology: An Introduction to Critical Theories of the Gift*. Abingdon-on-Thames: Taylor & Francis.

Thompson, E.P. 1967. 'Time, Work-Discipline, and Industrial Capitalism'. *Past and Present* 38: 56–97.

Throop, C.J. 2015. 'Ambivalent Happiness and Virtuous Suffering'. *Hau* 5(3): 45–68.

Unger, J.B., M.D. Kipke, T.R. Simon, S.B. Montgomery and C.J. Johnson. 1997. 'Homeless Youths and Young Adults in Los Angeles: Prevalence of Mental Health Problems and the Relationship between Mental Health and Substance Abuse Disorders'. *American Journal of Community Psychology* 25(3): 371–94.

Valverde, M. 1998. *Diseases of the Will: Alcohol and the Dilemmas of Freedom*. Cambridge: Cambridge University Press.

Veness, A.R. 1993. 'Neither Homed Nor Homeless: Contested Definitions and the Personal Worlds of the Poor'. *Political Geography* 12(4): 319–40.

Venkatesh, S. 2006. *Off the Books: The Underground Economy of the Urban Poor*. Cambridge, MA: Harvard University Press.

Vigh, H.E. 2015. 'Militantly Well'. *Hau* 5(3): 93–110.

Walker, H. 2015. 'Values of Happiness'. *Hau* 5(3): 1–23.

Ward, J. 2008. 'Researching Drug Sellers: An "Experiential" Account from "the Field"'. *Sociological Research Online* 13(1–2): 1–15.

Webb, A. 2012. *One Foot in Front of the Other*. New York: Skyhorse Publishing.

Wharton, A.S. 2009. 'The Sociology of Emotional Labor'. *Annual Review of Sociology* 35: 147–65.

Whiteford, M. 2010. 'Hot Tea, Dry Toast and the Responsibilisation of Homeless People'. *Social Policy & Society* 9(2): 193–205.

Whyte, W.F. 1943. *Street Corner Society: The Social Structure of an Italian Slum*. Chicago: University of Chicago Press.

Widlok, T. 2013. 'Sharing: Allowing Others to Take What Is Valued'. *HAU*, 3(2): 11–31.

Wilcox, D.M. 1998. *Alcohol Thinking: Language, Culture and Belief in Alcoholics Anonymous*. Westport, CT: Praeger Publishers.

Williams, T., and T.B. Milton. 2015. *The Con Men: Hustling in New York City*. New York: Columbia University Press.

Winance, M. 2010. 'Care and Disability: Practices of Experimenting, Tinkering with, and Arranging Peope and Technical Aids'. In A. Mol, I. Moser and J. Pols (eds), *Care in Practice*. Bielefeld: transcript, pp. 93–119.

Wolch, J.R., and S. Rowe. 1992. 'On the Streets: Mobility Paths of the Urban Homeless'. *City and Society* 6(4): 115–140.

Woodburn, J. 1982. 'Egalitarian Societies'. *Man* 17(3): 431–51.

———. 1998. 'Sharing is Not a Form of Exchange: An Analysis of Property-Sharing in Immediate-Return Hunter-Gatherer Societies'. In C. Hann (ed.), *Property Relations: Renewing the Anthropological Tradition*. Cambridge: Cambridge University Press, pp. 48–64.

Yaouancq, F., and M. Duée. 2013. *Les sans-domicile en 2012: une grande diversité de situations*. Paris: INSEE.

Yaouancq, F., A. Lebrère, M. Marpsat, V. Régnier, S. Legleye and Q. Martine. 2013. *L'hébergement des sans-domicile en 2012*, Paris: INSEE.

Zeneidi-Henry, D. 2002. *Les SDF et la ville: géographie du savoir-survivre*. Paris: Bréal.

Zigon, J. 2005. 'An Ethics of Hope: Working on the Self in Contemporary Moscow'. *Anthropology of East Europe Review* 24(2): 71–80.

———. 2009. 'Hope Dies Last: Two Aspects of Hope in Contemporary Moscow'. *Anthropological Theory* 9(3): 253–71.

———. 2011. *HIV Is God's Blessing: Rehabilitating Morality in Neoliberal Russia*. Berkeley: University of California Press.

———. 2019. *War on People: Drug User Politics and a New Ethics of Community*. Berkeley: University of California Press.

Zulyte, G. 2012. *Feels Like Home: Home-Making by Homeless Mothers in the Shelter in Lithuania*. Leiden: Leiden University Press.

Index

Printed in the USA
CPSIA information can be obtained
at www.ICGtesting.com
JSHW082239041223
52869JS00006B/81